Dublin Bay

NATURE AND HISTORY

Richard Nairn, David Jeffrey, Rob Goodbody

The Collins Press

FIRST PUBLISHED IN 2017 BY
The Collins Press
West Link Park
Doughcloyne
Wilton
Cork
T12 N5EF
Ireland

A CIP record for this book is available from the British Library.

Hardback ISBN: 978-1-84889-329-0

Design and typesetting by Fairways Design
Typeset in Minion Pro
Printed in Malta by Gutenberg Press Limited

Contents

Marsh fritillary on a marsh orchid at Bull Island *(John Fox)*

Foreword

Dublin Bay and its coastline are very different today from how they would have appeared when the first Vikings sailed up the Liffey in the ninth century. The changes to the bay since that time are man-made, both directly and indirectly. The Liffey has been canalised, a rail line was built across the southern shore and two long harbour walls have been constructed. One of these, the Great South Wall, caused Bull Island to form and it continues to grow. Refuse dumps have been transformed into the Poolbeg peninsula, East Point Business Park and large areas of Dublin Port.

In the past, changes occurred with little forethought as to how the bay and its environment would be affected. However, we live in very different times now and careful consideration of environmental impact is mandatory before development projects can proceed. There are also mandatory requirements to manage water quality and air emissions, for example.

Looking to the future, the bay will continue to change because of human intervention. In particular, sea level will rise as a result of anthropogenic climate change and adaptation measures will be necessary in response. Moreover, Dublin city and Dublin Port continue to grow, creating the need for major infrastructure projects including port facilities, housing, transport, power generation, water and waste treatment. Alongside these developments are rich habitats on the seabed, in the waters of the Liffey, in the bay and along the shore. One inevitably impacts on the other.

The challenge to simultaneously manage, develop and conserve Dublin Bay is formidable and requires an appreciation of both the bay's natural environment and its built environment. Each of these has many facets and it is difficult to gain an overall appreciation of the bay in all its complexity. This complexity is often described in dry and arcane environmental impact assessments required for development projects.

All change is challenging, and when change to Dublin's much-loved bay is imminent, strong emotions are evinced. The creation of the

Dublin Bay Biosphere in recent years, with its emphasis on people and the environment, is a welcome development. Beyond this, there has been a need for a concise and readable introduction to and overview of the bay. This book fills the gap. The collaboration between Richard Nairn, David Jeffrey and Rob Goodbody and the review of the book's chapters by a wide range of experts has created a rich synthesis of natural science and history to reveal many aspects of Dublin Bay and Dublin city. The book also references many sources and provides a stepping stone into a wide range of research and knowledge. It will be an invaluable and inspiring volume on Dublin Bay for many years to come.

Eamonn O'Reilly, Chief Executive, Dublin Port Company

Acknowledgements

We are grateful to Dublin Port Company and the Dublin Bay Biosphere Partnership for subventions which were vital to allow publication of this book. It grew out of a conference hosted by Dublin Port Company in 2015 to celebrate the 300th anniversary of the decision to build the Great South Wall. Eamonn O'Reilly, Chief Executive of Dublin Port Company, was a keen supporter of the project from the start and kindly agreed to write a foreword for the book. Tim Carey, Maryann Harris, Les Moore, Jenni Roche and Hans Visser also gave the book their full backing throughout.

John Fox enthusiastically took on a number of photographic assignments and his images are a key part of the book. Other pictures were provided by Brian Burke, John Coveney, Dublin City Council, Stephen Falk, Vincent Hyland, Cormac Lowth, Melanie McQuade, Richard T. Mills, Karl Partridge and Hal Sisk. Cormac Lowth also provided much information on maritime heritage of Dublin Bay and many excellent illustrations. Sam Hutchison and Nick Maxwell (Wordwell Books) sourced several historical paintings. We are grateful to Adams Art Auctions and the National Maritime Museum, London for permission to reproduce historical paintings and to the National Library of Ireland, The Royal Society of Antiquaries of Ireland, Dr Patrick Wallace, The National Archives at Kew, the British Museum and the British Library for other illustrations. The portrait of Captain William Bligh appears by courtesy of the National Library of Australia. Gordon Ledbetter provided the illustrations by, and the portrait of, Alexander Williams. The 1848 woodcut from Yarrell's *A History of British Birds* was kindly provided by David Cabot. Richard McCormick and Philip Lecane of the National Maritime Museum were very helpful in tracing other illustrations for the book. Nigel Monaghan of the Natural History Museum facilitated the photographing of fish specimens in the museum collections. Ed and Daphne Barrow kindly gave permission for use of aerial photographs by the late Peter Barrow. While every endeavour has been made to trace the ownership of illustrations and to acknowledge the source, the authors wish to apologise if any such acknowledgment has been overlooked. The authors would be grateful to hear of any such omissions so that due acknowledgment can be included in future editions.

We were especially pleased to be able to include some sketches by George Ivor Nairn (1859–1951), great-grandfather of Richard Nairn, who expresses his thanks to Linda Nairn and Diane Davison for making these available. Paul Francis painted the prehistoric view of Dublin Bay. Many of the historical maps in the book are from the Dublin Port Company archive, which contains an invaluable record of changes in Dublin Bay. Richard McCormick, Joe Varley and Cormac Lowth assisted with cataloguing this map archive, access to which was kindly arranged by Niall Dardis. Other historical maps were provided by courtesy of the library of Trinity College Dublin. Modern base maps for the book were expertly prepared by Matthew Hague. Most of the diagrams were drawn by Rebecca Jeffrey.

For information on recreational uses of Dublin Bay, we are grateful to Dermot Moynihan (Irish Underwater Council), Alec Elliott (Irish Sailing Association), Hal Sisk (sailing), Eugene Garrihy (Dublin Bay Cruises) and Niall Hatch (BirdWatch Ireland). Ger Morgan (Aquatic Services) and Tasman Crowe (University College Dublin) provided information on marine communities. Much information on birdlife was supplied by Niall Tierney, Olivia Crowe, Ricky Whelan and Steve Newton (BirdWatch Ireland). Various chapters were reviewed by David Cabot, Clare Crowley, Lisa Courtney, Tom Curtis, Robert Devoy, Cormac Lowth, Richard McCormick, Melanie McQuade, Derry Nairn, Micheal O Briain, Brendan O'Connor, Jack O'Sullivan, Jenni Roche, Karl Partridge, John Quinn, John Sweeney, Niall Tierney and Jim Wilson. For the improvements that they suggested we are extremely grateful.

Finally, thanks are due to our long-suffering wives and families who provided essential support and forbearance during the extended period of writing and editing.

1 | Introduction

In James Joyce's *Ulysses*, Stephen Dedalus 'closes his eyes to hear his boots crush crackling wrack and shells'. Joyce set much of the action of his famous novel in Dublin Bay. The story moves from the Forty Foot bathing place, where the character Buck Mulligan washes on Bloomsday morning, to Sandymount Strand, where Stephen ponders his world, and to Howth Head, where Leopold Bloom makes love to his wife Molly under the rhododendrons. Partly as a result of Joyce's writing, Dublin Bay has become one of the most famous coastal features in the world.

Sitting on a beach in warm summer sunshine, enjoying the sensation of sand and water running through our fingers, is for most of us our earliest experience of the coast. For countless generations of Dubliners this special moment of discovery probably took place in Dublin Bay, on Dollymount or Sandymount Strand, at Howth or in the little harbour of Sandycove near Dún Laoghaire. Adults retain a fascination with the open spaces of these shores and, as Rachel Carson wrote in her classic book *The Edge of the Sea*, 'in the recurrent rhythms of tides and surf and in the obvious attraction of movement, change and beauty'.[1]

Evening in Dublin Bay
(John Coveney)

Dublin Bay – Nature and History

Dublin Bay is the cradle of the city not only because the original town was born and grew to maturity on the shores of the bay, but also because the city is still nurtured by the coastal environment. The bay facilitates Ireland's trade through Dublin Port. It takes all the waste water from the city and surrounds. It protects the city against storms and it provides much-needed open space for people to escape from the urban jungle.

Dublin's history is intimately connected with the bay around which it grew. It was consolidated as a town by the Vikings who first beached their longships on the sandy shores of the bay in the ninth century AD. A thousand years later, great changes in the bay resulted from engineering schemes to deepen the channel for shipping in the port. Entering the modern era, the city and the port encroached on the bay in an eastward direction. Even today, the bay offers a glimpse of wild nature for those Dubliners who live and work in a bustling city. It provides people with a refuge from the noise and stress of modern life and a connection with an older order defined by nature.

Dublin Bay: location and place names

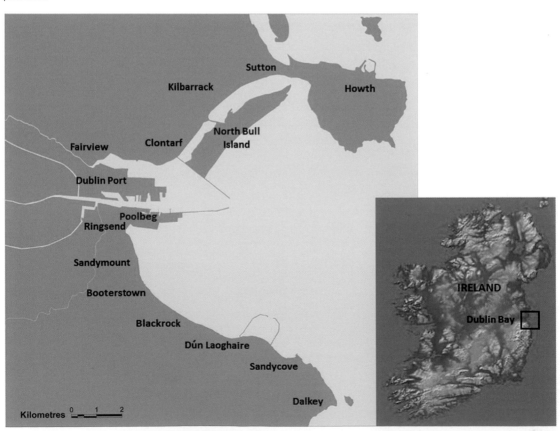

The arms of Dublin Bay stretch wide to embrace its citizens and to welcome visitors. The bay is much loved and enjoyed by the people of Dublin. Witness the crowds walking on Sandymount Strand at low tide on a fine weekend, spectators watching the kitesurfers on the seafront at Dollymount or the multitude of white sails in the bay on a summer evening. The paths around the bay provide increasing numbers of people with open space for walking, running and cycling. Generations of Dubliners have learned to swim or fish on its shores, and for millennia the bay has provided food for the city's population, from the cockles and mussels of Molly Malone's day to the fresh fish landed today in the fishing port of Howth.

Dublin Bay is such a familiar sight to most people that we find it difficult to imagine how it might have looked before the city began. Early maps provide useful clues. For example, we know that the River Liffey was much wider and shallower in earlier millennia, before it was confined between the quay walls. At low tide, the mud would have been too soft to support a person's weight and the only crossing was a wide shallow section of the river, with wicker mats staked to the riverbed, which came to be known by the Irish name of *Átha Cliath*, or 'ford of the hurdles'. The name *Dubhlinn* means 'black pool', referring to deeper water where the River Poddle enters the Liffey estuary. Thus, the names of the city itself related to the bay.

The river channel was a dynamic feature, changing its form as sand shifted around the bay. Maps from the seventeenth and eighteenth centuries show multiple channels emerging from the land, and these frequently changed their positions over time. The middle part of Dublin Bay was filled with extensive sandbanks, known as the North and South Bulls. At the upper levels of the beach, where the sand dried, it was blown ashore to form sand dunes on low-lying parts of the land such as Sandymount and Clontarf. In the inner, more sheltered parts of the bay, sand dunes would have been fringed by saltmarsh with winding channels and creeks.

From the arrivals of Viking longships to the massive container ships of today, Dublin Bay has provided a refuge for shipping when the winds on the Irish Sea blow strong. Dublin Port, which occupies the mouth of the Liffey, is the gateway for three quarters of the trade entering and leaving Ireland. Six ferry companies operate up to seventeen sailings a day to the UK and over a hundred cruise ships visit each year. The giant twin chimneys of the Poolbeg Power Station are an iconic feature of the city and the bay and one of the first things that visitors see as they arrive in Dublin by sea or by air. The Ringsend Waste Water Treatment Works cleans up all the sewage from Dublin and surrounding urban centres before the cleansed water is discharged into Dublin Bay.

Dublin Bay from the south
(John Fox)

In the midst of all this human activity, a living ecosystem carries on its miraculous engine of primary production, feeding, reproduction and nutrient recycling. The tide fills the bay twice a day, refreshing the shore and bringing seawater into contact with fresh water from the land. Some of the best examples of sand flats, dunes, saltmarsh, rocky shores, cliffs, islands and offshore sandbanks, all special European natural habitats, are found in Dublin Bay. Beneath the sands, countless millions of shellfish, worms, crustaceans and other creatures feed on the plankton and detritus carried in from the sea and organic matter brought down by the rivers. Great flocks of migratory birds, in their tens of thousands, feed in the area between the tides, arriving from as far afield as Arctic Canada and tropical Africa. Marine mammals, including seals, porpoises and dolphins, are resident in parts of the bay and larger relatives such as whales make occasional visits. Dublin Bay had the first designated bird sanctuary in Ireland and it now has more designations than any other place in the country. The latest of these is its recognition by UNESCO as a biosphere. We believe that a scientific understanding of the biological and chemical drivers of the ecosystem is essential to any decisions about its management.

In this book, we have attempted to weave together the history of the city and the ecology of the bay in which it is set. We have given special attention to the role of elements, such as nitrogen, and the importance of detritus, as these are key factors in the bay's ecosystem. The human and natural components of the bay are so closely intertwined that they have learned to coexist and, in some cases, even to depend on each other. For example, the natural processes in the bay break down our sewage effluent, which is then recycled by marine decomposers. Indeed, the disposal of raw sewage from the city in previous centuries probably generated some of the rich organic matter in the mudflats near Bull Island that now support high densities of marine creatures eaten by the thriving bird populations. The brent geese that fly in long lines across the city each day in winter have learned to exploit amenity grasslands as a replacement for the mudflats that were infilled as the urban area expanded eastwards.

Dublin Port, with the city in the background *(John Fox)*

Although Dublin Bay is one of the best-studied ecosystems in Ireland, we still scarcely understand how this natural area functions or what the long-term effects of development might be. We are only just beginning to appreciate that the birds we see in Dublin Bay move frequently both within and outside its boundaries. We see new sand dunes forming on the south side of the bay, but we know little about how this will affect sediment movements in the rest of the bay. We need to understand how our activities are affecting the bay's ecosystem, from disturbing birds to dredging shipping channels, and the longer-term implications of climate change, which are already affecting us all.

In this book we seek to answer some of these questions, by learning from centuries of historical experience and by interpreting the research that has taken place in and around Dublin Bay over the years. We have tried to make the science of ecology and the academic study of history accessible to the general reader. These two threads are inseparable in those parts of the book where we explore historical ecology, a branch of science that uses the knowledge gained from old documents, maps and photographs to help interpret the present patterns in nature, whether it is the origins of a rich habitat like Bull Island or the disappearance of a key species like the native oyster from the coastal ecosystem. It explores how nature has influenced, and been influenced by, political, economic and cultural change over a long period. Natural history in Ireland is also unavoidably a history of culture and society, involving the utilisation and exploitation of nature as well as its study.[2]

While the human history of the bay is considered throughout the book, Chapters 2 to 5 are largely concerned with nature and the natural processes that are the basis for life in the sea, on the shorelines and coastal lands around the bay. Chapter 6 explores the birdlife of the bay. Chapters 7 to 10 record the history of human involvement with the bay from earliest times to the modern era. The final chapters, 11 and 12, consider how the bay has been managed and what the future holds for this vital resource.

In his novel *Finnegans Wake*, James Joyce wrote the immortal words, 'riverrun, past Eve and Adam's, from swerve of shore to bend of bay'. The great bend of the bay from Howth to Dalkey is the setting of this book. For thousands of years, Dublin Bay has been a conduit for carrying ships in and out of the capital city and for trade with other countries. Today it is a familiar watery fringe to the largest urban area in the country, while the port at its centre is a barometer of the national economy. The importance of Dublin Bay is recognised by the European Union and the United Nations, and its value to all of us is immeasurable. We hope that this book will excite an interest in the bay among modern Dubliners and visitors alike, for whom it is an economic asset, a life-support system and an invaluable recreational resource.

2 | The Coastal Environment

South Dublin Bay from
Booterstown *(John Fox)*

While every coastal complex is different, Dublin Bay has many familiar natural habitats, including sandy beaches, mudflats, saltmarsh, sand dunes and islands. The coast is a dynamic and constantly changing environment with many contributory factors, not least of which is the human influence, which comes mainly from the urban area.

In this chapter, we explore the physical factors that influence how ecosystems function in Dublin Bay. To reveal its complexity, we consider the six main factors that influence the Dublin Bay environment. The living components and how they interact with one another and with their environment are explored in Chapters 3 to 5.

Dublin Bay Profile

Dublin Bay encloses an area of about 296 square kilometres (km^2). This includes the intertidal zone of about $16km^2$. The true benthic (sub-tidal) area ($175km^2$) ranges in depth from 25m to a large inner area less than 5m in depth. This information is compiled from that used for the computer model of Dublin Bay, which led to estimates of dispersion of the Liffey plume and associated pollutants.[1]

A rough calculation of the quantity of water entering and leaving Dublin Bay on a single high spring tide is 768 million cubic metres (m^3) of seawater, enough to fill 123,000 Olympic swimming pools. This may be compared with the flow of the Liffey at $10m^3$ per second ($432,000m^3$ in 12 hours), a ratio of almost 1,800:1.

This suggests that river-borne materials should be efficiently dispersed, but, because it is less dense than seawater, river water literally floats as a coherent plume across the northern sector. Because the tidal flow in the Irish Sea is predominantly south to north, and moving water has momentum, there is a tendency for a circle of water to rotate in a clockwise direction in the bay.

The length of the mainland shore from Sorrento Point, Dalkey to the Nose of Howth, including the Liffey banks to the tidal limit at Heuston Bridge weir, is approximately 65km. All shoreline calculations are approximate, as they may be hugely extended by including all minor inlets and docks.

The main factors affecting the environment of Dublin Bay. As the environment is so complex, analysis is easier if we first consider each factor separately. Then the interactions between factors may be considered. This can lead to the design of ecological experiments.

The Irish Sea

The contents of seawater

The composition of full seawater and typical river water are compared in the diagram on page 11. Despite the dramatic differences in chemical make-up, most components may be disregarded as environmental factors. Marine organisms are perfectly adapted to this medium. Only in the saltmarsh habitat does salinity figure as a key variable.

To prepare a solution roughly comparable with seawater, dissolve 3.5 grams of common table salt (sodium chloride) in 1 litre of water. Sea water is slightly denser than fresh water, allowing fresh water to float – in the absence of tidal or wind mixing – in the confined waters of the mouth of the Liffey.

The presence of sulphate as a major ingredient is important in mudflats, where it may be chemically modified. Bicarbonate in seawater is part of a complex chemical exchange between atmospheric carbon dioxide and the world's oceans. It is currently known that atmospheric carbon dioxide absorption is leading to increasing acidity of seawater. This has damaging effects on marine creatures with calcium carbonate parts, especially shellfish.

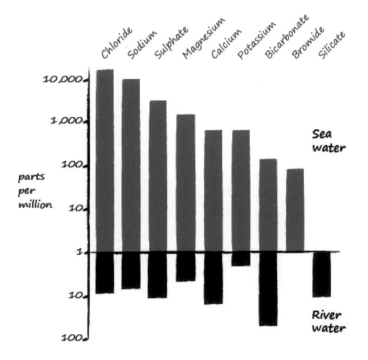

The composition of seawater compared with river water.

The potassium content is of academic interest, as it contributes a very low level of radioactivity to seawater worldwide through the presence of the isotope K^{40}. Isotopes are forms of elements with different nuclear masses but the same chemical properties. This provides a background value against which all other sources of radioactivity may be judged. Sea water is normally relatively free from suspended sediment, but Dublin Bay water can sometimes be quite turbid. Phytoplankton and zooplankton – tiny microscopic plants and animals – are the major particulates.

How tides work

Tides are puzzling to many people. Unless you use the sea regularly, it can be difficult to understand why sea level rises and falls, at different times and by different amounts each day. But the tides are a key to understanding marine life in the sea and on the shore. Tidal currents carry into the bay the plankton and marine detritus that provide the essential 'fuel' for all marine animals, from shellfish to whales. The twice-daily rise and fall of the tide exposes the beaches, where great flocks of wading birds probe for their prey beneath the surface of the

11

Bull Bridge at high tide (left) and at low tide (right) *(Richard Nairn)*

Digging for bait on Sandymount Strand at low tide *(Richard Nairn)*

sand. High tides wash piles of seaweed to the top of the beach, where they are covered by blown sand and provide fertiliser for strandline plants to germinate.

The rise and fall of the tide is due, firstly, to the rotation of the moon around the earth once every 12 hours. Every day we experience two high tides and two low tides. They are caused by the gravitational attraction of the moon and the sun on the earth's oceans.

The second reason for tides is the phase of the moon. When the moon is full or new, the gravitational pull of the sun is aligned with that of the moon, increasing the attraction. The rise of the tide is greater and the fall lower, in what is termed a 'spring' tide. When the moon is at half size the difference between high and low tide is the least and this is known as a 'neap tide' period.

Finally, tidal variation is caused by the slightly elliptical orbits of the moon around the earth and the earth about the sun. This means that the amplitude of a tide has seasonal variation. In a practical sense, both spring and neap tides have slightly lower amplitudes in May, June and July, with full amplitude restored in August. It is, however, possible to calculate the times of high and low tides for a given location, together with the amplitude for each tide. Tide tables for each port are essential for mariners and of great value for all of us who venture into the intertidal zone. The Irish Sea is relatively small (103,600km^2) compared with, say, the Baltic (377,000km^2). Here we can imagine the tidal wave entering from the Atlantic between Carnsore Point, Wexford and St David's Head in Pembrokeshire. The surge moves northwards so the time of high tide becomes later at more northerly east coast ports. The flood (or rising) tide continues for about six and a half hours, some water escaping through the North Channel, the remainder returning by a reversal of the flow as the ebb (or falling) tide. It takes about 12 months for the water of the Irish Sea to be totally renewed by Atlantic seawater. Hence the water of this sea is depleted of nutrients and slightly less saline than the wider Atlantic Ocean.

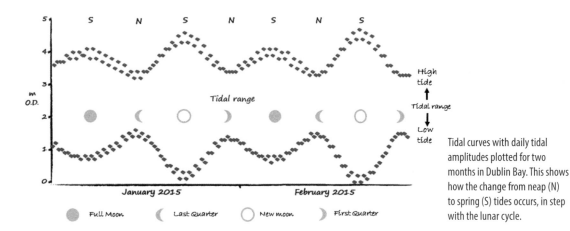

Tidal curves with daily tidal amplitudes plotted for two months in Dublin Bay. This shows how the change from neap (N) to spring (S) tides occurs, in step with the lunar cycle.

The diagram above shows the daily tide heights for two months, so the smooth transition between spring and neap is obvious. In Dublin Bay, and in the Irish Sea, the rise and fall of tides generates a very large turnover of water compared with inputs from rivers. It is a characteristic of Dublin Bay that the tidal flow is asymmetric; the falling part of the cycle is about one hour shorter than the rise. This means that current speed is about 15 per cent faster on the fall (ebb). Tidal flow in the Irish Sea as a whole generates a clockwise rotation of water in Dublin Bay, which has a profound effect on the distribution of sediment from the Liffey. In post-glacial times – the last 13,000 years – tidal currents have redistributed material from a terminal moraine situated between Carnsore Point and St David's Head. The bottom current has sorted sediment by grain size, so that only fine sand predominates in Dublin Bay and the middle reaches of the seabed. This material continues to flow in to Dublin Bay, accumulating mainly at the shoreline.

The Liffey estuary with Poolbeg
peninsula in the foreground
(Peter Barrow)

Rivers and their catchments

The discharge of sediment from a major river into the sea creates what is
known as an estuary. The River Liffey, joined by the River Dodder to the
south and the River Tolka to the north, are the rivers that discharge into
the estuary of Dublin Bay. The highest point of the tide in the Liffey is at
Islandbridge weir, and before the water passes that point, its properties
are very different from seawater. All the elements of salinity are close
to zero, but the river water is rich in sediment. The silt sediment is
derived from the erosion of rocks and particularly glacial sediments in
the valley floor. The other material is organic, and it includes variable
amounts of fine peat from the upper catchment and an autumnal input

14

of leaves from deciduous trees and other plants. The Liffey is a very modified and controlled river, with the large Pollaphuca Reservoir, and a weir at Leixlip. Annual rhythms of sediment transport by the river are discernible, but the system is less responsive to short periods of high rainfall. In contrast, the Dodder and the Tolka rivers are both subject to frequent flooding.

The principles of sediment transport by moving water are explained in the diagram below. When suspended in still water, gravity forces a particle to travel in the direction of the centre of the earth. The rate of sedimentation is determined by the density and diameter of the particle. Most inorganic particles have similar densities, so diameter is the key dimension. A sand grain will fall through water within a few minutes, a silt grain will take many minutes, and a clay particle (diameter less than 63 micrometres) will take many hours.

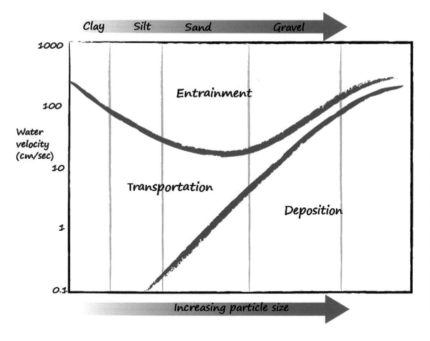

Sediment transport and deposition at a range of current speeds. The smaller the grain size, the longer it remains suspended and the slower a current must be before deposition is possible. Entrainment means that particles already sedimented may be re-suspended for further transport.

When the water is moving, at the speeds common in estuaries and coastal zones, a number of things become clear. First, sand is barely transported by a river current, but may move very close to the bottom. Second, the main material transported and deposited is silt. Small amounts of clay in suspension never get a chance of deposition. Third, the main opportunities for deposition occur when current stops, especially at the turn of the tide or when an obstacle reduces current speed. Fine organic matter has a small diameter and low density so should not settle in an estuary. However, particles tend to flocculate (or clump together) when they come into contact with the relatively concentrated inorganic solution of seawater. In addition, they are often adhering closely to silt particles. In practice, detritus tends to behave in a similar way to silt. The estuarine reaches of rivers are great deposition zones for organic matter and silt.

Sewage is another source of fresh water and nutrients added to the tidal water. In the case of the mouth of the Liffey, waste water from the sewage treatment plant at Ringsend is discharged together with the slightly warm water from the ESB's Poolbeg generating station (now with added capacity provided by several gas-turbine powered generators). This plume of water does not mix immediately, but floats on the underlying water mass. It probably combines with seawater in more turbulent conditions beyond the harbour walls. Since the year 2000 sewage treatment arrangements have been upgraded. Two pumping stations have been built, at Dún Laoghaire and Sutton, which transfer untreated sewage from south and north via two steel pipelines laid under the bay. They terminate in an enlarged and upgraded treatment works at Ringsend. The main consequence is that although the works is treating much more sewage, the discharge of particulates into the Bay has been greatly reduced. The properties of the waters in an estuary may be compared in the table across.

In this simplified comparison, five characteristics of water are compared using four sizes of water drops: the larger the drop, the more important the factor. The table shows that the estuarine zone and, to a lesser extent, the coastal zone generally are full of gradients. From an environmental point of view, mobile organisms can select niches according to their preferences and tolerances. As examples, shoals of grey mullet feed at the edges of the plume of sewage/cooling water, while Atlantic salmon must cross the gradient in salinity from sea to river in the estuary. From an environmental monitoring point of view, scientists are aware that these gradients exist and the positions of boundaries are continuously moving with tidal currents. This means that any measurements of water quality must be qualified by position and tidal state before the data can be interpreted. This makes estuarine monitoring much more complex than monitoring river or lake water quality. Full-strength seawater is clearly salty, but always has low

	Seawater	Cooling water	Sewage	River water
Salts	⬤	⬤	⬤	⬤
Inorganic particles	⬤	⬤	⬤	⬤
Organic particles	⬤	⬤	⬤	⬤
Nutrients	⬤	⬤	⬤	⬤
Temperature	⬤	⬤	⬤	⬤

Simplified comparison of the waters of the coastal zone

values for particulates and nutrients. The annual temperature curve for seawater (winter minimum about 8°C, summer maximum about 15°C) is moderate compared with river water, which also explains the moderating effect of the sea on coastal land. Coastal mist is also a consequence of this difference in temperature.

Cooling water

Generating electricity involves passing high-pressure, high-temperature steam through a turbine. The steam is ultimately cooled in a condenser, transferring heat to an unlimited supply of estuarine water. However, it must be of good quality and unlikely to cause corrosion damage to the bronze condensers of the turbine system. It is also important that fouling, either by algal growth or by shellfish such as mussels, is prevented. Because of these engineering demands, discharged cooling water may contain traces of chlorine and a little dissolved copper, in addition to being several degrees warmer than ambient water.

The estuary forms a potential reactor for the mixture of waters listed above, but one factor that may partially prevent this is the density differences between seawater, river water and even sewage and cooling water with their higher temperatures. In the Liffey we tend to find that fresh water travels to the sea literally on the back of a falling tide. When the tide turns there is more turbulent mixing, which continues while the rising tide is flowing in the opposite direction to the flow of the river. Estuarine conditions allow for the sedimentation of silt and organic

*Cooling water outfall of the
Poolbeg generating station
(Richard Nairn)*

matter, especially in inshore areas. Nutrients (organic carbon, organic
or inorganic nitrogen and phosphorus) may be used immediately –
usually those dissolved in the water – or stored in sediment.

Rocks around the bay

The rocky buttresses of Howth Head and Dalkey Hill, which form the
northern and southern arms of Dublin Bay, are made of the hardest
rocks. Some of the oldest known rocks in Ireland are found at Howth
Head. These are from the Cambrian period, some 500 million years
ago. They were laid down as shales and quartzites in a primeval ocean
that separated two continents and slowly closed during the Ordovician
period about 450 million years ago. The crust of the earth on one side
of the divide was being consumed beneath the other and the resulting
friction would have caused earthquakes and volcanoes. The evidence
for this is found at Portrane on the north Dublin coast and on Lambay
Island, where a distinctive green-flecked rock called andesite outcrops.

Dalkey and Killiney are underlain by the same granite that forms
the spine of the Wicklow Mountains. This is best seen on the shoreline
between the Forty Foot bathing place and Bullock Harbour, where great

blocks of granite resist the erosive power of the waves. At Dalkey quarry, which supplied the building stones for Dún Laoghaire Harbour, the great depth of granite can be appreciated, although it is thought that it may reach down many kilometres into the earth's crust. It was once molten rock that originated below the earth's surface and was slowly exposed as erosion removed the softer rock layers above. During the Devonian period (about 400 million years ago) the granite of the Dublin Mountains was injected deep within the earth's crust. The pressure and heat from this process baked the surrounding rocks and turned them into a type of compressed rock called schist, which can be seen today at Killiney Bay. The molten granite slowly cooled as it rose in the earth's crust, forming the typical speckled white rock that was widely used as a building material in the city of Dublin.

In the centre of the bay, the limestone that forms the low-lying centre of Ireland meets the Irish Sea. However, this rock is deeply buried beneath layers of glacial sands and gravels with fluvial sediments in the central river area. During the Lower Carboniferous period the area was covered by warm, shallow tropical seas where corals, crinoids and shellfish-like creatures called brachiopods lived. The fault separating the limestone from the much older rocks of Howth Head may be readily

Gulls roosting on granite bedrock at Bullock Harbour (*Richard Nairn*)

seen from the shore at the southern end of Sutton Strand and in the cliff at Balscadden Bay, Howth.

If we could cut a cross-section across the limestone in Dublin Bay we would find a major buried channel, the route of the pre-glacial Liffey, first identified by Anthony Farrington in 1929.[2] Away from this channel the bedrock lies at shallow depths below ground level across the central city. The buried channel turns south of the present River Liffey course just to the west of Heuston Station at Islandbridge and then northwards under the Guinness brewery and on towards Broadstone. It then veers north-east towards the North Circular Road area and the East Wall. Here the channel is about 1.5km wide. It then turns south-east towards the sea, running diagonally across the Alexandra Basin and the Ringsend peninsula. This suggests a river meandering across tidal sandflats as it approaches the sea. The ancient channel walls and floor are well defined here by the many boreholes that have been drilled for port development works.

The bedrock lies at more than 40 metres below the surface at Ringsend. The old channel is approximately 2.5km wide at this location. It is believed that the buried channel extends on out into Dublin Bay in a south-easterly direction. As yet there are insufficient boreholes to model the channel much beyond the Great South Wall.

An Ice Age legacy

During the last Ice Age (only about 20,000 years ago) a glacier flowed down the Irish Sea carrying rocks from Scotland, including a distinctive bluish microgranite from Ailsa Craig. This ice met glaciers flowing from the Irish midlands. When it melted it deposited glacial till, or boulder clay, which is well exposed along Killiney beach. Glacial till is widely distributed across central Dublin. These sediments can vary greatly in thickness, from a few metres to more than 20m. The boulder clay contains groundwater. The presence of marine sediments in the glacial materials provides evidence that the sea overran the area now occupied by the east of the city of Dublin. As the ice retreated, the sea again took over the area, laying down a thick sequence (of up to 40m in depth) of intertidal and estuarine deposits overlying glacial till in the Liffey channel downstream of Butt Bridge.[3]

Sea level change

The abandonment of the buried channel by the modern River Liffey for much of its passage through the city centre is due to processes of erosion and deposition related to changes in sea level during the late glacial and post-glacial periods. As the ice retreated, the original channel was re-excavated to almost its original depth (40m) at a time of low sea level, and glacially derived clays and gravels were deposited. Then began a long period of sea level rising in the bay, although the sea level probably rose and fell many times in between. Overlying the till and glacial gravels is a firm to stiff laminated clay with shells deposited in an intertidal or estuarine environment. It has an average thickness of 3–5m but thickens to over 20m in the vicinity of the power station. Then there were foreshore deposits of gravel and sand, followed by offshore deposits of marine clays and sands. At the top of the sequence are the recent mud deposits of the River Liffey. The pre-glacial channel was effectively filled up with these sediments.[4]

After the Ice Age

As the last glaciation finally began to retreat from Ireland, about 13,000 years ago, the Irish Sea was a very different place. The thick glaciers that covered the northern part of the earth had locked up large amounts of the water in the oceans and global sea level was at least 100m lower than it is today. We might imagine the bay as a wide marshy area of

Riparian woodland similar to that which filled Dublin Bay after the Ice Age *(Richard Nairn)*

land between the hills of Howth and Dalkey. Initially, this would have been covered in tundra vegetation, a bit like parts of Iceland today. Meltwater emerging from the front of the glaciers may have formed large subdivided rivers with freezing water finding its way to a sea that still had floating icebergs.

As temperatures gradually rose, the river valley would have been filled with woodland trees such as birch, with willow and alder in the wetter parts. Here, multiple channels wound their way through tangled branches. Herons and otters would have fed in the shallow water with its abundant fish populations. This prehistoric landscape is explored further in Chapter 7.

Climate

In the context of western Europe, the climate of Dublin Bay is moderate. Nevertheless, seasonal variation drives changes in ecosystem activity. In winter there is a big difference between air and sea temperature. Low-temperature episodes in the intertidal zone are offset by the rising tide. In summer, intertidal salinity may rise with prolonged sunshine, until restored by either tidal cover or rainfall. Equally, prolonged rainfall at low tide may reduce salinity briefly.

Rising daily temperatures in spring permit many biological processes to happen in tandem. We can observe spore release of green algae, reproduction in intertidal fauna and increasing microbial activity in sediment, leading to nutrient mineralisation. Late spring to early summer sees the germination of intertidal annual plants and a rising biomass (the term that ecologists use to describe the volume or weight of living material) of algae. Animal numbers rapidly reach a peak, then steadily increase in biomass. By late July/early August, algal and higher-plant growth peaks. Seed and spore production occurs and die-back begins.

Wind is a constant factor on all coasts. But the east coast of Ireland is predominantly a 'lee shore' in the face of the prevailing south-westerly wind. However, onshore winds occur often enough to raise tide heights by at least one metre, causing minor flooding of seafront roads. Storm-driven waves at spring tides in winter may demolish newly accumulated sand dunes.

Climate change

The main basis of climate change science is the observed increase in atmospheric carbon dioxide concentrations over the last 150 years. That is the period of western industrialisation and fossil fuel use. Compared with nitrogen or oxygen, carbon dioxide has a greater capacity to absorb long-wave radiation emitted from the surface of the earth. In this way, carbon dioxide is like the glass of a greenhouse; the more there is, the less heat escapes from the earth into space. The outcome is an observed increase in heat globally, mostly seen as increases in land temperature, although land temperatures have risen more sharply than ocean temperatures in recent decades. However, most of the excess heat energy trapped by the enhanced greenhouse effect has been transferred into the oceans. It has been mixed through the great volume of the oceans in a way that cannot occur on land. Two consequences of this global warming are the thermal expansion of seawater and the melting of land-based ice, leading in the long term to a rise in sea level, currently estimated as 3.2mm per year.[5]

Terrestrial climate scenarios depend on latitude and general geography. The first predicted change for Ireland was that winters would be warmer and wetter and summers warmer and drier.[6] If this proves to be generally correct in the long term, summer conditions may be the most taxing for coastal ecosystems. Higher intertidal salinities may prevail and a slow drift northwards of plant and animal species would occur. This may not represent a major restructuring of the coastal ecosystems. A second prediction is that extreme weather events would occur more frequently because of the higher amounts of energy in the ocean–atmosphere system. Climate change is discussed further in Chapter 12.

Catastrophic events

A catastrophe is an unexpected event in which normal environmental factors are suddenly transcended. They are usually rapid in onset and limited in duration. In ecological terms the communities affected do not have time to adapt and mass mortalities may be an outcome. Catastrophes may be the result of natural or human-caused phenomena.

Storms and floods

Storm surges are one of the most damaging coastal and estuarine phenomena in temperate regions. The 1953 surge, which affected eastern England and the Netherlands, arose as a storm drove a mass of water from the North Sea southwards into the narrow neck of the English Channel. A spring tide had just passed, and recorded tidal heights in the storm were in the order of two metres above those predicted. In the

Netherlands many lives were lost and in England large areas of farmland were inundated with seawater.

The ingredients of this surge were the strength, duration and direction of the wind; the state of the tidal cycle; the shape of the shoreline; and the decreasing depth of the seabed. In the winter of 2013–14 a similar, but less severe, event occurred. At the same time the west coast of Ireland was battered by high waves on top of a high spring tide. This led to comb-down of dunes that had accumulated over centuries, as indicated by the archaeological evidence that was revealed.

What are the chances of a similar event in Dublin Bay? The worst-case scenario is a high spring tide coinciding with storm force winds from the south-east. Heavy rain, producing high volumes of river water, increases the potential flood risk. Wave height is a consequence of the distance that waves can travel over the sea surface – the so-called 'fetch' of the waves. The longest fetch is diagonally across the Irish Sea. Strong winds from this quarter are rare. A strong southerly wind might pile high spring tide water against the neck of the north channel, but it is not clear where the worst floods would occur. What is routinely seen is minor flooding on high spring tides, which indicates greater vulnerability. In the face of predictions of increased frequency of extreme weather events and progressively rising sea levels, a wise policy would be to protect infrastructure. Sand dune systems and other vulnerable habitats will recover in time if conditions are right and human activities allow.

A storm at Bullock Harbour
(John Coveney)

How we affect the coastal environment

Contamination

The growth of Dublin city and its effects on the bay are described in Chapters 7, 8 and 12. Contamination of estuarine and coastal waters is a constant factor associated with cities. It arises from discharge of sewage, discharge of industrial waste, spillage or leakage of cargo or ships' lubricants, freshwater drainage from city streets and roofs, and warm water from power stations. After some fifty years of scientific study, technical development and regulation backed by environmental monitoring have minimised the most adverse effects of deliberate contamination. An interesting feature of contamination is that it is reflected not only in the waters of an estuary, but also in the sediments. For example, it is possible to detect traces of mercury in River Liffey sediment, probably originating from long-vanished paper mills on a tributary. Catastrophic accidents are another matter that may only be addressed by contingency plans.

Contaminants can be divided into two categories: a) potentially harmful substances or micro-organisms; b) nutrients of potential value to plants. In either case science is needed to determine if the concentration of the substance is biologically significant. Only when significant concentrations of contaminants are detected may they be regarded as 'pollutants'.

Oil pollution

Catastrophic pollution by spilt oil was a real hazard to coastal waters until international co-operation resulted in tightening of regulations in the oil industry. Fortunately, very few minor oil spills have occurred in Dublin Bay. However, since Dublin is a major oil trans-shipment port, an oil pollution contingency plan has been in place for many years. If a spill occurs, wind and tide will disperse it widely. Containment by booms and recovery of the oil is a first priority, but is difficult to achieve in practice. Fugitive oil has a number of fates. Lighter fractions may evaporate or actually dissolve in water. Even at low concentrations, dissolved hydrocarbons may be toxic to plankton. More serious is the chance of food web concentration, in which the amount of hydrocarbon increases at each step of the chain. For example, the links in one chain would be plankton→invertebrate→fish→bird or mammal, with the bird and marine mammal populations being the most seriously affected.

The bulk of the oil will float, and move with the current, with increasing amounts being emulsified with time as a result of wave action. The small droplets of oil in water often combine with silt particles and are added to the sediments. They may be ingested by filter or deposit feeders and again enter a food web. At one time emulsifying chemicals were deliberately sprayed onto oil slicks to 'disperse' them, but all they did was to hasten the slick to the sediment. Also in many cases the oil/ dispersant mix was actually more toxic than the oil alone! Current flow and wave action tend to drive slicks inshore, where they are grounded. Contamination of bathing beaches can be an economic disaster for local people. The quick and expensive solution is to scoop up contaminated sand and spread it in a suitable place. A slick that drifts on to a saltmarsh is effectively immobilised, and no attempt should be made to remove it. Micro-organisms exist on shorelines that efficiently decompose hydrocarbons under aerobic conditions. This process has now developed into a technology in which a suitable culture in a nutrient medium is sprayed on to a landed slick and time takes its course. A problem not yet solved is the treatment of birds directly fouled by floating oil. Many mortalities usually result, in spite of efforts to clean birds with detergents. In Dublin Bay this fact alone must encourage authorities to maintain their guard against spills.

Amenity pressures

Dublin Bay is the largest public amenity area on the east coast of Ireland in terms of the number of people it can accommodate. The greatest numbers simply walk or cycle the promenades above high-tide mark. These year-round users leave virtually no impact, not even disturbing roosting birds. Beaches attract large numbers and huge densities of summer visitors. The impact of these visitors and their vehicles has been much debated internationally and will be discussed further in Chapter 11. All the other users of the amenity have more specialised needs. Yacht and sailing clubs have established premises around the bay. Water quality is an important consideration for small-boat sailors and other water contact sport participants, such as swimmers, sub-aqua divers, sport fishermen and beach users. The main issue is managing sewage treatment to minimise pathogenic microbes, including viruses.

Golf links are well established on Bull Island. This has amounted to the replacement of one amenity resource with another – to be discussed further in Chapters 5 and 11. Education about the bay is largely concentrated at Booterstown Marsh and Bull Island. Although protected, both sites are accessible, especially for watching the remarkable numbers of migratory birds. The sheer range and scope of amenities in the bay both enhance the quality of life of people in the city and attract visitors. In our view the slight collective impact on the ecosystem is offset by the benefits to well-being and people's health. Clearly, these amenities must be managed as a priority alongside other economic needs such as port development.

The promenade at Clontarf
(*John Fox*)

How ecosystems work

An ecosystem is a community of living organisms in conjunction with the non-living components of their environment (for example air, water and mineral soil), interacting as a system. More recently, the idea of 'ecological goods and services' – worth about three times global GDP

– has been introduced. Estuaries and wetlands are the most valuable of these.[7] In a given ecosystem, organisms are classified according to their ecological function: primary producers (such as plants); consumers or predators (such as birds); and decomposers (such as bacteria). Energy flows through this system, together with minerals and other substances (see diagram on facing page).

Practical methods of determining these flows are relatively simple. For example, in many coastal habitats, taking a core sample of appropriate diameter (surface area) will enable all the animals attached to or buried in the seabed and any plants in an area to be counted. Numbers of animals may be converted to weights (biomass) or energy equivalents. Plants are treated in the same way. When this sampling is repeated at (say) monthly intervals, growth (equals energy capture or loss) may be measured. If chemical analysis of organisms is performed, flows of minerals, for example nitrogen or phosphorus, or other substances may be estimated. This approach totally fails to take mobile animals such as fish and birds into account, but they can be counted by different methods. Water samples provide measurements of detritus and plankton, but it is difficult to combine these with other living things directly.

Solar energy is the only sustainable source of energy at earth's surface and plants are the only organisms capable of fixing it. Energy is embodied in carbon-to-carbon chemical bonds. Common examples are sugar, starch and cellulose. At its simplest, a grazing animal, for example a snail, a limpet or a brent goose will consume plants. In turn they will be consumed by their particular predators, the carnivores. Energy is lost through these transactions as faeces and as metabolism plus body heat loss in warm-blooded vertebrates.

Animal faeces, together with the dead parts of animals and plants, represent a secondary source of energy, termed 'detritus'. Detritus is also an important carrier and reservoir of nitrogen. Detritus plays a pivotal role in aquatic ecosystems, where it may also be imported or exported with the flow of a river or the turn of the tide. This is an important source of organic carbon and thus energy for many animals and microbes. It also contains valuable organic nitrogen, which is the main limiting factor to growth in coastal communities. Research into coastal ecosystem dynamics is important in fishery and wildlife management and in monitoring marine pollution.

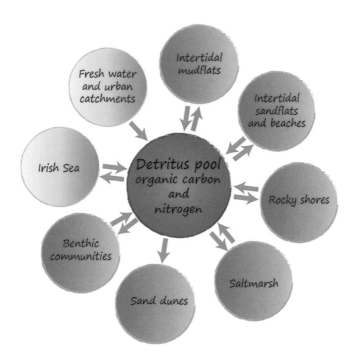

Detritus in Dublin Bay. The diagram indicates how most of the habitats described consume or produce detritus.

What is a habitat?

A habitat is a unique environmental complex, defined by settings or levels of several environmental factors. Each habitat accommodates a community of organisms. These communities – plants, animals, and micro-organisms – are adapted to survive and flourish under the defining conditions. Within habitats there are 'niches' for plants, animals and micro-organisms. This concept includes the particular non-living complex together with the interactions with living organisms. To paraphrase a zoologist's definition, 'habitat' is an animal's address, 'niche' is an animal's profession.

In the Dublin Bay tidal ecosystem, four groups of habitat can be recognised. The sub-tidal habitat is always immersed in seawater and continually exposed to the tidal currents of the Irish Sea. There are three transitional habitat sequences which are mainly intertidal, but a link to land habitats may be justified in ecosystem terms. The sequence most subject to wave action is the transition from rocky shore to cliff or island. The link to the intertidal and seabed habitats is through the feeding of birds and subsequent transfer of nutrients. Also subject to strong currents and waves is the transition from intertidal sand flats to beach and sand dune. Finally, in intertidal areas sheltered from waves and where tidal currents are minimal lies the transition from mudflat to saltmarsh.

Linkage between these habitat sequences is provided by the same tidal rhythm and the supply and renewal of detritus as a carrier of organic carbon and nitrogen. This justifies regarding the whole of Dublin Bay as a single ecosystem. The broad habitat groups of marine (below low tide), intertidal (between low- and high-tide marks) and terrestrial (above high-tide mark) are described in the next three chapters.

3 | Marine Life

The sea is the life-support system for most of the wildlife in Dublin Bay. It powers the ecosystem of both the deeper water and the area between the high and low tide marks. It is also probably the least-understood part of the bay as much of it is out of sight and out of mind. For centuries, the fisheries of Dublin Bay and neighbouring parts of the Irish Sea fed thousands of city dwellers and provided much-needed employment on fishing boats. These fish populations, with the abundant seabirds and marine mammals, are all part of a diverse marine ecosystem.

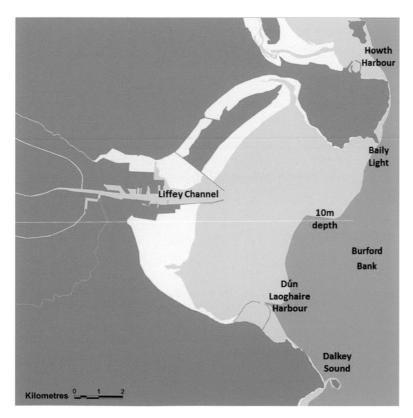

Dublin Bay marine areas. Shallow water between low water mark and 10m depth are shown in light blue.

The world of plankton

In the introduction to his classic book *The Open Sea*,[1] Sir Alister Hardy explained that the strangeness to us of life in the oceans is not just because most of it is out of our sight. The plants and animals that live below the surface are so different from our familiar neighbours on land that they could be from a different planet. The word plankton comes from the Greek word *planktos*, which means drifting or wandering beyond its own control. This drifting habit distinguishes plankton from the swimming creatures – fish, seabirds and marine mammals *or nektos*. It also separates it from the *benthos* – those animals that live on the seabed or buried in the sediments. Nearly all the small animals we find on the shores of Dublin Bay have spent some part of their lives drifting among the plankton in the surface layers of the sea. Shore crabs begin life as miniature larvae floating far out in the sea. Here they are among the eggs and juvenile forms of fish, jellyfish and millions of other tiny creatures. The plankton is a mixture of microscopic animals (zooplankton) and plants (phytoplankton) and the numbers of species and individuals are beyond most people's comprehension. There may be over 50,000 microscopic plants known as diatoms in a single cupful of seawater. The weight of single-celled plants drifting over an area of sea the size of a typical garden is equivalent to a crop of potatoes. Many of the planktonic plants and animals rise to the sea surface at night, sinking again by day, followed by the fish shoals that feed on them.

Navigation mark near the Kish Lighthouse *(John Fox)*

The production of phytoplankton and a chlorophyll standing crop has been studied in the western Irish Sea and here the season lasts 3–4 months in the summer. In more northerly waters the season is shorter at two to three months.[2] The Dublin Bay prawn drifts as larvae in the plankton of the Irish Sea. The greatest numbers of larvae are found at a depth of 18–27 metres by day, ascending by approximately 9 metres around dusk.[3] In Dublin Bay phytoplankton blooms occur in high-salinity waters due to the mixing of seawater, which is low in nutrients, and nutrient-rich river waters. The average annual flux of phytoplankton carbon from the River Liffey has been calculated at 23.5 tonnes of carbon per year, of which half was accumulated or remineralised in the river estuary and did not enter the bay.[4]

Jellyfish

The warm summer temperatures often bring plenty of jellyfish into the sheltered waters of Dublin Bay. These beautiful animals drift with the tides and winds but are usually dead or dying by the time they strand on the beach.

The compass jellyfish is common in summer *(John Fox)*

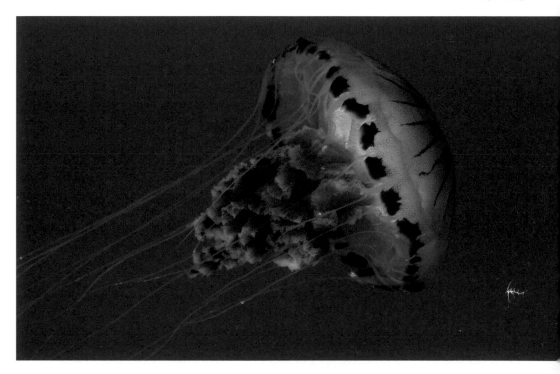

The common moon jellyfish feeds by trapping tiny plankton all over its surface. In summer there are many larger barrel jellyfish in the Irish Sea. The bell-shaped body can measure up to a metre across. There are occasional visits to Dublin Bay by other more dangerous species such as the Portuguese man o' war, which is actually a colony rather than an individual. This colony can kill a person with the poison in its sting. All jellyfish can sting and they should not be touched even when stranded on the beach. Most jellyfish begin life as polyps that break off from a colony and become free-swimming *medusae* – in effect tiny jellyfish – in the plankton. As the jellyfish grow they migrate towards the sun, which brings mature adults into sheltered spawning areas such as Dublin Bay. After breeding is finished the jellyfish are often dispersed by winds and tides, possibly because their ability to swim in one direction declines as they near the end of their lifespan. This is when large numbers of jellyfish come ashore on beaches such as Dollymount and Sandymount strands.

Life on the seabed

The water in Dublin Bay is mainly Irish Sea water with a relatively small contribution from the Liffey and other catchments. The floor of the bay is mainly clean, fine sand, derived from middle Irish Sea sediment, with the addition of silt from fresh water. The sand is 'clean' because it is relatively free from organic matter. The sediment shifts about with the tides and all burrowing animals need to stabilise their burrows.

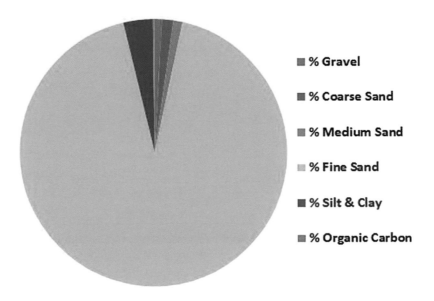

- ■ % Gravel
- ■ % Coarse Sand
- ■ % Medium Sand
- ▨ % Fine Sand
- ■ % Silt & Clay
- ■ % Organic Carbon

Average composition of sediments on the floor of Dublin Bay

The biological make-up of the bay is complex, because there is continuity between the sea, the intertidal zones, the estuarine zone and the fresh water beyond tidal influence. The benthic zone is below the lowest recorded low tide mark and this is occupied by a diverse community of fish and smaller animals living either on the seabed or buried just below the surface.

Energy supply to benthic organisms is from two different sources: phytoplankton and detritus. Phytoplankton is at its lowest over winter, growing rapidly in spring. At this time of year dissolved nutrients in seawater are at their highest and the water temperature is rising rapidly.

Phytoplankton growth outpaces its consumption by zooplankton or other predators. By the summer, predation and lack of nutrients cause population growth to cease, even though water temperatures are near their yearly maximum. In some seasons there may be a short autumnal increase in population, before it drifts down to the winter minimum.

Because detritus arises from many different sources, it is difficult to estimate which are the most important at any particular time of year. Faecal pellets are produced by all the animals in the ecosystem and are accompanied by a rich bacterial population. Detritus is imported from (and exported to) adjacent water masses. Inshore communities make their contribution, and so do freshwater sources, especially in autumn.

A study of animal communities living on the seabed of Dublin Bay was carried out by a team from the Benthos Research Group, University College Galway in August–September 1989.[5] They divided the fauna into three communities, which differed slightly in species composition. However, the main picture was of densely packed burrow-forming invertebrates that fed largely on detritus. In the most widespread community, the team counted 17 different species with some 5,700 individual animals per square metre. While it comprised mainly polychaete worms, the community also included bivalves and crustacea.

One of the most abundant species on the seabed is the sand mason worm which is present in all the three communities and which is now known to be a key species in the ecology of the bay.

The sand mason worm lives in clean sand below low water mark where its crown of tentacles waves in the tide searching for food particles in the water. The worms collect particles of sand and broken pieces of shell, selecting fragments of just the right size for building the tubes that protect their soft bodies. The worms are up to 30 centimetres in length, with many segments that are yellow, pink and brown in colour, although the bushy gills are coloured blood red. Some shorebirds, such as bar-tailed godwit, that wade in water up to 10cm deep, can feed on sand mason worms at extreme low tide.

In June 1989, an event occurred that was directly connected with the ecology of the sand mason worm. A large mass of unpleasant-looking brown material drifted ashore from the deeper water. Covering most of the 5.5km of Dollymount Strand, the Bull Island beach, it was up to 30cm deep and several metres wide. The press made much of the event, wrongly likening it to raw sewage. The slimy brown material was a fine, branched, brown seaweed with the scientific name *Ectocarpus siliculosus*.

Sand mason worm on the seabed *(Vincent Hyland)*

This little seaweed is recorded occasionally on the rocky shores of Howth and the granite shores of south Dublin Bay. The key question was why should a rocky shore species grow so prolifically, yielding some 1,000 tonnes of dry matter on the beach? The question was partially answered by sending out a team of divers to collect samples and take photographs in the benthic area immediately east of the beach. They found that each strand of seaweed was originally anchored to a tube of the sand mason worm. At a certain point in the growth of the plant it became too buoyant and broke free. For the previous three weeks the wind in the bay had been exceptionally light. The absence of strong wave action had permitted the delicate structure to accumulate. The other key question was where did the nutrients, mainly nitrogen, for this production come from? The answer must surely be that nitrogen is liberated by each sand mason worm when it consumes protein-rich organic matter for its own needs. The sand mason liberates an ammonium-rich 'urine', which is an ideal nitrogen source for *Ectocarpus*. There was a minor outbreak in 1990, but on the whole this nuisance has not recurred and it seems to be a feature of very calm and warm spring periods.

Fish in the sea

Several surveys of the Lower Liffey and the Tolka estuaries by Inland Fisheries Ireland have found that sprat, sand goby and juvenile mullet are by far the most common fish here, with sand smelt and, occasionally, cod also prominent. In May and June 2013, a number of beam trawls were taken within a study area stretching from Alexandra Basin West to the Dublin Bay Buoy.[6] This survey was undertaken to assess the main benthic fish and mobile invertebrates within and adjacent to the dredging area for the shipping channel. Fourteen fish species were captured in the trawls, although many of these would not be well known to anglers. The trawls also contained at least 25 species of invertebrates, mainly mobile species such as crabs and shrimps, but also starfish, brittle stars, sea slugs and many other small animals. Most of the fish found in this study were marine migrant species such as plaice and dab, which use estuaries primarily as nursery grounds but usually spawn and spend much of their adult life at sea. Some of the fish, such as Nilsson's pipefish and sand goby, are more at home in estuarine conditions as they can tolerate a wide range of salinity. There were also a few species of marine stragglers, such as scaldfish, which are occasionally found in the lower reaches of estuaries. The type of sampling gear used in this study would not have captured the more mobile fish species on the seabed such as lesser spotted dogfish, cod, and large flat fish (also known as demersal species). Nor would the trawls capture faster-moving pelagic species such as herring, mackerel and sand eel in the upper layers of the sea.

The lesser sand eel is one of the most abundant pelagic fish in Dublin Bay. They have a silvery appearance and can live in quite shallow water near high tide mark or move out to deeper water. In summer, great shoals of sand eels move into shallow water to spawn. Eggs are laid in the softer sand, where they stick to sand grains. Each female can produce up to 20,000 eggs, which will hatch within a few weeks. Sand eels are an important component of the diet of many seabirds, including razorbills, guillemots and terns (see Chapter 6). They are also hunted by seals and porpoises. This makes them a keystone species in the estuarine ecosystem.

Salmon smolts travel to sea from the Liffey in the spring to early summer period (March to May), while a small number of adults (spring salmon) return in February–March, and grilse (salmon that have spent one winter at sea) return in summer and autumn. Two other rivers that flow through Dublin, the Dodder and Tolka, also have smaller

Grey seal feeding on a plaice
(Richard Nairn)

Common tern carrying a sand eel back to its nest *(John Fox)*

populations of salmon and sea trout. The lower reaches of the Dodder are best for sea trout, and in 2010, Inland Fisheries Ireland (IFI) scientists recorded juvenile salmon in the lower reaches of the Tolka, suggesting that there may be some salmon spawning in this river too.

Recreational fisheries

Sea angling is a popular pastime in Dublin Bay, and growing year by year. Angling from small boats is often concentrated around harbours such as Howth, Dún Laoghaire or Bullock Harbour, where boats can be hired. The main species fished are mackerel (in summer), and some pollack. All the piers are used to fish for mackerel, with particular concentrations of anglers on Dún Laoghaire piers and the Great South Wall in Dublin Port. Herring are also taken from piers, and some mackerel are still being caught as late as December. Bass are taken mainly from shore or from kayaks and they have also become more common in recent times.

Lesser spotted dogfish is very commonly caught by line fishermen in Dublin Bay, while smooth-hound, another member of the shark family, has become quite a common visitor in the last few years during late summer and early autumn. The species is mainly being caught (using crab as bait) in deeper water outside the bay, although an occasional catch has been reported from the Great South Wall. Spurdog, which were extremely common off Howth about two decades ago, are now very rare, having declined dramatically in the whole Irish Sea area over the past few decades. Rays are not generally caught within the bay but may be fished on the offshore banks such as the Burford and Kish. Flounder, plaice, dab, gurnard, whiting, coalfish, haddock and codling are also caught on these shallow banks. Thornback seems to be the most common ray species in the area, but spotted (Homelyn), cuckoo and blonde rays are also known in this part of the Irish Sea.

Commercial fisheries

Commercial fishing is quite limited today in the open waters of Dublin Bay, and none is undertaken within the main shipping channel, due to the need for navigational safety. Traditionally, the bay was the site of three types of commercial fishing: drift netting for salmon; inshore trawling for rays and plaice; and potting for brown and velvet crabs, lobster and whelk. Drift netting for salmon ceased in January 2007 following the countrywide ban on the practice, while trawling declined in the 1980s due to the increase in the size of fishing vessels and the perceived lack of fish in the bay. Small-scale pot fishing for crab and lobster is still carried out on rocky seabed areas on the northern and southern approaches to the Bay around Howth and Dún Laoghaire.

Trawling in the waters off Howth *(John Fox)*

The main fishery around the Kish and Bray banks is for whelks, which are primarily landed into Dún Laoghaire and Howth harbours by small boats. The surrounding area is extensively trawled for haddock, plaice and spurdog, although very little trawling occurs inside the 20m-deep contour area around the banks.

Marine mammals

The top deck of a ferry leaving Dublin Port is an ideal vantage point to look for marine mammals. When the ship is crossing the bay towards the Kish lighthouse, you may get a glimpse of a small black triangular fin or the curved back of a porpoise as it surfaces briefly for air. The harbour porpoise is the smallest and the commonest cetacean found in Irish waters. In Dublin Bay, it reaches some of the highest densities so far recorded in Ireland. In 2008, Simon Berrow and his colleagues from the Irish Whale and Dolphin Group carried out a targeted survey of harbour porpoise in the Dublin Bay area.[7] Zigzagging across the outer bay, they made an estimate of 138 porpoises in the whole of Dublin Bay. One of the best places to see harbour porpoises from land is the cliff path around Howth Head. Their small curved backs appear again and again in the fast-flowing tides that surge around the Baily lighthouse and into Dublin Bay. There are also regular sightings of porpoises from the rocks above Dalkey Sound, where the tide races through from Killiney Bay to Dublin Bay. It may be that their prey, small shoaling fish, are more concentrated or easier to catch in these tidal races.

Harbour porpoise off Dún Laoghaire *(John Fox)*

There are also many records of dolphins in Dublin Bay. The most frequently reported species is the bottlenose dolphin, and three individuals appeared to take up residence in the Dalkey/Killiney Bay area in 2011. Many members of the public watched their breaching displays from the road, train, boat or sea kayak and this celebrated group even made it on to the RTÉ television news. Minke whales, smallest of the baleen whales, are occasionally recorded in the Dublin area. They usually surface briefly to breathe (blow), showing the small dorsal fin with a part of the back. They are sometimes seen from passing ferries entering or leaving Dublin Port. The larger whales feed by filtering large volumes of seawater through their mouths where the closely spaced plates of baleen act like a sieve to separate the tiny planktonic organisms from the water. Humpback whales, once thought extinct in Irish waters, have been sighted a number of times in the Dublin area in recent years. In July 2010 a humpback whale crossed the path of the Irish Ferries vessel *Ulysses* south-east of Howth Head.

Minke whale *(John Fox)*

There are two common species of seal in Irish waters – the harbour seal and the larger grey seal. Both can be seen in Dublin Bay, but they can be difficult to tell apart, especially when the animals are young. All seals spend part of every day in the sea feeding and part of the day on land, where they rest, digest their food and replace the oxygen that they need in their blood when they perform deep dives. Lying on rocks or beaches is known in the seal world as 'hauling out'. In Dublin Bay there are regular seal haul-outs on the northern tip of Bull Island and in Dalkey Sound. In the latter location, the mainly grey seals are very tolerant of visitors and will even swim around kayaks with great curiosity. On Bull Island they are more wary because they are often chased by dogs here and they normally retreat to the water for safety. Some grey seals also haul out on Ireland's Eye.

Grey seal with pup at Dalkey Island *(Richard Nairn)*

Breeding (or pupping) by either seal species in Dublin Bay itself is unusual as the pups are quite vulnerable to disturbance. Occasionally grey seal pups are born on Dalkey Island or Howth Head. Young pups are sometimes found on Bull Island. However, the island of Lambay, 11km to the north of Howth, offers very secure breeding places and many pups are born here each year. The grey seals give birth to their pups mainly in caves and on cliff-bound beaches in the autumn months. The white-coated young animals are very vulnerable as they must remain on land, suckling from their mothers, for up to three weeks before they moult the white coat and take to the sea. Harbour seals, in contrast, often give birth in shallow water and the pups can swim almost immediately. Until the 1970s both seal species were regularly hunted by fishermen as they were seen as serious competitors for valuable fish such as salmon. Since

1995 they have had the protection of the European Habitats Directive and numbers of both species have recovered.

Rachel Carson wrote that 'the face of the sea is always changing. The surface waters move with the tides, stir to the breath of the winds and rise and fall to the endless forms of the waves. Most of all, they change with the advance of the seasons.'[8] The sea is the vital link between all the habitats and species in Dublin Bay. Its tides wash the shores and feed the animals that live there. Sediments are eroded from the cliffs and deposited on the beaches, where the finer sand is lifted by the wind to form sand dunes. These shorelines and the lands near the coast are explored in the next two chapters.

Harbour seal at Bull Island
(John Fox)

4 | Shorelines

I n *Ulysses* James Joyce describes Stephen Dedalus taking a walk on Sandymount Strand. Even in the century since Joyce wrote that passage, the beaches of Dublin Bay have changed – sometimes dramatically. The massive industrial structures of the port now dominate the landscape when viewed from either north or south and the sandy shorelines have moved in response. Today, daily tides and easterly storms move the sand around and change the shape of the bay in such a gradual way that most people hardly notice. Some of the changes in the bay have also had a profound influence on its wildlife.

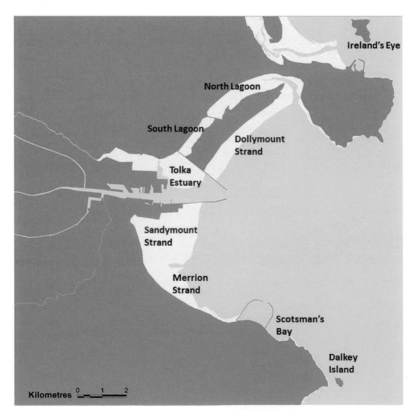

Dublin Bay with intertidal areas shown in yellow

Dublin Bay is a large sheltered inlet of the Irish Sea protected to north and south by rocky headlands. The area between the low and high spring tide marks, known as the intertidal zone, ranges from steep rocky shores to wide, open sand flats, mudflats and saltmarshes. There is a remarkable diversity of shoreline types, from very exposed to highly sheltered conditions, and the flora and fauna reflect this diversity.

Shoreline life

In Dublin Bay, the area between the tides is dominated by sandy habitats. However, there are other intertidal habitat types – mudflats, saltmarsh, mussel beds, rocky shore and sea walls – that are often overlooked. Sand dunes, rocky shores, cliffs and islands – which are largely above high tide mark – are discussed in Chapter 5.

Life on sandy shores

At first sight the extensive sands of Dublin Bay look lifeless and barren, but the large numbers of birds feeding at low tide and the people who regularly dig for bait here suggest otherwise. After an easterly storm the strandline is often awash with a wide variety of shells and other marine life that gives some indication of the hidden variety to be found in the bay. Dig just a few centimetres below the surface of the wetter sand and a rich variety of marine life is exposed. Larger mollusc shells such as cockles, tellins and razorshells and a bewildering variety of marine worms emerge from their sandy burrows. The reason a beach appears to be so devoid of life is simply that the sand is unstable compared with a rock surface, so the animals must live within the beach rather than on it.[1]

Bait-digging in the Tolka Estuary *(John Fox)*

Over the last century or so, many naturalists have collected shoreline samples in Dublin Bay. One group, the conchologists, who study shelled animals, have found Dublin Bay a rich collecting ground over the years. One of the earliest of these marine biologists was Albert R. Nichols, who in 1899 produced a list of the marine shellfish of Ireland.[2] He was followed by Rowland Southern, who made a special study of the marine worms of Dublin Bay and adjoining coasts, which he published in 1910.[3] Many other studies have been undertaken by staff and students of the Dublin universities, including an account by Brian West of the fauna of the intertidal flats and beach around Bull Island.[4] This thorough study distinguished between the animal communities found in the sheltered mudflats and sandflats on the landward side of the island and those found on the more exposed beach on the seaward side facing Dublin Bay.

It was not until 1982 that a comprehensive account of the intertidal life of the whole of Dublin Bay was produced, by James Wilson of Trinity College Dublin.[5] Wilson has an unrivalled knowledge, accumulated through nearly four decades of study, with numerous publications, on marine molluscs and their connections with the pollution status of the bay. His most extensive study of the bay was undertaken by simply digging out a square of sand (a quadrat) measuring one quarter of a square metre, at intervals of 250 metres on a grid covering the entire intertidal part of the bay. By digging down to 25cm below the surface at each of these quadrats, Wilson managed to systematically sample a total of 313 sites in 1977. His results gave a remarkably clear picture of what lay below the flat sands of Dublin Bay. The 74 species of macrofauna (larger animals) he uncovered allowed Wilson to classify four main biotopes or communities of animals.

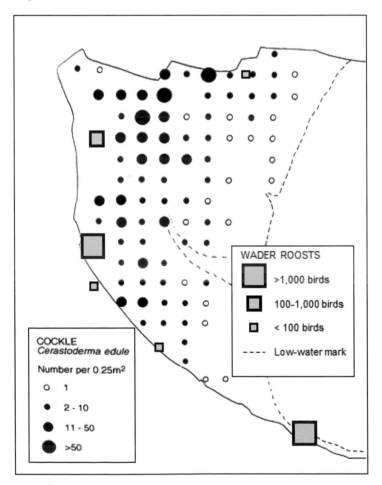

Map of cockle density in south Dublin Bay (after Wilson 1982) with roosts of wading birds

The first of these biotopes was at the lowest edge of the sands – a place only exposed for a very short time twice a day at low water. Here the sand was well washed by wave action and was characterised by ragworms, sand mason worms and thin tellin shells. The second community was found in the middle and upper shores, which contain rather siltier sand, inhabited by the cockle, the Baltic tellin, and by various polychaete worms. The third zone, the muddy lagoons to landward of Bull Island, were characterised by the peppery furrow shell and locally abundant populations of the laver spire shell and the crustacean *Corophium volutator*. Occasional mussel beds were found in this third zone, but only where post-glacial gravels were revealed. The final major biotope in the bay was represented by the muddy sands in the Tolka Estuary, where ragworms were especially characteristic and where few bivalves were recorded.

Although they can only be seen under a microscope, there is known to be a rich population of flora and fauna living *between* the sand grains on beaches. This is a community of tiny, microscopic organisms, known as 'meiofauna'. Between roughly spherical sand grains there is a space

Simplified and generalised food web based on intertidal habitats. At high tide mobile benthic species may move in to feed.

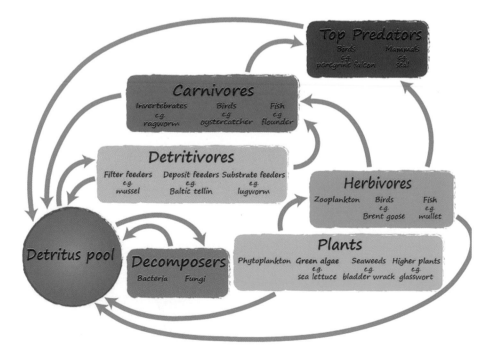

of up to 40 per cent of total volume. The space is filled by either water or air. The interstitial community includes bacteria, fungi, micro-algae, protozoa and a rich meiofauna of microscopic animals. Each wave crashing on to a beach allows water to be replaced and the possibility of traces of detrital organic matter carried by seawater to be captured by the biofilms of bacteria surrounding each grain. When a grain dries, the biofilm remains as a coat, and may be transported with the blown grain. The meiofauna is believed to be an important link between organic detritus and the larger organisms.

Wilson noted that there was 'little evidence of any estuarine influence on Dublin Bay as a whole, and the fauna of that area enclosed by the harbour walls and the Bull Island causeway differed little, within limits of habitat, from that outside'. He made special mention of the inner Tolka basin, which had much less fauna than the rest of the bay. He believed this impoverishment was due to the high silt content and the pollution load accumulated in the sediments rather than to the fresh water brought down by the Tolka River. In the 1970s, when his sampling was carried out, parts of this area could be described as 'abiotic' or without life, while the rest of Dublin Bay showed little evidence of pollution. By comparison with the impoverished nature of the Tolka Estuary at that time, the lagoons behind Bull Island were among the richest zones of the bay, both in terms of diversity of marine life and biomass. It is not surprising that this area also has the highest densities of bird life in winter as they are attracted to feed mainly on marine worms and shellfish.

To interpret the patterns of marine animals in the intertidal area, their feeding habits need to be understood. The pioneering work of James Wilson was later subjected to more detailed analysis by Steffen Roth of the University of Jena in Germany during a research period at Trinity College Dublin.[6] Although there is still considerable uncertainty about exact feeding habits and diets of many marine animals, each of the 74 species sampled by Wilson in 1977 was assigned to a trophic guild (or feeder type) to group the sample data into functional communities. The animals were classified into the following categories: carnivore, omnivore, commensal, deposit feeders, substratum ingesters, suspension feeders, suspension/deposit feeders, suspension/carnivore, and herbivore (grazer). The number and weight of animals in each group was calculated. The abundance and biomass values of each species with the same feeding type were added for each of the sample sites and the principal trophic structure was then determined for each of Wilson's

313 sample sites. Roth's analysis suggests different animal assemblages in the north and south bays, a difference which Wilson had been unable to detect. Deposit feeders were restricted to the muddy lagoons and to some upper shore sites. Sediment ingesters such as the bristle worm and the much larger lugworm were much more widespread.

Empty cockle shells are very common on the surface of the beaches at Sandymount and Dollymount. Cockles live their entire lives buried in clean sand using their big fleshy foot to pull themselves under the surface. They can burrow deeper in the sand to avoid being eaten by a passing flatfish such as a plaice or a bird such as an oystercatcher. The most vulnerable parts of the cockle are its soft siphons, which are like two hosepipes stretching to the water above the sand. Using one siphon as an inflow and the other as an outflow, the shellfish constantly filters seawater through its body. From the water, it filters out tiny planktonic food items and organic detritus. The ridges and furrows on the shell of the cockle help it to anchor itself in the mobile sand. Cockles are so plentiful on Sandymount Strand that part of the beach is called Cockle Lake.

Life on muddy shores

The environment of muddy shores differs profoundly from freely draining and aerobic sands. A few millimetres below the surface, the mud is black, indicating the presence of iron sulphide. This means that oxygen is absent. The reasons are twofold. First, fine inorganic silt grains have very small spaces between them, which trap water. This does not permit drainage between tides. The second reason is the organic detritus, deposited together with silt, which is a rich source of energy for marine bacteria. They rapidly utilise dissolved oxygen in seawater, and then change to living without oxygen. Several important ecological effects result from this change.

The fauna of the mudflats in the Bull Island lagoons was described by Brian West, who noted that animals living in the finer muds, where the organic content is at its highest, face the problem of lack of oxygen as the anaerobic layer is often only a few millimetres below the surface.[7] The invertebrates here survive either by possessing physiological adaptations that allow them to survive temporarily in airless sediments or by maintaining pipelines (or siphons) to the surface. Commonest species in the mudflats are the tiny spire shell *Hydrobia* and the shrimp-like crustacean *Corophium*. A huge variety of microscopic worms live here too, together with the larger ragworm, which is one of the preferred

Cockle shells and live mussels on Sandymount Strand
(Richard Nairn)

Curlew feeding on a lugworm
(Karl Partridge)

prey items of the wading birds. The muddiest areas are where the tidal movements are slowest, allowing the finer particles to settle out of the seawater. These are generally in the most sheltered areas of Dublin Bay such as the mouth of the River Tolka, the lagoons on the landward side of Bull Island and the inner parts of Sandymount Strand near Irishtown. Booterstown Marsh also has some fine muddy shores, but it is strongly influenced by fresh water at low tide, which makes it brackish with a different type of plant and animal community.

The Bull Island lagoons

The development of Bull Island in the nineteenth century created an extremely sheltered area between the island and the mainland of Clontarf. The area known as the Bull Island lagoons, north-east of the wooden bridge, was originally a single shallow creek. The building of a solid causeway across this creek in 1964 was motivated by Dublin Corporation policy to provide access to the greater part of Dollymount Strand for amenity reasons. Before the causeway, the northern end was a relatively remote place, accessible only via the wooden bridge or by boat across Sutton Creek. Before 1964 tidal waters from the two ends of the Bull Island channel met and mixed at a point between the Naniken Brook and the Santry River. This meeting point was a place of minimum flow and a site of sediment deposition. The pattern of saltmarsh development on either side of the channel suggests this. Nevertheless, the main pattern of saltmarsh growth for the next century was parallel to the main axis of the island. As nearly 200 metres breadth of saltmarsh was laid down in that period, it may be deduced that a considerable volume of silt was entering the system and being captured or deposited. Since the origin of this material is primarily the River Liffey, there is no reason to suppose the annual volume of silt available for capture has altered.

When the causeway was constructed, its location was determined by the meeting point of the tides. Although large-diameter concrete conduit pipes were laid in the main line of the channel, these rapidly became choked with silt. The causeway created two independent lagoon-like basins, each fed by separate freshwater sources and inflows of tidal water. Fifty years later, each has its own characteristics.

The south lagoon receives tidal water from the Liffey and the Tolka rivers. Because of its smaller size, and lower silt content in the tidal water, it is a less efficient silt trap. Most sediment accumulation is associated with the existing saltmarshes. In the event of a serious oil spill in the port area, it is most probable that it would be contained in this lagoon, the causeway acting as a useful barrier.

The north lagoon receives seawater of a different character, with silt-bearing Liffey water entering Sutton Creek on a rising tide. Because of its larger size, the tide entering this lagoon slows until it is almost still at its southern end. Silt deposition is active for about 1.5km from the causeway. Many measurements of deposition rates have been made. Most indicate that about 1cm of fine sediment is being deposited each year (with about 225,000 cubic metres being deposited since the causeway was built). The surface of this silt patch has been colonised by an interesting mosaic of glasswort, brown seaweeds and the usual green algae of the mudflats. It is clearly a precursor of new emergent saltmarsh. At the present rate of progress, some 50 hectares of emergent saltmarsh will develop in the next

Muddy shore at Bull Island south lagoon with green seaweeds *(Richard Nairn)*

50 to 100 years or so.[8] This is not a large area in the context of the north lagoon, and represents a restoration of habitat lost both in the construction of the causeway and subsequent reinstatement of St Anne's golf course.

Physical laws enable us to predict the theoretical rate of sediment deposition from current speed, and particle size and density. However, the critical factor is generally the rate of loading of the system with fine-textured particulate material. It is important to realise that this loading process may be very seasonal. For example, autumnal leaf fall, associated with decomposition generally, will lead to a much higher loading with organic matter. Stormy winter seas will carry more sediment of all kinds, as will turbulent rivers after heavy rainfall.

In a coastal inlet such as Dublin Bay the typical scenario is one in which the tidal current is slowed to speeds of less than one metre per second, perhaps even coming to rest as the tide turns. This presents a 'window' in the tidal cycle when a rain of sediment will descend through the water column to alight on the bottom. This period ends as the current accelerates with the ebbing tide. Once material has been deposited in quiet water, it is not readily resuspended. The current required to resuspend it is much greater than those encountered during sedimentation episodes.

Resuspension does, however, occur in a number of special circumstances. For example, small waves being driven over the mudflat as the tide falls may entrain sediment which is later carried out to sea; cutting back channels into the saltmarsh, again by a falling spring tide; winter or other fresh water flood conditions, such as occurred in June 1993. Thus, wherever fine sediment is encountered in the intertidal shoreline it always overlays coarser material. This is typically the 'fine sand' characteristic of the offshore sediments.

Plants of the mudflats

Green seaweeds are abundant on some of the mudflats, especially in the northern part of Dublin Bay. They were first recognised as a nuisance in the nineteenth century, and Adeney attributed them to the discharge of sewage.[9] He wrote: 'The effect of such discharge, for example, upon the growth of the green sewage weed *Ulva latissima,* or sea lettuce, during summer seasons cannot be exactly estimated. Under the old conditions of things this weed grew plentifully in different parts of the harbour, especially in the shallow portions on the north side of the deep channel; and considerable quantities were deposited by tidal action along the

Clontarf foreshore during the summer. These deposits underwent a more or less rapid putrefactive decomposition, and at times became very offensive from the formation of sulphuretted hydrogen.'

A more recent investigation by David Jeffrey and his colleagues, between 1992 and 1995, discovered the cause of high algal biomass in certain discrete areas. Highest production was generated on areas of mudflat in the south lagoon, in the same place each year. Laboratory experiments showed that these anaerobic muds generated ammonium, which diffused to the mud surface. It is likely that protein in organic detritus is decomposed by marine bacteria. Thus, green algae probably depend on anaerobic mud beneath them for their nutrient supply.[10] This work influenced the design of the new Ringsend treatment works, which greatly reduces the release of particulates into Dublin Bay. Most of the remaining particulates now originate from the River Liffey.

A taxonomic study on the algae was carried out by Peter Pitkin of Trinity College Dublin.[11] He sampled the shoreline from the mouth of the Tolka at Fairview to Sutton Creek and found the highest densities of green algal mats in the most sheltered section between the Bull Wall and the causeway to Bull Island. As the tide rises, most of the mat floats free from the mud surface and drapes its long fronds around any obstacle, such as a post. Most of the green weed here is the tubular form of *Enteromorpha*, which is a filamentous alga. A total of 32 species of green algae have been recorded from the Dublin Bay mudflats. While many records of algal biomass according to season are available, the detailed ecology of each species has yet to be worked out.[12] Biomass peaks between late June and early July, with values ranging between 75 and 150 grams dry weight per square metre of mud. Species of *Enteromorpha* provide much of the biomass, but a rather uncommon alga called *Vaucheria litorea* is conspicuous in the north lagoon.

Although it was probably much more widespread in the past, a small patch of eelgrass still grows on the beach close to Merrion Gates on the south side of the bay. Most eelgrasses suffered widespread decline in the 1930s, possibly due to a fungal disease. Eelgrasses are of botanical interest: first, because they are perennial plants related to the freshwater pondweeds; second, they play an important role in southern temperate waters below the tideline, providing breeding and feeding grounds for fish. In Dublin Bay eelgrass forms an important part of the diet of brent geese when they arrive in August and September (see Chapter 6). They still graze the remaining patch at the Merrion Gates, even upending at high tide to reach the nutritious plants, but the biomass above ground is soon consumed.[13]

Glasswort (or *Salicornia*) is an annual plant, germinating in dense stands on mud close to the upper neap tide range and it is a pioneer for saltmarsh vegetation. It is a wild plant that has recently become a fashionable food in delicatessens. Just north of the Bull Island causeway, there is a '*Salicornia* Flat', which was studied here over one full growing season by Brian Madden.[14] He found that, on germination in late April–early May, there were some 5,000 seedlings per square metre (m^2) dropping to 1,000 per m^2 at peak biomass. Inspection revealed 'bitten off' seedlings, suggesting predation, possibly by flounder. The seeds, which remain attached to the dead plants, are a food source for ducks such as teal, in addition to the common invertebrate animals *Hydrobia* and *Corophium*. Remains of dead plants eventually enter the organic detritus pool.

Pioneer saltmarsh of glasswort at Booterstown *(Richard Nairn)*

Another glasswort bed has recently developed at Booterstown. An important feature of glasswort is that the whole bed acts as an efficient sediment trap. The seedlings are at the mud surface on germination, but buried in sediment at the end of the season. At least 1cm of sediment is accumulated between May and September. The *Salicornia* Flat is clearly an early stage in the formation of saltmarsh.

Another pioneer plant on the mudflats is the common cordgrass, which is a product of hybridisation in the 1890s between an American species and a closely related European species of perennial grass. It was quickly realised that this grass had the capability to rapidly colonise coastal mudflats and create a dense sward that was seen as potential new land. At Bull Island there is evidence that the cordgrass was planted in straight lines along the upper saltmarsh on the northern side of the golf courses.[15] It was first recorded on the island in 1934. The building of the causeway in the mid-1960s caused some rapid siltation, and disturbance of the plants almost certainly caused their spread. In the 1970s, it was suggested that this spread of cordgrass might 'lead to the elimination of the mudflats', so Dublin Corporation began a programme of controlling the grass by digging up and removing the plants. When this proved ineffective, herbicides were used at various times between 1973 and 1997, but Mark McCorry found that the covering of cordgrass actually increased on a sampled area between 1989 and 1997, despite the control efforts.[16] McCorry also sampled the invertebrate diversity beneath clumps of cordgrass and found that the fauna here was just as abundant and species-rich as areas that were covered with the native glasswort.[17] Attitudes to cordgrass have changed significantly since the 1990s and control measures are no longer considered either necessary or feasible in Dublin Bay.

Mudflat micro-organisms

Decomposition of algal mats depletes the oxygen in the underlying mudflats, accompanied by a range of sulphur-metabolising microbes which utilize sulphate in seawater. Most conspicuous are white masses of *Beggiatoa*, which look like spilt vanilla ice cream. The white appearance is due to masses of elemental sulphur within the filamentous chains of this bacterium. Also present are large patches of purple sulphur bacteria. Decomposition of algal mats is often very smelly and the odours include hydrogen sulphide and dimethyl sulphide. This latter volatile substance is a major contributor to the oceanic sulphur cycle, restoring sulphur to the atmosphere from the ocean. What is more, this material in the atmosphere assists the formation of water droplets and hence is connected to global water balance.

A further microbial consequence of anaerobic sediment is that it provides a refuge for organisms which generate *Botulinus* toxin, namely *Clostridium* species. This can lead to cases of botulism in seabirds from time to time, especially in warm summers. This presents no direct medical hazard to people, but the presence of dying sea birds can be very distressing.

A final consequence of the deposition of silt and detrital organic matter together is the accumulation of metals such as zinc, lead, copper and cadmium. All these metals bind to organic matter and have highly insoluble sulphides. Therefore zinc, which is ubiquitous in urban areas because of galvanised surfaces, may be carried to a mudflat site bound to organic detritus. When this decays or is consumed, the zinc ion may become bound to the sulphur. Enrichment of this kind is well known in estuaries and is the reason why deliberate discharge of such potentially toxic metals is prohibited.

Saltmarsh

Saltmarsh is a unique habitat type where terrestrial plants and animals have adapted to frequent flooding by high tides and can tolerate high salt content in the soil. One of the best places to study a saltmarsh is on the north side of the causeway to Bull Island, where the whole sequence from the first pioneer plants to the high marsh can be seen in one place. There is also an example of the pioneer phase outside the railway near Merrion Gates, which is worth watching as it develops.

Saltmarsh zonation

Just above the *Salicornia* Flat some permanent vegetation appears, possibly separated by a low 'cliff', 20–30cm in height. The 'cliff' is cut by small waves breaking at high water neap tides. The next coloniser is a low-growing perennial grass, *Puccinellia maritima*. Its leaves are commonly grey with deposited silt, and it is a very effective silt-trapping species. Usually it is accompanied by other perennials, typically greater sea-spurrey and sea plantain. Beneath these species there is about 30cm of fine silty sediment, with a relatively low organic matter content, arising from root penetration and the deposition of organic detritus. This vegetation and its accompanying soil is described as 'lower saltmarsh'. This is one of the areas most favoured by wading birds for roosting at high tide. As the seawater creeps in across the mudflats at Bull Island, great jostling flocks of dunlin, redshank, knot and bar-tailed godwit push up among the vegetation into the creeks and pools of the saltmarsh. Here they sometimes continue feeding on saltmarsh invertebrates, but most will spend the next few hours resting, digesting and preening their all-important plumage.

In the next zone, sea thrift joins sea plantain and a few other species including sea arrowgrass and sea lavender. The vegetation is positively lawn-like, but the leaves are mainly those of plantain and thrift. A little saltmarsh grass may still coexist in the lower hollows of this 'middle marsh' zone. The sediment here contains more organic matter. The plants are long lived, slowly growing upwards as sediment continues to accumulate.

Lower saltmarsh at Bull Island
(Richard Nairn)

The 'upper marsh' is demarcated at its lower edge by the appearance of another fine-leaved grass, red fescue. From its tentative, dwarfed first appearance it may be seen to gain in stature as the zone extends upwards to its boundary with dune vegetation at the highest point that spring tides reach. It is interesting that red fescue is a plant shared with the sand dunes.

While it retains some 'middle marsh' species, other characteristic plants in this zone are sea milkwort and two salt-tolerant rushes, the conspicuous sea rush and the small, fescue-like saltmarsh rush. The fine sediment in this zone is very thin, feathering out to nothing at the uppermost boundary. Organic matter content is relatively high. The 'levees' at the margin of channels are colonised by sea purslane, a relatively recent incomer to the Bull Island. The soil provides ample nutrients for this salt-tolerant plant, and is fairly well aerated.

Middle saltmarsh at Bull Island
(John Fox)

Soil structure

The structure of the soil supporting the sequence of saltmarsh zones may be described as a wedge of fine sediment and organic matter, itself overlying the sloping surface of the sand island. The soil and vegetation complex is shown in the diagram opposite, which is derived from a metre-by-metre study of the Bull Island marsh surface. The upper surface of the wedge is initially smooth, as may be seen in the younger, northern section of the marsh. But eventually drainage channels cut into the surface. These are sinuous in form and as they deepen they admit inflowing tidal water with its suspended sediment. As in a major river that overtops its banks, silt and detritus are deposited to form a raised 'levee' at the creek margins. This is a sub-habitat for plants in its own right.

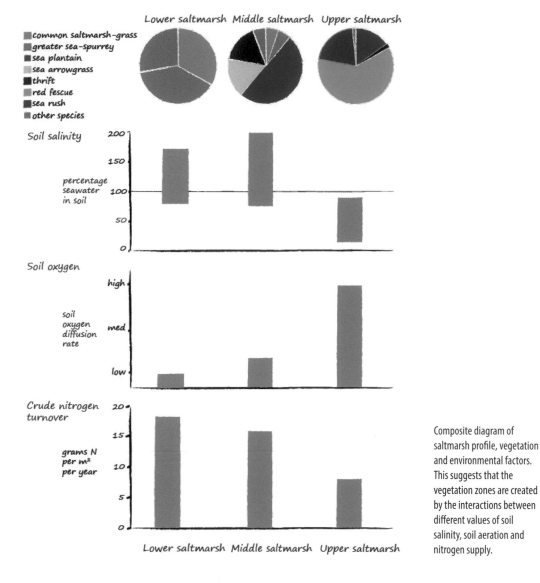

Lower saltmarsh Middle saltmarsh Upper saltmarsh

■ common saltmarsh-grass
■ greater sea-spurrey
■ sea plantain
■ sea arrowgrass
■ thrift
■ red fescue
■ sea rush
■ other species

Soil salinity

percentage
seawater
in soil

Soil oxygen

soil
oxygen
diffusion
rate

Crude nitrogen
turnover

grams N
per m²
per year

Lower saltmarsh Middle saltmarsh Upper saltmarsh

Composite diagram of saltmarsh profile, vegetation and environmental factors. This suggests that the vegetation zones are created by the interactions between different values of soil salinity, soil aeration and nitrogen supply.

Plant interactions

Saltmarsh soil formation is a complex process but it can be broken down into a series of interactions, shown in the diagram above. These interactions suggest that a number of soil properties may influence the zones of vegetation that change with height of the marsh surface. They are salinity, soil aeration and soil fertility. The weight of vegetation (biomass) in the lower marsh is similar to that on the *Salicornia* Flat, except that the root-to-shoot ratio is much larger. Shoot and underground biomass continue to rise in the middle marsh, attaining values of about 3kg per square metre. Biomass then declines in the upper marsh. Exceptionally high root biomass such as this is elsewhere associated with highly stressed plant communities such as those in Arctic and arid zone conditions.

The high salt content (salinity) of the saltmarsh soil leads to considerable stress for the plants that grow there. Its magnitude and distribution on Bull Island was first described in 1975–76 by Elizabeth McNamee of Trinity College Dublin with the help of the late Professor H. Weibe of Utah State University, USA. He was a world-renowned specialist in plant–water relationships, and brought with him newly developed equipment for his sabbatical year in Dublin. This enabled the rapid determination of soil water salinity at the rooting depth of each vegetation zone.

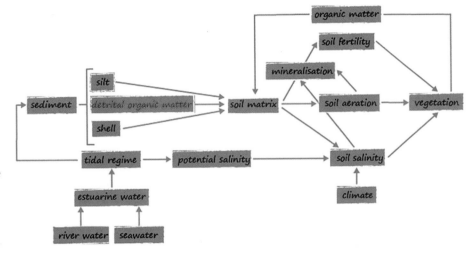

Suggested soil development diagram for saltmarsh on Bull Island. Several different environmental factors combine with plant growth to generate the factors expressed in the diagram on page 59. Soil formation is a dynamic process and will continue in the face of climate change.

The lower and middle marsh have salinity values from slightly below seawater salinity to substantially above. In fact, a doubling of seawater salinity was recorded in middle marsh soil. In total contrast, the salinity of upper marsh soil never attained seawater levels. This data reveals that rainfall may effectively reduce salinity in all zones, while in the upper zone the effect of rainfall-derived groundwater is apparent. Long periods of summer sunshine, with only slight inundation by high spring tides, greatly increases salt content. This is relieved in August when full seawater again covers the whole marsh. At the same time an index of soil aeration was determined. Lower and middle marsh soils were largely devoid of air, while upper marsh soil was well aerated and similar to other terrestrial soils.

Booterstown Marsh

Booterstown Marsh was once part of the intertidal area of Dublin Bay until it was cut off by the building of the railway embankment in the 1830s (see Chapter 8). During the first half of the twentieth century the marsh was drained and cultivated – the potato ridges can still be seen when the water level is low. Oil spills in 1982 on the Trimblestown stream and, more severely, in 1985, led to deoxygenation and contamination of the marsh. The vegetation became dominated by sea club-rush, which could withstand the brackish conditions. The rediscovery of a rare species called Borrer's saltmarsh grass, following some works on the drainage, enhanced the conservation status of the marsh. In response the flap valves were removed, allowing a free flow of salt water that is rich in oxygen. This reduced the area of the sea club-rush, but also caused a decline in the rarer Borrer's saltmarsh grass. Apart from the formation

Booterstown Marsh with wader roost on the island and a DART train passing *(Richard Nairn)*

Rocky shoreline at
Sandycove.
(Richard Nairn)

in 2006 of the two mud islands for roosting birds at high tide, no major
work has been undertaken on the marsh in recent years. However, a
viewing area was made on a small pocket of land just to the north. The
long-term future of Booterstown Marsh is far from clear, although it
now forms an important high tide roost for wading birds.

Life on rocky shores

Rocky shores are the habitats where most science students first explore
marine biology. The plants and animals show clear zones, parallel to
the tideline, and the species found here are dependent on the degree
of inundation by the tide and the degree of exposure to waves. Rocky
shores are usually in exposed locations where they are regularly lashed
by strong waves, so animals and plants need to be strongly attached or
living in crevices or under boulders to avoid being washed off into the
sea. In Dublin Bay, the main rocky shores are on the south side of the
bay between Seapoint and Dalkey and on the north side from Sutton
around Howth Head. The hard surfaces of most of the harbours and

sea walls also provide artificial habitats for similar plant and animal communities.

These shores are often subject to the most energetic waves and currents. On the Howth peninsula the intertidal shore stretches upwards to exposed rocks and cliffs above the direct effects of the tide. This should perhaps be regarded as an extreme example of a terrestrial habitat, where salt spray is added to a situation where regular drought occurs and the rock may be hot in summer. The most commonly observed 'plants' are a small group of lichens – the orange *Caloplaca*, the yellow *Xanthoria* and the black *Verrucaria*.

Seaweeds are a hugely important component of rocky shore ecosystems. They provide valuable food sources for a wide range of marine animals, including barnacles, tunicates, anemones and polychaete worms. Sea urchins and sea cucumbers graze on the larger weeds. Smaller fragments of seaweeds are eaten by planktonic feeders such as copepods. In the water, bacteria and fungi feed on dissolved organic matter, including sugars and amino acids that are released into the sea as the familiar mucus on the surface of seaweeds. Seaweeds also provide vital shelter for smaller animals, preventing them being washed off by waves. To appreciate this, simply lift one of the curtains of brown seaweeds growing near low water mark and notice the myriads of animals, from scuttling green crabs to fixed limpets, barnacles and anemones. The fronds of the weed are a valuable substrate for encrusting animals such as tube-building worms. As the weed decomposes in the sea it adds to the organic detritus that is such a key component of the coastal ecosystem. Finally, stranded seaweeds on the beach also quickly decompose and are eaten by masses of invertebrates, notably the familiar sandhoppers.

Brown and red seaweeds may be regarded as 'honorary plants' as they have no known relationships in evolutionary history to flowering plants, or to each other. However, they possess common characteristics such as cellulose cell walls and chloroplasts. Thus they play a part in primary production. They all have a similar basic structure with a holdfast that anchors the developing plant by penetrating minute crevices in the rock surface and expands as growth progresses. A stalk-like stipe then develops, which bears a flat leaf-like thallus, and the whole structure above the holdfast is flexible in the moving water.

In the brown seaweeds, between the cells there are massive concentrations of colloidal alginate, which has a great capacity for absorbing and retaining water and serves to protect cells against drying out. Alginates are the basis of an important industry on the Atlantic coast of Ireland.

The thallus erodes with wave action, shedding material to the detritus pool. During reproduction, seaweeds liberate considerable volumes of spores into the sea, contributing to the diet of filter feeders. The commonest brown seaweeds in the upper intertidal zone are spiral wrack and channel wrack. Both have thick cell walls and recover well after drying and re-immersion in seawater.

The production in this zone is comparatively low. Between the brown algal stipes may be found occasional plants of shorter living green algae, including the broad thallus of sea lettuce and the filaments of *Enteromorpha*. These may extend down the shore into the lower zone if space allows. A common animal living in this zone is the periwinkle. Two more brown seaweeds dominate the middle intertidal zone – bladder wrack and knotted wrack, which have a higher biomass and offer better cover for fauna. Typical animals found in this zone are barnacles, anemones and limpets. A third brown seaweed, serrated wrack, is characteristic of the lower intertidal zone. This species does not recover from desiccation and must be covered most of the time by seawater.

In areas of high wave energy, animals also have to cling tightly to the rock surface to avoid being washed into the sea. Barnacles are ancient relatives of shrimps, crabs and lobsters, all classified as crustaceans. They remain glued to their rock base by a glycoprotein cement. The body is protected by a tough membrane surrounded by six calcareous plates. At the apex of this pyramidal structure are two valves that open only at high tide. Then modified legs emerge and start to beat rhythmically to enable filter feeding. Reproduction entails two planktonic larval stages before settlement close to existing adults. Close packing of individuals is a successful strategy, both to discourage competition and promote effective reproduction. Limpets are their main competitors for space.

Brown seaweeds on a rocky shore *(Richard Nairn)*

Most people have eaten mussels in a seafood restaurant at some time. The familiar blue-black shells are very common on rocky shores but mussels also settle on beaches, especially where there is a layer of gravel under the sand or mud. Sticking out between the two shells (or valves) are some strong threads known as the byssus. These are used to anchor the shell to the rock like the guy ropes of a tent. Mussels sieve large volumes of seawater, filtering out small food particles. They usually occur in dense colonies (or mussel beds), with the later arrivals attached to other shells rather than to the rock or gravel below. Dense mussel beds, such as those that occur on the edges of the channels leading out of the North Bull lagoons, support a diverse community of invertebrates including sponges, hydroids and anemones. Mussels can exist in some polluted waters and are common on hard surfaces in ports and harbours. One of the best areas to see mussels is on the large granite boulders on the shoreline between Dún Laoghaire and Dalkey. Several waders, notably oystercatchers and curlews, have strong bills that are used for opening mussels, while gulls frequently drop the shells from a height onto rocks to break them open.

A UCD student project at Seapoint (south Dublin Bay) and Rush (north Dublin) found that the size of the mussels themselves affects the structure of the mussel bed and hence the niches available for other species to occupy. It was also found that sediment loads in the seawater may affect the types of associated species.[18] Another UCD study compared the encrusting animal communities on natural rocky shores and artificial structures such as piers in Blackrock and Dún Laoghaire. In general, vertical urban structures were more densely populated than vertical natural surfaces, except in the case of mussel beds. However, flat natural rock faces appeared to have more dense communities than horizontal urban structures. Species diversity also differed, with vertical structures holding a greater range of species than horizontal surfaces. The species that tended to occur in greater densities on natural rather than artificial surfaces were limpets, dog whelks, periwinkles and barnacles.[19] Differences in the biodiversity on artificial and natural structures are often attributable to differences in the complexity of the surfaces in terms of small cracks and crevices and larger features such as rock pools. Research is ongoing to find engineering solutions to improve the degree to which artificial structures mimic natural ones as surrogate habitats for marine species.[20]

Mussels and barnacles on an exposed rocky shore
(Richard Nairn)

The Bull Wall

Marine life on the Bull Wall, built on the north side of the Liffey in the nineteenth century, was studied by Brenda Healy of UCD in the 1970s.[21] She described the loose structure of the wall, which leaves spaces between the rocks resembling miniature caves at low tide. The seaweed zones of the Bull Wall are typical of rocky shores, with flat wrack dominating near the high water mark, bladder wrack and serrated wrack found lower down. Green seaweeds are common too.

The moon rising over the Bull Wall *(John Fox)*

Most of the rocks are covered with barnacles and limpets, with large quantities of mussels on the lower levels. In the sheltered crevices beadlet anemones can be found. The outer section of the Bull Wall is covered at high tide and here the dominant seaweed is knotted wrack. Mussels are also plentiful here, but sponges become more obvious on the underside of rocks. The steep gradient and absence of rock pools are the main differences between the habitat on the wall and that on natural rocky shores.

Beachcombing on the strandline

One of the most productive areas for a beachcomber walking the shores of Dublin Bay is the strandline, where much of the flotsam and jetsam of the sea is deposited. After a big easterly storm the high tide mark in

Dublin Bay can be littered with seaweed and shells of all kinds including cockles, tellins, wedge shells and razorshells. Occasionally the stranding of deeper-water animals such as a large starfish or spider crab suggests that the seabed has been disturbed by gales. The litter of the urban area is also a feature of the strandline – all kinds of plastic containers, drink cans, polystyrene sheets, fishing debris and pieces of timber come ashore and are often wedged between the boulders on the sea walls and rocky shores. The stranded seaweed on a beach has a special function when it becomes buried by blowing sand. It contains the seeds of coastal plants and, as it decomposes over the following year, it provides an ideal seedbed for the growth of strandline plants. These – the foundations of coastal lands – are described in Chapter 5.

5 | Coastlands

The habitats of coastal lands are those that are above the highest tides but still strongly influenced by marine sediments, shaped by both erosion and deposition and by the salt-laden winds that blow constantly across them. The more natural habitats, such as sand dunes, cliffs, islands and coastal heath, are the main focus, but there are also many urban habitats, such as golf courses, parks, quay walls and coastal buildings.

Sand dunes

Imagine for a moment that you are enjoying a picnic on Dollymount Strand on a fine summer's day. The tide is out and a wide flat beach stretches out before you. Then the wind begins to blow from the sea and fine sand starts to lift into the air and swirl around. It gets into everything – your eyes, your camera, even your sandwiches. It blows along the beach in great gusts, settling wherever there is an obstacle around which it can gather. As the sand sweeps around the tip of Bull Island, it encounters some plants on the strandline that actually thrive with burial in moving sand. These are the typical strandline plants – searocket, sand couch grass and sea sandwort. These pioneers are followed by the dune-building grasses – lyme grass and the sand burial champion, marram grass. Here the embryo dunes begin to form, first as annual heaps of sand and then, if they survive the winter storms, consolidating into foredunes. Similar foredunes can also be found in a few parts of south Dublin Bay – at Booterstown, Irishtown and Poolbeg.

On the beach

Of all the habitats discussed in this book, beaches and sand dunes possess unique amenity values in the public mind. Protection and management of these must be achieved in parallel with coastal protection and science-based nature conservation. However, the environmental factors are beyond our control. These critical factors are the continuing supply of sand by coastal currents; periods of fine, dry summer weather; and moderate winter storms, especially those coinciding with high spring tides.

We first met the sandflats of Dublin Bay in Chapter 4. Here the sandy seabed material is transported into the intertidal zone by coastal currents. What might be described as a flow of sand slowly progresses northwards from the terminal moraine at the southern end of the Irish Sea. It travels as sand waves on the seabed. Part of this flow diverts into Dublin Bay, flooring the sea bottom and ending up on the beaches. Ultimately this same material may, in periods of fine, dry weather, be blown by wind to form sand dunes at the top of the beaches. In a wet summer, sand grains adhere together and will not move along the beach.

Historically, several sandy beaches were located around Dublin Bay, but some of them have either been obliterated by the building of coastal

Aerial view of Bull Island from the south-west. The main dune ridges can be seen to the right of the golf course and the saltmarsh to the left. *(Dublin City Council)*

A sandstorm on Dollymount Strand *(John Coveney)*

roads and port structures or their source of sandy sediment has been cut off. The beach that used to fringe the Clontarf shore has now been replaced by Bull Island and by the present Dollymount Strand. Other sandy beaches occur on the south side of the bay at Sandymount and Merrion and new beaches are already developing above the average high tide level at Booterstown, Irishtown and Poolbeg. All of these beaches are intimately connected with the sand dunes that develop above the tide and these beach systems exchange sand with the dunes in both directions through deposition and erosion. This is a natural process and erosion needs to be accommodated to prevent the beach being depleted of sand from this source. If hard coastal protection measures are put in place the beach normally deflates and sand is removed from the coastal system, eventually undermining the coastal protection.

Dune development

Although beach sand is largely the same fine sand that floors the bay, the upper parts of the beach contain 8–10 per cent calcium carbonate, arising from broken seashells. These shell fragments erode to the same dimensions as grains of sand.

A good way to understand how beaches develop and evolve into dunes is to imagine the behaviour of individual sand grains, in responding to water and wind. If this sandy material remains wet between tides, it will tend to stay fixed at low tide, one sand grain firmly adhering to the next by capillary forces. The upper part of the beach, above the reach of neap tides, may not be wetted by seawater for days at a time. When the upper surface of the sand drains free of seawater, and solar heating plus wind circulation permits total drying, a grain is free to move. Sand grains are close to spherical as a result of the tumbling action to which they have been subjected since each particle was eroded from its parent rock. When this mass of spherical particles is acted on by gentle wind pressure, their first motion is to roll downwind. As wind speed increases, rolling suddenly changes to hopping. The impact of a landing grain gives another grain sufficient energy to take off. Eventually the whole floor of the beach is a moving curtain of sand, seldom above knee height. Sand transport ceases abruptly if rain falls, wind ceases or local wind speed is reduced by an obstruction. On the generally sea-smoothed beach the only obstructions are provided by tide-borne debris, distributed along

Embryo dunes at the north end of Bull Island (*John Fox*)

71

the latest high tide mark. This material is a mixture of seaweed and other organic substances, flotsam and jetsam from the sea and beach litter.

With a suitable onshore breeze, a small ridge of sand develops, centred on the line of debris or strand-line plants. The fate of this embryo ridge then depends on the wind and the tide. If a high spring tide is accompanied by a high wind, so much wave energy may be generated that the ridge will be demolished. However, the upper part of the foreshore will have been nourished and the next ridge may be a few centimetres higher. Alternatively, if the ridge survives into the late spring, seed of annual plants, buried in the sand, germinate and a growth sequence described in the diagram opposite culminates in the development of a new permanent foredune ridge. Plant growth encourages more sand accumulation.

The dependence of embryo dune development on the presence of beach debris raises the question of the wisdom of beach-cleaning by local authorities. It raises questions of the balance between health-and-safety issues, aesthetics and the need for dune development, which assists in coastal protection. Beaches and dunes are interdependent in their long-term development, and the conservation of the total sand mass must be regarded as a whole.

The sand dunes of Bull Island are among the most extensive examples of this habitat type in Ireland[1] and they are all the more valuable because we know their age precisely. Looking at a plan of Bull Island and considering its history (Chapters 9 and 10), we know that the six ridges that have developed since the sand spit emerged in the early 1800s can be dated to 1869, 1902, 1906, 1936, 1960 and 1983. This intermittent appearance of ridges is probably dependent on the complex of climatic factors mentioned above coinciding in a number of years when all factors were favourable for uninterrupted growth. In 1982 an embryo ridge survived into 1983 and Peter Fay, his appetite for dunes whetted by his undergraduate thesis at Trinity College Dublin,[2] began a doctoral study on its further growth.[3] Apart from describing in detail the topography, soil characteristics and vegetation of this dune system in his first thesis, Fay made a fundamental contribution to the question of nitrogen supply. The 1906 ridge is the one feature that can be traced the full length of the island. Its formation must have been a signal event in the island's development, transforming it from a more or less nondescript, flat sandbar to a more hospitable place for summer sunbathing.

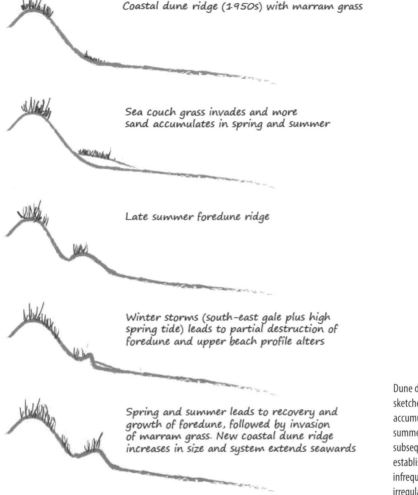

Coastal dune ridge (1950s) with marram grass

Sea couch grass invades and more sand accumulates in spring and summer

Late summer foredune ridge

Winter storms (south-east gale plus high spring tide) leads to partial destruction of foredune and upper beach profile alters

Spring and summer leads to recovery and growth of foredune, followed by invasion of marram grass. New coastal dune ridge increases in size and system extends seawards

Dune development. The sketches indicate stages in sand accumulation and colonisation in summer, winter comb-down and subsequent regrowth to a more established foredune. This occurs infrequently, hence the long irregular intervals between the building of a main dune ridge.

Plant adaptations to dune conditions

When a stable foredune community has become established, with its characteristic tussocks of sea couch grass, this is a sign that the water between the sand grains of the dune is no longer wholly saline. A transition then begins with an invasion by the marram grass community. This is the most successful sand-binding grass in both hemispheres of the temperate zone. It can be seen to intercept sand by markedly reducing wind speed. Furthermore, it can match the pace of accumulation by upward growth of the shoot system by up to a metre per year. As a dune surface becomes higher, it moves away from the freshwater table of the dune, as shown in the diagram. At both edges, the freshwater lens outcrops through the foredune on the seaward side and through the uppermost zone of the saltmarsh.

Marram roots extend down to the lowest summer levels of the water table. In order to determine the biomass of these roots, Peter Fay had to core down to a depth of 2m to sample them completely. He used lengths of 10cm plastic water pipe, driven in with a sledgehammer and extracted with a modified car jack.

Plant water use strategies

The reason why dunes are so dry is that even fine sand has a low water-storage capacity. All dune plants must therefore practise an economical water-use strategy. Some plants are long-lived and simply tolerate drought by deep roots and rolled or folded leaves, as in marram grass and sand couch grass. Water may be stored in fleshy roots or succulent leaves, as in sea spurge and dandelion. The latter is also a rosette plant, its whorls of leaves generating a moist boundary layer, which reduces evaporation. Other modifications to leaves include hairiness, which is common, and waxy or reflective cuticles, of which spurge is the best example.

A final strategy is pursued by the winter annuals, such as dove's-foot cranesbill. There are several examples of these plants in the dunes. They germinate in autumn and overwinter as annuals, flower in spring and produce seed before May. The most conspicuous and attractive is the early forget-me-not. Their habitat is the 'young fixed dune', where the grassland is slightly open.

Sea rocket on the strand line at Bull Island *(Richard Nairn)*

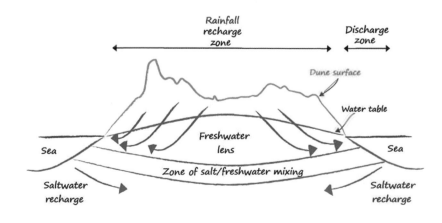

Diagram of the water table beneath a dune system of the Bull Island type. The mass of fresh water, derived from rainfall, is supported by the more dense seawater underlying the island.

Dune succession

If we remember that the embryo dunes are currently being formed from beach sand, while the innermost ridges date from the nineteenth century, it would be reasonable to expect change in the dune soil, the flora and the fauna as we move further back from the beach. The vegetation of the dune complex at Bull Island was described by Professor John Moore of UCD in 1977.[4] He followed an imaginary walk from the strandline across the dunes to the mature grassland closest to the mainland. He also noted that the two golf clubs had modified much of the dune grassland on their fairways by adding fertiliser and by continuous mowing, which produces vegetation more characteristic of dry suburban lawns. The succession of plant communities across the dunes is best studied along a transect in which a continuous strip of plant cover is recorded to show changes with distance from the beach. Simultaneously the level of the ground surface is recorded to correlate plants and topography. At regular intervals the organic matter content and calcium carbonate content of surface soil are measured. Finally, the total nitrogen content of vegetation is determined using specially cut plant samples.

Looking at the topography, it can be seen that the ridges are fairly evenly spaced and are separated by parallel hollows. Where these hollows are close to the water table they are known as dune slacks. The biggest slack in this section is the Alder Marsh on Bull Island. Its floor is in fact lower than the high tide mark of ordinary tides. In winter it frequently floods, and for most of the year the water table is within a few centimetres of the surface. It is backed by the 1906 ridge, with the 1937 ridge on the seaward side. For some 30 years this marsh was on the seashore but it is now a wonderfully rich, wet grassland.

It holds a stunning display of the marsh helleborine, and a variety of other marsh orchid species. It is also the breeding place of a thriving population of a rare butterfly, the marsh fritillary, whose caterpillar feeds on the extensive devil's-bit scabious. Recent work at Bull Island suggests that the Alder Marsh is drying out as the water table gradually drops. Standing water levels during the winter have also been affected and the marsh has not been flooding as extensively in recent winters. It is thought that these changes have been occurring too rapidly to be explained by natural habitat succession. A recently completed research project by Fiona Devaney studied the hydrology, vegetation and restoration prospects of the Alder Marsh at Bull Island.[5] The drying

Devil's-bit scabious (blue colour) in the Alder Marsh at Bull Island *(John Fox)*

out may be caused by groundwater abstraction within the island and possibly by the invasion of the non-native shrub, sea buckthorn. A glance at the diagram on page 74 indicates the danger of saltwater intrusion into groundwater by over-extraction. Collecting and storing rainwater would be a better source of fresh water for green maintenance.

Soil characteristics

It has been remarked on for many years that as dunes age the calcium carbonate content declines and the organic matter content increases (see the diagram on page 78). This has been cited as evidence of soil evolution in dunes worldwide. It represents the interaction between climatic and biological factors. Seashell carbonate is decomposed over time by acids in rainfall and those secreted by plant roots. The rates of decomposition depend both on rainfall and annual temperature. This implies that decomposition rates on the Irish east coast are substantially lower than those on west coast dunes. The effects of the increased organic matter content are largely concerned with soil surface stability. This means that soil will no longer erode under strong gale conditions, and requires rabbit burrowing to create disturbance. Soil that is rich in organic matter has better capacity to retain water and nutrients, compared with raw sand.

Dune nitrogen economy

In the late 1950s a group from Bristol University experimented with nutrient applications to the sand dunes and discovered that adding nitrogen-containing fertiliser improved plant growth considerably. Neither phosphate nor potassium addition alone would stimulate growth.[6] Since then, much attention has been devoted to research related to nitrogen economy of dune systems as a whole.

In 1982 an embryo ridge survived into 1983 and Peter Fay began a doctoral study on its further growth.[7] He examined in detail the nitrogen economy of foredunes and the main dune ridge at the Bull Island. Much to his surprise, the biomass, including the massive underground roots, contained more nitrogen than the oldest community, the 'dune pasture'. So a picture emerged of nitrogen entering the dunes 'with a bang', rather than building up with time. Further work demonstrated that beach sand was a comparatively plentiful source of the element, compared with weathered sand of older dunes.[8] In fact, this is the major source for foredune and main dune, where biological nitrogen fixation has not been detected. A clear link with detritus deposited on the beach was indicated. Fay was so worried that this was an effect of urban contamination that he collected samples from beaches in Connemara and on the Wicklow coast for comparison. These samples yielded yet higher levels of nitrogen.

Marsh Helleborine *(John Fox)*

However, in older communities beyond the reach of blown beach sand, the biological fixation of nitrogen is the most important process for balancing the constant leaching of nitrogen from the dune system. In most zones leguminous plant species occur. These range from clovers and vetches to common gorse. What they have in common are root nodules containing a colony of *Rhizobium* bacteria. The bacteria incorporate nitrogen from the air into amino acids using energy from the plant. This link is so direct that it ceases when the plant is producing nectar in midsummer. The nodules decay in autumn, and release fixed nitrogen to the soil. In the meantime, they nourish the plant. Dunes are a veritable laboratory for nitrogen fixation studies, as several other systems exist. One day we may be able to assess their relative importance to the system.

Sand dune animals

The invertebrate animals of sand dunes are quite poorly studied, but we do know that the dunes are a rather unfavourable environment for small animals. This is because the vegetation cover is often sparse and there is generally low organic matter in the soil. However, there are some animals that are dune specialists and those found on Bull Island were described by Martin Speight in 1977.[9] One species that has an interesting behaviour is the spider-hunting wasp, which can be seen running backwards and forwards over the bare sand with a particular jerking gait, vibrating its antennae rapidly as it seeks out a spider. The spiders are stung to death and then stored in a burrow for the larvae of the wasp to eat.

Some of the small animals found on the Bull Island dunes are quite rare. For example, the white satin moth, which occurs on willows in the Alder Marsh, has been found at only one other location in Ireland. The marsh fritillary butterfly is rare in Europe and has special legal protection. The curiously named hairy woodlouse is found in Ireland only on Bull Island, at Howth and at Portmarnock; elsewhere in Europe this species is not found further north than Portugal. A very specialised

Composite diagram of dune topography and soil features. This shows a classic system with the decline in calcium carbonate and the increase in soil organic matter obvious within a century of development.

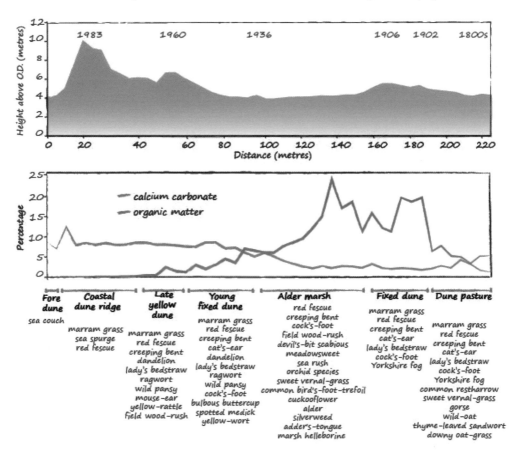

fly, *Salticella fasciata*, is well established in the dunes on Bull Island, which are among the most northerly known locations for the species.[10]

Although we have some knowledge of the biodiversity of the dunes, it is certainly incomplete and we do not have enough information to enable the construction of a quantitative food web. We can only guess at the importance of species in either transferring energy or limiting minerals. The well-defined bands of dune vegetation must be largely ignored when considering fauna. We can only think in general terms for two reasons. First, no detailed studies have been carried out in particular zones: while collections have been made to illustrate biodiversity from several types of site, e.g. the Alder Marsh on Bull Island, these have been one-off, non-quantitative or census-type collections. Second, many animals are obviously mobile and their habitat or home range may embrace many or all vegetation zones.

Marsh Fritillary butterfly
(John Fox)

However, it is possible to examine the feeding habitats of various animal groups to get some idea of the complexity of life in the dunes. Many insects are herbivorous. Obvious examples are the leaf-chewing caterpillars, the leaf-sucking aphids and bugs, and the nectar-seeking bees and adult butterflies. Seeds are also important food sources for some ants. One group of insects that has been receiving more attention in recent years is the bumblebees. These attractive animals depend on the food plants that they find in the dunes. For example, the moss carder bumblebee is the most notable species in this group recorded on Bull Island, followed by the red-tailed bumblebee. Both species were defined as 'near threat' in the 2006 *Regional Red List of Irish Bees*.[11] The moss carder bumblebee is in decline across Europe, and on the south-east coast it is only recorded in good-quality dunes.[12] It is believed that coastal habitats and flora-rich urban areas are supporting the populations of this sensitive species. The primary producers are a limited range of specialised higher plants, bryophytes and lichens. The key herbivores are probably the wide range of mollusc species. The biomass of this diversity of snails would be a worthwhile study in any temperate dune system.

Moss carder bumblebee
(Stephen Falk)

Looking at dunes for a long number of years, we can see large changes in the populations of rabbits and Irish hares. A peak population of rabbits was present in the 1970s, before the viral disease myxomatosis completely wiped out the population. Rabbits, probably now resistant to the virus, are again present on Bull Island. Robert Lloyd Praeger mentions in *The Way that I Went*, published in 1937, that an unexpected result of the protection of Bull Island was that hares increased so rapidly that 'they threatened to devour the island and, for the sake of its other inhabitants, large numbers of them had to be captured and removed'.[13] Today, it is thought that the hare population has been reduced to a very few individuals, but the cause is far from clear. Disturbance by uncontrolled dogs is suggested as one reason. It is thus difficult to assess the overall effect of these largest herbivores on the vegetation. Here it is probably small.

Mice, including both the long-tailed field mouse and the house mouse, probably eat seeds and fleshy plant roots. The house mouse has a curious history on Bull Island. In 1895, a zoologist called H. Lyster Jameson caught a glimpse of some unusually pale-coloured mice in the dunes and, on trapping a sample of these, he argued that their colouration acted as camouflage against the sand and thus natural selection had favoured this variation. In 1931, 'Jameson's mice', whose skins were now in the Natural History Museum, were examined by Eugene O'Mahony, who concluded that the sandy-coloured specimens were from a different subspecies, which he called the North Bull house

Hare on the saltmarsh at Bull Island *(John Fox)*

mouse.[14] He later decided, with no evidence, that they were identical to a subspecies of house mouse from Egypt, known as *Mus musculus orientalis,* and that they must therefore have been introduced. A further re-examination of the skins by the zoologist James Fairley in 1970 poured cold water on this theory – he noted that Jameson's specimens contained many colour variations and that the mice from Bull Island were no different from those found elsewhere.[15] So the North Bull house mouse turned out to be a fictional character after all.

Decomposers

The biomass of decomposers in the dunes is not known, but their known biodiversity is considerable, and it includes small oligochaete worms and several isopods, including the common wood louse. Many insects, especially larval forms, are also dependent on dead organic matter. Finally, it should be noted that the greater number of fungal species recorded from Dublin Bay are found in dune systems. When the balance of biomass consumption in dunes is ultimately worked out, it may well be found that most energy is transferred directly from plants to decomposers. This hypothesis is based on the observation that many herbivores are insects – sap suckers, leaf chewers or nectar feeders. Their biomass is probably quite small and most plant biomass is unscathed by grazers. However, the increasing rabbit population could alter things radically by impacting on the vegetation.

Carnivores

It is hard to link the highly mobile large carnivores strictly to the dunes. Clearly the kestrels and peregrine falcons that are frequently seen here will seek prey from dunes, saltmarsh, mudflats and purely terrestrial habitats. This is probably true also of blackbirds, song thrushes and other smaller land birds that feed on a variety of invertebrates and plant foods. A limited number of breeding birds are found in dunes because of the scarcity of nest sites. It is thus important to ensure that dune sites are as free from disturbance as possible during the nesting season (see also Chapter 6).

Cliffs

The ancient rocks of Howth Head have withstood the attacking power of the Irish Sea since the retreat of the last Ice Age and now form dramatic cliffs that are a familiar sight from the city fringe. With their vertical gradient from rocky shore to clifftop, they illustrate how the plants and, less obviously, the animals occur in zones. This is clearly seen close to the water level as brown seaweeds give way to black lichens in the splash zone and bright yellow lichens higher up the rocks. Their nutrients are derived from the sea and from the droppings of the cormorants, shags and gulls that often roost on such ledges near the water level.

Above the rocky shore spray zone, with its lichens, is a narrow zone of salt-loving plants growing in soil-filled rock crevices. These plants, and their soil, are regularly doused in seawater, but they are also exposed to rainfall and fresh water running down the cliff face. They include sea pink, sea campion and sea plantain. Where the slope of the rock face is moderate, at about 30 degrees, soil from the glacial drift deposits may overlie the rock and form a base for longer-lived vegetation. This takes

Cliffs at Howth Head *(John Fox)*

the form of wind-tolerant scrub, mainly wind-pruned blackthorn. An associated plant is the naturally prostrate form of the common broom, which is very wind-tolerant. When grown in garden conditions, this plant retains its prostrate habit. The steeper rock faces are bare of soil and vegetation, but provide numerous sites for nesting seabirds (see Chapter 6).

The cliff path from Balscadden in Howth to Sutton Strand is regarded as one of the finest coastal walks in Ireland. The high section from Balscadden to the Baily Lighthouse lies above the scrub zone, with dry heath above. It is an ideal viewing platform for observing nesting birds, cetaceans and seals at sea. A number of uncommon plants can be seen from the path. Some appear to be out of ecological context, but this can be explained by the biogeography of Howth. For example, two plants common in the Burren in County Clare – bloody cranesbill and wild madder – are rarely found in coastal situations. The former has a northerly distribution, up to Scandinavia; the latter's distribution extends into southern Europe. Howth is virtually the most northern location for both species on the east coast of Ireland.

Close to where the path crosses the road to the Baily Lighthouse, there is a patch of another coastal plant, spring squill. It is distributed along both eastern and western shores of the Irish Sea, but its overall distribution extends from Norway to Spain and Portugal. Finally, a more common plant is sheep's bit, which is conspicuous beside the path and has attractive bright blue flowers in summer. It is notable that the cliff vegetation of Howth is designated in its own right as a European Union Special Area of Conservation under the Habitats Directive.

Heathland

Immediately above the cliffs of Howth is a heath plant community that is as remarkable as those inundated with seawater. The word 'heath' is of ancient origin, deriving from Old English, but also related to German and Dutch. Heathland plants are challenged by four extreme environmental conditions: very low soil fertility; regular fire and drought; and acid soil. This high level of selection has led to a very low biodiversity of specialised plant and animal species. Dry heaths are endangered in Europe and most remaining examples are protected as Special Areas of Conservation under the European Union Habitats Directive. Because it is also an attractive open space in Howth, the area is protected by a Special Amenity Area Order.

On Howth, three plant species dominate the heathland: heather (or ling), bell heather and autumn or western gorse. The glory period is in August, when all are flowering, and when the purple shades of the heathers are a perfect foil for the gold of the gorse. Heather is also present in raised and blanket bogs. There is some evidence that the heath and bog forms (ecotypes) of heather are distinct morphologically. The leaves of heath forms are hairier, for example. Bogs and heaths share the characteristic of ultra-low fertility. In Howth, this is a product of the Cambrian rocks, depleted of nutrients in the ancient past and metamorphosed by heat and pressure to give today's quartzite and slate. Soils derived directly from these rocks are simply a mix of coarse rock fragments and peat-like organic matter. These are known as skeletal soils. Elsewhere on Howth are soils developed from more distantly derived glacial materials. These tend to bear grassland, bracken or birch woodland with European gorse.

The distribution of skeletal soils tends to follow the high ground, with glacial soils scraped into hollows. Thus, at the top of the eastern sea cliffs there is heath, with a band of grassland containing many coastal

Heathland above the Baily Lighthouse, Howth Head
(John Fox)

species between heath and the true cliffs. Heath fires are a regular feature, occurring at intervals of between five and 15 years, depending on how dry the weather has been. In ecological terms it is accepted that this is a natural response to minimal fertility. Ash from burning renews nutrients for a fresh generation of plants. The plants, in turn, have three particular characteristics: inherent flammability; capacity to regenerate after burning; high capability for efficient absorption and utilisation of nutrients, especially phosphate and nitrogen.

Flammability is a strange property for plants in a temperate climate. For example, heathers have thick cell walls when mature, relatively low water content and a high content of flammable volatile compounds. A natural source of ignition is a lightning strike in a summer thunderstorm – the probability of this occurring is perhaps once in 50 years. The more frequent occurrence is certainly either careless or destructive behaviour by people. The ecology of fire has been studied comprehensively in many parts of the world, and is no longer regarded as an unnatural catastrophe, but as part of a long-term cycle in heaths, some coniferous woodlands and eucalypt woodlands. The practical question for landowners and local authorities is how to manage fire in dry heath. The simple answer is that, in an area of about ten hectares, optimum conditions from a biodiversity perspective are to have three or four different ages of heath. The best way of achieving this is to break up the area with rides or broad walking tracks, which will serve as fire breaks and allow access to firefighters on foot. The intensity of fire depends on the fuel density and the direction and speed of the wind. A fire in an old stand of heath,

Ling heather *(Richard Nairn)*

with much fuel, which burns against the prevailing wind, may consume all the living plants and much of the soil organic matter. Regeneration will be slow, and may depend on seed blown in from unburnt areas. In contrast, a fire burning downwind in a six- to ten-year-old stand will probably leave much living material and a substantial bank of seed in the soil. In the following few weeks a dense crop of heather seedlings will appear, interspersed with new shoots of autumn gorse. Stocky seedlings of the gorse may appear later. Five years afterwards, little trace of the burn will remain.

In contrast, a severe burn may result in a succession of 'fireweeds' appearing. These have wind-dispersed seeds and take advantage of the burst of nutrients released by a severe burn. After a few years the fireweeds die out, and the heathland shrubs reassert themselves. The greatest danger to heath from fire is the occurrence of a series of severe fires, with total loss of organic matter from soil. Residual fertility would be eliminated, and the water-storage capacity of the soil greatly reduced. Under these conditions revegetation might take decades to occur, without expensive assistance. Gorse fires are a completely different matter from heath fires, but are often confused on Howth. Gorse invades former agricultural grassland on comparatively fertile drift soils. Fires are used to limit the spread of the shrub, but this technique must be carefully controlled.

Surviving low fertility requires: carrying effective fungal mycorrhiza, which colonise a large soil volume; having a high root-to-shoot ratio; slow growth rates, enabling maximum use of absorbed nutrients, especially phosphate; and low tissue concentrations of phosphate. Autumn gorse also develops nitrogen-fixing root nodules. This makes it independent of external sources of nitrogen, and it is probably a significant contributor to the nitrogen supply of other woody plants such as the heathers.

The main reason why drought is a constant factor in the heath environment is the poor water-storage capacity of the soils. When there is a brief gap in rainfall, soil moisture is rapidly exhausted by plant transpiration. Heath plants do not die, but they shut down water loss in much the same way as the sand dune grasses discussed earlier in this chapter. This part of eastern Ireland only receives 700mm of rainfall

Gorse and heather
(Richard Nairn)

each year, but rain days are numerous. A brief shower may restore the water deficit rapidly. Alternatively, the summer sea fogs of Howth may supply 'occult water', which condenses on leaf hairs and may be later be absorbed into plant tissue or run down the stem to the roots.

The same factors that led to low fertility have generated acid soil. This simply means the absence of minerals such as calcium carbonate or the common clay minerals. To the plant, low pH in the rooting zone means high levels of soluble aluminium, which is toxic to some plant species.

The environmental selection pressures are so strong that all common lowland plants are excluded. However, none of the three dominant heath species survives if the environment alters. This may be readily observed at the edges of the heath community, where even small traces of glacial drift soils are present. Here there are grasses, bracken and even birch trees, which overwhelm and displace the heath flora. Some rare plant species are found on Howth Head – green-winged orchid, bird's-foot, hairy violet and betony. These species are confined to very thin drift soil, marginal to the heath as strictly defined.

The animals of cliff and heathland are small and difficult to observe. A number of rare invertebrates have been recorded from Howth Head – the two-winged fly *Phaonia exoleta* occurs in the woods at the back of Deerpark and has not been seen anywhere else in Ireland, while the ground beetle *Trechus rubens* is found on storm beaches on the eastern cliffs. A hoverfly, *Sphaerophoria batava*, known from only a few Irish locations, is present in the heathland habitat at Howth Head.

Islands

Islands have a romantic image in many people's minds. They are associated with isolation from society and with adventurous people who live a more elemental lifestyle. Surrounded by water, islands can seem like a small world of their own, with well-defined boundaries. For plants and animals, islands offer a refuge from the more intensive land use of the mainland, where only some species can adapt and survive alongside modern human civilisation. Seabirds frequently thrive on islands because of the absence of ground predators, such as foxes, and the relative freedom from human disturbance. Seals also favour uninhabited islands where they are less likely to be disturbed by people and their dogs.

Islands are relatively rare in and around Dublin Bay, but where they occur, they offer safe refuges for larger animals, and some unimproved habitats. The main rocky islands – Ireland's Eye and Dalkey Island – lie off the headlands of Howth and Dalkey respectively, and are essentially extensions of these promontories. Bull Island in the northern part of the Bay is now technically no longer an island as it is linked to the mainland by a bridge and a causeway. It is described in detail earlier in this chapter.

Ireland's Eye

Ireland's Eye, located just north of the Howth peninsula, is a triangular platform of ancient Cambrian greywackes and quartzite rocks. Its highest point is only 69m above sea level, but it has impressive cliffs on the north and east sides. Of particular interest is the stack, or column of rock, that is almost completely separated from the main island. The Vikings used the word *Ey* for island and so it became known as Erin's Ey and ultimately Ireland's Eye. The island was also formerly

The eastern end of Ireland's Eye
(John Fox)

known as *Inis Faithlenn*. On the north side there is a large cave that has a high enough ceiling to allow a boat to enter. There are extensive areas of maritime grassland and bracken on the island slopes and the swathes of bluebells are an impressive sight in early summer. Much of this vegetation is enriched by deposits of seabird guano over many centuries. The only buildings are a ruined church dating from the sixth or seventh century and a Martello tower built in the early 1800s. A climb to the summit at the northern end gives an excellent view of the whole island. Some of the most impressive seabird colonies in the Dublin Bay area are found on Ireland's Eye (see Chapter 6).

Grey seals are a regular feature on the rocks around Ireland's Eye, but pupping is relatively rare in comparison with the larger island of Lambay to the north, which has many suitable beaches and caves that are rarely disturbed. Ireland's Eye attracts a large number of visitors in summer and there are regular small -boat services from nearby Howth Harbour. In dry summers, the vegetation on the island is sometimes set alight and many birds' nests are destroyed.

Dalkey Island

Dalkey Island, which guards the southern entrance to Dublin Bay, has an ancient history. The name of the island and the neighbouring mainland are derived from the Irish phrase *deilg-inis*, meaning 'thorny island'. One view is that this may be a reference to the thorn shape of the island rather than a description of its vegetation.[16] The 'ey' in Dalkey may be derived from the norse word *Ey*, meaning island. There is evidence on Dalkey Island of a promontory fort which had sea on all sides except the landward side, which was protected by a fortified ditch. Archaeological excavations were undertaken in the 1950s by David Liversage,[17] who argued that the earliest settlement on the island belonged to the 'Larnian Culture', a mesolithic culture, named after Larne near Belfast, and found only on sites close to coasts and estuaries in western Scotland and eastern Ireland. The evidence was found in two kitchen middens, piles of discarded shells, sealed by an extensive black layer in which archaeological material from the Neolithic to the early Christian period were intermixed, including Bell Beaker pottery from the later Neolithic period. The remarkably well-preserved early Christian ruins of St Begnet's church are a prominent feature, while the Martello tower that crowns the summit of the island is associated with stonework that once held the swivelling base of defensive canons.

Dalkey Island seen from
Coliemore Harbour
(John Coveney)

There are several smaller islets alongside the main island, the largest of which are Maiden's Rock (to the north) and the Muglins (to the east). There is a freshwater well on the western side of the main island, which may have allowed people to live here in the past. The main habitats found on Dalkey Island are semi-natural grasslands (Yorkshire fog grassland and short-turf maritime grassland); dense bracken; granite outcrop; rocky shores and granite cliffs; and some disturbed ground around the buildings. Some of the plant species on Dalkey Island will tolerate, or perhaps require, a considerable degree of trampling and disturbance and so benefit from grazing.[18]

A small herd of feral goats finds sufficient grazing to live on Dalkey Island throughout the year. Although they tend to run away from visitors, the goats are probably descended from domestic animals that were once used by occupants of the islands. Rabbits are also part of the mammal fauna here, and between them the goats and rabbits graze the coastal grassland to a short sward. Seals have become a significant feature in Dalkey Sound in recent years. These are almost exclusively grey seals and there have been occasional records of their white-coated pups in autumn. The seals are relatively tolerant of boats and will even investigate swimmers and kayaks, which are regular visitors.

Several gull species breed among the bracken slopes and a few pairs of shelduck and oystercatcher are generally present in summer. Of special interest are the terns that breed on Maiden Rock at the northern end of Dalkey Sound. Common terns are regular breeders, with occasional nests of Arctic tern and the rarer roseate tern. BirdWatch Ireland has established a nestbox scheme here and this has given them shelter, encouraging greater numbers of terns to breed (see Chapter 6).

6 | Birds

Birds are among the most attractive and popular animals and their close proximity to people in Dublin Bay makes them easy to study and enjoy. Most birds do not recognise our subdivision of Dublin Bay into separate habitats, as set out in the last three chapters. Instead, they move freely around the bay in search of food, refuge and breeding places. For this reason, we have devoted a separate chapter to the birds alone.

Despite being surrounded by urban development, Dublin Bay has some of the largest and most impressive bird populations in Ireland. It holds internationally important numbers of four species of waterbirds in winter and nationally important flocks of a further 18 species. The majority of these species are waders and gulls.

Black guillemots on the South Wall of Dublin Port *(John Fox)*

The wintering flocks of brent geese are among the most approachable of their species, given that they breed in the Arctic wilderness of northern Canada. There is a large breeding tern colony within the confines of Dublin Port and tens of thousands of terns from all over the Irish Sea gather to roost on Sandymount Strand at the start of their long annual migrations to Africa. This roost of terns in Dublin Bay is the largest and most spectacular in Ireland and Britain.[1] The seabirds that breed on the cliffs of Howth Head, Ireland's Eye and Lambay feed in the shallow waters of the Bay where fish abound. Dublin Bay offers many opportunities for birdwatching just a short walk or bus ride from the city centre.

Early birdwatching in Dublin Bay

The early inhabitants of Dublin probably saw the arrivals and departures of the birds in the bay as a sign of the changing seasons. They also treated them as food. Prehistoric settlers would probably have collected seabirds' eggs in summer from the cliffs of Howth and the offshore islands and perhaps also harvested some of the fat-rich seabird chicks for winter food, as was common on other coasts of Ireland.[2] Excavation of the middens (or empty shell heaps) at Sutton and in the Viking heart of Dublin has revealed remains of several coastal bird species. The excavations at High Street and Wood Quay show that, by the Anglo-Norman period, the inhabitants of the early city were trapping wild geese and ducks on the estuary wetlands, along with wintering waders such as plovers, snipe and woodcock.

There is scant written record of the birds in Dublin Bay until 1772, when John Rutty published his *Essay towards a Natural History of the County of Dublin*.[3] His notes on the birds of the county give details of the status of each species with a reference to the value of each as food. By the mid-nineteenth century natural history was developing as a pursuit of the leisured classes. A landmark publication of this time was William Thompson's *Natural History of Ireland* (1849–51),[4] the first three volumes of which were devoted entirely to birds. Thompson, a resident of Belfast, relied on many local ornithologists all around Ireland to keep him informed of the status of common species as well as the occurrence of rarer specimens. One of his regular correspondents, R.J. Montgomery, wrote in 1849, 'the Sanderling appears in Dublin Bay in small flocks, on the sea-side of the North Bull, where I never saw more than, I should think, from fifteen to twenty at a time'. Today, Dollymount Strand remains one of the best areas to see sanderling following the tide edge in Dublin Bay. Of the purple sandpiper, Thompson records how 'Mr W.S. Wall, bird preserver, Dublin, presented me in 1833 with an immature specimen which was shot by himself at the lighthouse beyond the Pigeon-house Fort, Dublin Bay.' Purple sandpipers still occur each winter on the piers and rocky shores around Dublin Bay from Dalkey to Howth.

THE SANDERLING.

Sanderlings
(William Yarrell 1848)

Thompson was a fine observer in his own right. He could also be quite lyrical. He wrote, 'In the silence of a fine starry night, when nought else is heard, the cry of the Curlew, consisting both of the simple and the long-drawn tremulous whistle, uttered from a great height in the air, has a very fine effect', and added, 'the calling and answering of these birds by night is often heard over the city of Dublin.' Another of Thompson's correspondents in Dublin, John Watters, published *The Natural History of the Birds of Ireland* (1853),[5] but Watters was more interested in the romantic images and songs of the birds than in recording their status, as Thompson did so accurately. Thompson wrote: 'Mr J. Watters, jun., informs me that during the night, he hears great flocks of wildfowl pass over the house where he lives (in Crow-street), in the midst of the city of Dublin, particularly early in winter and spring. Between ten and eleven o'clock, on the night of 20th March 1850, flocks of wigeon continued to pass over for nearly three-quarters of an hour, the loud calls of which afforded evidence of their species.'

One Dublin ornithologist who seems to have been virtually forgotten was Alexander Williams (1846–1930).[6] Praeger fails to mention him in his encyclopaedic book *Some Irish Naturalists* and there is no reference to him in the historical review in Clive Hutchinson's *The Birds of Dublin and Wicklow*.[7] Williams was originally from Drogheda but moved to Dublin as a youth. His family were hat manufacturers, but following a decline in this trade, he and his brother began a taxidermy business in Dublin's Dame Street, where they sold mostly bird specimens. Some of the specimens mounted by the Williams brothers are still on display in the Natural History Museum in Dublin's Merrion Street. The backgrounds of these display cases were painted by Alexander Williams himself – he was an accomplished artist and a member of the Royal Hibernian Academy. Williams was a dedicated naturalist and birdwatcher and his unpublished diaries give a fascinating day-to-day account of the bird species that he encountered in Dublin Bay and further afield.[8] He wrote many articles for the journal *The Irish Naturalist*, among them a 1908 paper entitled 'Bird life in Dublin Bay'.[9]

In one of his most interesting observations, Williams records: 'a colony of the Lesser Tern (now known as the little tern) has existed for many years in varying numbers, nesting under many difficulties [on Shelly Banks beach in South Dublin Bay]. Unfortunately, in recent years bicyclists in increasing numbers and youngsters have found their way to the bank, chiefly on Sundays, often accompanied by dogs, and the nests have frequently been raided.' Williams then gives a brief account of what must have been the earliest bird conservation project in Dublin Bay: 'arrangements have been made to place a watcher on the Shelly Bank, and it is hoped that the birds may now have a better chance of their numbers increasing.'

Williams was also especially knowledgeable about the birds that used a now-vanished island on the north side of Dublin Bay:

Alexander Williams
(1846–1930)

On Clontarf Island and in its vicinity my late brother Edward and myself for years had many opportunities of becoming acquainted with the appearance and habits of nearly every species of bird that frequented the shores of Dublin Bay. The early frosty mornings of September used to find us wading along the sandy margins of the streams that skirted the island, searching closely among the flocks of Dunlins for the Little Stint or the Curlew Sandpiper, and sometimes late into moonlight nights lying among the long grass and listening to the confused cries of the multitudes of sea-fowl spread all over the island to the water's edge. The rising of the tide away down at Sutton and Dollymount, and the covering up of the mud-flats and feeding-grounds, both by day and night, brought great flocks of birds up the Bay, and gradually as the tide approached high water they crowded on Clontarf Island. On a day in winter it used to be a great delight to watch through a field-glass the movements of this great collection of wild-fowl.

Williams eloquently described the appearance of a bird of prey at the high tide roost:

This scene of repose and enjoyment would sometimes suddenly change, the birds at the same instant becoming violently agitated, and springing into the air in masses, wheeling and curving as the different flocks swept away from the island, their loud call-notes and alarm cries making a babel of musical sounds. The startled

Foraging Bar-tailed Godwit on the edge of the tide *(John Fox)*

onlooker might gaze in surprise, thinking a boat had suddenly appeared to cause so great a disturbance, but the quick eyes of the birds had discerned their natural enemy, the Peregrine Falcon, high overhead, coming from his eyrie over the rugged slopes of Ireland's Eye, where the Falcons have bred for years, and in a few seconds he might be seen in a long swooping flight in search of his prey, alarming and putting up every flock of birds from Howth to Clontarf.

This was a time when shooting birds was an acceptable method of examining their plumage and obtaining specimens for taxidermy. Williams writes: 'Owing to the want of cover for shooters few of the rarer birds have been obtained on the island. A friend once on a moonlit night obtained a Little Stint by firing at random at a flock of Dunlin. My brother secured some Curlew Sandpipers more than once from a boat at the tail of the Bank.' Thompson referred to the shooting of green sandpipers at Clontarf and also of the purchase of one of these rare birds from 'a hawker in the metropolis'. A late nineteenth-century ornithologist, H. Blake Knox, who lived in Dalkey, regularly took his boat out on Dublin Bay in pursuit of rarities. He recorded quite casually that he shot five or six black-throated divers, now a rare winter visitor to the Bay. His most valuable written contribution was a paper in the *Zoologist* journal (1866) on the migratory birds of County Dublin.[10]

Knots and Bar-tailed Godwits drop into a high tide roost in South Dublin Bay
(John Coveney)

By the late nineteenth century, ornithology was growing in popularity as a separate interest from shooting. Richard Barrington, a resident of Fassaroe near Bray, County Wicklow, was a leading ornithologist of this period. He was one of the pioneers of the study of bird migration and he set up a network of correspondents, mainly lighthouse keepers, all around the coast of Ireland. Over two decades, he systematically collated records of birds seen and collected by the keepers at these remote stations. Realising the importance of night migration, he recorded how thousands of birds were attracted to the bright lights, where they often met their deaths. He corresponded with both the keepers of the Baily Lighthouse on the point of Howth Head and the keepers on the Kish lightship, stationed on the sandbank that marks the outer limits of Dublin Bay.

His famous book, *The Migrations of Birds as Observed at Irish Lighthouses and Lightships* (1900),[11] contains records from 1881–97 as well as measurements of about 1,600 wings that the keepers sent to him for zoological examination. This collection is now housed in the Natural History Museum. Barrington's invaluable book also records original observations for each year of the survey. At the Baily, he notes in September 1888, 'large numbers of sea gulls follow the Hopper barges daily at all seasons in the neighbourhood of this station. These barges come out from Dublin to discharge mud and one carries the rubbish swept off the streets.' Many hundreds of migratory songbirds were also recorded by the lightkeepers. For example: 'Kish Bank Lightship – March seventeenth 1890, one Skylark killed striking at 11pm going NW. March eighteenth, several Skylarks with Thrushes about the lantern at 11pm. Howth Baily – October seventeenth 1892: some Starlings struck lantern at 11pm, one caught'. Barrington also produced a guide to the birds of the Dublin District for the 1908 meeting of British Association of Science.[12]

Modern ornithology in Dublin Bay

One of the best-known ornithologists of the early twentieth century was Father Patrick Kennedy, a Jesuit priest who became a teacher of classics at Belvedere College, Dublin. He was a leading member of the Dublin Naturalists' Field Club and its president in 1941/42. Father Kennedy used the new medium of radio to raise awareness about the birds of Dublin Bay. In 1953, his popular little book *An Irish Sanctuary – Birds of the North Bull*[13] did much to awaken the interest of Dubliners to the wealth of birdlife on the edge of the city. It was also largely due to Kennedy's efforts that Bull Island became Ireland's first bird sanctuary, designated under an order signed by the Minister for Justice in 1931. In his book, Kennedy outlined the reasons for this designation, including this far-sighted vision:

> The reason which outweighed all others for the choice of the North Bull was the educational and cultural value of having a bird sanctuary so near to the city of Dublin with its schools, colleges and universities. Nature study is an important part of education, and teachers could take their pupils either in groups or classes to study wild birds and their habitats at close quarter. The well-known fact that birds quickly recognise the absence of danger makes this possible. Birds know the difference between a man with a gun and a man with a pair of field glasses; where there is no shooting they are not easily frightened.

From then until his death in 1967, Father Kennedy led a series

Brent geese on the saltmarsh at Bull Island. Note the numbered leg-rings. *(John Fox)*

of campaigns to prevent reclamation of Dublin Bay for various developments (see Chapter 11).

Shortly after Kennedy's death, the Irish Wildbird Conservancy (IWC) was formed by the amalgamation of three smaller conservation and ornithological bodies, some of which had existed since the previous century. The foundation of the IWC coincided with a renewed interest in the birds of Dublin Bay. While wildfowl counts at Bull Island had been carried out at intervals since 1951, it was not until the early 1970s that an energetic young ornithologist, Clive Hutchinson, organised systematic winter counts of all waders and wildfowl around Bull Island. This intensive study was part of the IWC Wetlands Enquiry, summarised in Hutchinson's landmark book *Ireland's Wetlands and their Birds*.[14] His comments on Dublin Bay in the 1970s make interesting reading today. Hutchinson records that at the time, Bull Island was under continuing threat from local authorities.

> Dublin Corporation commenced the dumping of domestic refuse on the saltmarsh several years ago but has halted operations pending the production of a scientific report on the area by [the research institute] An Foras Forbartha. Dublin Port and Docks Board has proposed plans which involve converting part of the channel into an enclosed lagoon and reclaiming much of the

mudflat outside the island.

He urged 'the utmost vigilance to ensure the survival of this remarkable wetland'.

One of the main issues that exercised conservationists in the 1960s and 1970s was the building, by Dublin Corporation, of a causeway at Bull Island. Hutchinson remarked:

> [I]n 1964, a causeway from the mainland to the mid-point of the island, which has been under construction for several years, halted the tidal flow through the channel. Without the scouring action of the tide silting followed on each side of the causeway, saltmarsh succession resulted and several fertile clumps of cordgrass established themselves on the mudflat.

The ornithologists were so alarmed by this dramatic change in the Bull mudflats that 'a programme of bird counts was initiated in September 1967 to monitor the numbers of all wildfowl species on a continuing basis.' For his paper on the first phase of this programme, Hutchinson drew on earlier unpublished counts at the North Bull in the 1950s and 1960s organised by the Dublin-based ornithologist George Humphreys and the Irish Wildfowl Committee. This allowed him to produce the first graphs showing long-term changes in the birds at this site.[15]

Hutchinson, an accountant by profession, was a good organiser as

Roosting waders and gulls at the Bull Island saltmarsh (John Fox)

well as a prolific researcher and writer. Shortly before he returned to his native Cork to set up an accountancy practice, he published a very useful account of the birds of the two counties of Dublin and Wicklow,[16] in which he noted that at Bull Island 'the long series of duck counts, carried out over twenty years, produced no evidence of decrease in the numbers of any species apart from the occasional fluctuations from one year to another. Indeed, three species, Teal, Pintail and Shoveler, have increased over this period. Teal may have increased because of the increased food supply provided by the spread of *Salicornia*.' This suggests that ornithologists' fears that the building of the causeway would imperil the wetland were overstated.

The 1970s was a period of intensive study of Bull Island by academics from Trinity College and University College Dublin. This resulted in the 1977 publication of a remarkable book about the island, its environment and ecology, edited by David Jeffrey, with contributions from expert authors.[17] The launch of the book *North Bull Island* coincided with a memorable seminar held at the prestigious premises of the Royal Dublin Society. Clive Hutchinson wrote a chapter for the book on the birds of Bull Island. Going beyond his earlier accounts of numbers of common wildfowl and waders, he also summarised the less frequent

Waders mass together in a roost at high tide at Merrion Strand *(John Coveney)*

species – seabirds and land birds – that could be seen around the northern part of Dublin Bay. Another chapter, by Roger Goodwillie, explored the ecology of wildfowl and waders, 'to put them into some sort of perspective within their chosen environment'.

By the 1980s, the academics had expanded their horizons to embrace the whole of Dublin Bay. A programme of lectures at UCD resulted in a book entitled *Managing Dublin Bay*,[18] which contained a chapter on the waterfowl of Dublin Bay by Micheál Ó Briain,[19] then a zoology student at UCD. Ó Briain was undertaking a detailed study of the ecology of the brent geese that used the bay and surrounding coastal grasslands. He noted that 'a unique feature of Dublin Bay is that it is a suburban environment where the birds are habituated to humans – more so than in other estuaries. They are the most studied birds in Ireland, which is not surprising, as they occur in such numbers and [are] such a conspicuous feature of the suburban coastline.'

Further details of the bird populations can be found in a paper by Olivia Crowe[20] and in the regular reports of the Irish Wetland Bird Survey.[21] In total, some 63 waterbird species have been recorded in Dublin Bay. Overall, the numbers of waterbirds have remained relatively stable, although enormous numbers of gulls in some winters temporarily elevate the peak numbers. Published data give an average peak of 31,700 birds over the five winters 2006/07 to 2010/11.[22] Any site that regularly supports more than 20,000 waterbirds is considered to be of international importance in a European context. In Dublin Bay, the most common species are black-headed gulls, dunlin, oystercatcher, golden plover, knot, light-bellied brent geese and redshank. The bay also holds significant numbers of bar-tailed godwit, black-tailed godwit, curlew and shelduck.

The most recent survey work by BirdWatch Ireland, undertaken as part of the comprehensive Dublin Bay Birds Project, included low-tide and rising-tide surveys carried out on a monthly basis between 2013 and 2016. In every month, the total number of birds recorded was greater during the low-tide survey than the rising-tide survey. This is probably because the numbers are difficult to estimate accurately when birds are roosting in tightly packed flocks. Both surveys showed a build-up in numbers to a midwinter peak, with the highest number recorded on a single survey day at 34,241. In total, 64 waterbird species were recorded across all these surveys.[23]

Birds and their ecology

Most of the writings on birds in Dublin Bay concern the species present and changes in numbers. To understand what brings such large numbers and diversity of birds here year after year we need to probe a little deeper into their behaviour and ecology. The main attractions of the bay for the birds are rich food resources, safe roosting places and nesting sites. To illustrate the lifestyles and ecology of the wide variety of birds in Dublin Bay, we have chosen brent goose, oystercatcher, kittiwake and common tern as representatives of the wildfowl, waders and seabirds. But we start by describing each group as a whole.

Wildfowl

Swans, geese, ducks and grebes are generally categorised as wildfowl – a leftover from the days when they were all legal quarry for shooters. Only one goose species, the light-bellied brent goose, occurs regularly in Dublin Bay and this is described in more detail below. It is easy to see a variety of ducks in the bay, ranging from the large, conspicuous shelduck to the small teal that hide in the saltmarsh creeks on Bull Island. In fact, the main concentrations of ducks in Dublin Bay are found in the saltmarsh and lagoons that fringe the island. There are also significant numbers of wigeon, mallard, pintail and shoveler here. The numbers of shelduck reached a peak in the 1990s and 2000s but declined again in the period 2001–2008. By contrast, wigeon declined by about a half up to 2000 and then further declined so that by 2008 there were few left here. This reflects international trends and may be linked with climate change; less sea ice in the northern hemisphere allows the birds to overwinter further north. Other species have fluctuated over the decades but some have declined. On the more open waters of the bay small flocks of fish-eating red-breasted mergansers and great crested grebes dive for their prey.

Brent geese: city visitors

Brent geese are mainly black and grey in colour with a distinctive white rump, which is visible in flight. Those that winter in Ireland are from a race with pale bellies; those found in Britain are mainly from the dark-bellied race. The two races breed in quite separate parts of the Arctic and, while they may meet in winter, mixing or interbreeding are rare. Brent are almost exclusively coastal in winter, favouring estuaries and other sheltered shores. Like many of the geese and swans, the young

Brent geese on coastal grassland at Clontarf *(John Coveney)*

birds stay with their parents over winter, following them on migration and learning from them about the best places to feed. The long lines of geese that fly daily across the city are moving from overnight roosts on Bull Island to daytime feeding areas. Normally, one of the experienced adults takes the lead in these daily commuter flights, with the younger birds falling in behind. Micheál Ó Briain noted that Dublin Bay was a stop-off area for the geese on migration, highlighted by the observation of an individual ringed bird seen on Strangford Lough, Dublin Bay and the Kerry bays all within the space of a week in early October 1986.[24]

As the days shorten and the temperatures drop in autumn, the first brent geese arrive in Dublin Bay after a 5,000km migration from Arctic Canada with a short stopover in Iceland. The most important food for the geese to regain condition after the long flight is a marine flowering plant called eelgrass. It is found in only a few places in the muddiest parts of the bay, with the largest patch close to the Merrion Gates at Sandymount. The links between brent geese and eelgrass were studied in detail by Micheál Ó Briain in the 1980s.[25] He measured the biomass (weight of organic matter) of the eelgrass, both above and below the sand, before the geese arrived in September. He then recorded the depletion of the eelgrass and the number of goose-hours that were spent consuming this protein-rich food. By November, the small patch of vegetation was completely exhausted and the geese moved on to feeding on green seaweeds and saltmarsh plants.

Brent geese are essentially vegetarians and they need to graze more or less continuously during daylight hours to keep their bodies in good condition for the long migration to the Arctic breeding grounds. As the population wintering in Ireland has grown steadily, the amount of intertidal feeding habitat in Dublin Bay has been exceeded and the geese have gradually moved on to feeding on coastal grasslands, including parks, sports pitches and other open spaces all around Dublin city. This phenomenon has been seen in other parts of the winter range, but nowhere is the adaptation to urban living so complete as in Dublin. Micheál Ó Briain seen this behaviour as early as the 1980s.[26] Another UCD ornithologist, Lorraine Benson, studied this habit of grassland feeding in the winter of 2006–2007 and she catalogued up to sixty different sites in Dublin, some of them more than 10km from the shorelines of Dublin Bay.[27] There are now over a hundred inland sites around the city with flocks of geese. The geese have learned this behaviour over several generations, passing on the essential information to their offspring, who stay with the parents throughout the winter. By night, the majority of the geese fly back to the saltmarsh on Bull Island, or swim on the waters of Dublin Bay, for safety from ground predators and people. Long V-shaped skeins of geese cross the evening sky heading out to the bay.

Brent geese feeding on spilt agricultural products in Dublin Port *(Richard Nairn)*

The study of energetics looks at the balance between food resources and energy consumption, a challenge that these long-lived birds face daily. The mathematics of this balance for the brent goose has been carefully calculated by scientists from Exeter University, led by Stuart Bearhop, both for the wintering sites in Ireland and on the migration staging grounds in Iceland. The research has been greatly assisted by the fact that a high proportion of the birds in the brent goose flocks are individually marked. This programme of catching and marking the birds with large numbered coloured rings has been organised by a voluntary team of enthusiasts who are members of the Irish Brent Goose Research Group. The team assembles several times a year to use their skills in cannon netting on various Dublin sites as they try to outwit the wary geese.

As the winter progresses the geese begin to break up into smaller flocks and disperse widely in search of scarcer food resources. By now they are even found on rocky shores and harbours, where they find some green seaweeds on the hard surfaces. In a recent development, brent geese have discovered that the quays in Dublin Port offer a further source of food. Agricultural products such as soya meal and maize are unloaded from the ships using large cranes and some of the material inevitably falls on the quay walls. The geese gather in large flocks on the water of Alexandra Basin in the port and, when the workers have left, they fly up to the quay wall to feed intensely on this protein-rich food. It probably helps them to build up body condition for the long flight back to the Arctic.

Waders

The waders are highly adapted for feeding in estuaries, with long legs and bills of different lengths suitable for reaching their preferred prey buried in the sand and mud. Clive Hutchinson and John Rochford summarised the occurrence of waders at Bull Island in the 1970s.[28] More recent data for the whole of Dublin Bay is available in the results of the Irish Wetland Bird Survey and the Dublin Bay Birds Project, both organised by BirdWatch Ireland. The most numerous species are dunlin, oystercatcher, knot, golden plover, redshank and bar-tailed godwit. Among the most impressive sights are the large roosts of waders, swirling flocks of knot, dunlin, oystercatcher and godwits that settle at high tide in the area of Merrion Strand and the Bull Island saltmarsh.

An oystercatcher calls from a rock (John Fox)

Oystercatchers: waders of beaches and grassland

One of the most distinctive of the waders seen throughout the year in Dublin Bay is the oystercatcher. With its smart black and white plumage, bright orange/red bill and pink legs it is difficult to confuse with any other species. Oystercatchers feed mainly on worms and shellfish, including cockles in sandy shores and mussels in rocky areas. However, they also occur in muddy areas such as the lagoons on the landward side of Bull Island, and here they have been found to select marine worms such as ragworms as the main prey.[29]

On Sandymount Strand, the oystercatchers concentrate on cockles and a clear correlation has been found between the density of these shellfish and the density of the waders.[30] John Quinn, now professor of zoology at University College Cork, also found that oystercatchers are more likely to move inland to feed on earthworms after rain, when the ground is soft and easier to probe. Larger numbers of birds feed inland when high tide is in the middle of day and is covering their intertidal foraging areas on Sandymount Strand. Quinn also found more of the waders feeding inland later in winter as cockle stocks become depleted. He noticed that the birds feeding inland tend to have finer-pointed bills than those on the shore. This is a known dichotomy in coastal areas generally. However, the fact that more of the inland feeders have pointed bills suggests that some individuals probably specialise in using these grasslands and that repeated probing in soil causes less wear and tear on their bills when compared with those that spend their time hammering open the tough shells of cockles.[31] One other interesting finding was that immature oystercatchers move to feed inland earlier in the winter,

Oystercatchers marked with yellow rings on Sandymount Strand *(John Fox)*

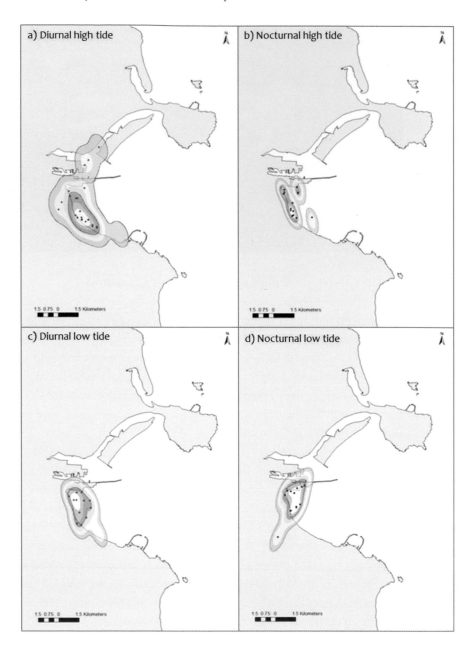

a) Diurnal high tide

b) Nocturnal high tide

c) Diurnal low tide

d) Nocturnal low tide

Radio-tracking locations and estimated home ranges of four oystercatchers in Dublin Bay in 2014 *(Courtesy of BirdWatch Ireland)*.

suggesting that earthworms are easier than shellfish for these birds to catch.

Recent research by BirdWatch Ireland, using colour-ringing of oystercatcher, redshank and bar-tailed godwit in Dublin Bay, has uncovered other secrets of the birds' lives. The main ringing site is on the shore of Merrion Strand near Booterstown Marsh, and cannon-nets have been used to catch and mark a large sample of several hundred birds with distinctive yellow plastic leg rings, each bearing a unique code, just like a car registration. From the more than 2,500 resightings of these birds (normally using a telescope) it has been found that there is a remarkable consistency in their daily movements and that the vast majority of the oystercatchers that roost at high tide on south Dublin Bay also feed here at low tide. In fact, the distribution of the bulk of resightings corresponds closely with the main density of cockles recorded by James Wilson thus supporting the findings of John Quinn that oystercatchers depend heavily on this shellfish (see map on page 46). The BirdWatch Ireland research has also included radio-tracking and satellite-tracking of some of the oystercatchers, curlews, redshanks and godwits, each of which was fitted with a small transmitter. The results show that individual birds are remarkably faithful to the same sections of shoreline throughout the winter, suggesting that they cannot easily shift elsewhere if disturbed. The colour-ringing of oystercatchers in Dublin Bay has also resulted in a large number of resightings elsewhere. This shows that the majority of these birds move north in spring to breed in Scotland, Iceland and Scandinavia.[32]

Disturbance of birds in the bay

On sunny weekends, when the tide is low, thousands of people flock to the beaches of Sandymount and Dollymount strands. A study of

Dog chasing black-tailed godwits. (Dogs should be kept on a lead when on the beach or dunes.) *(John Fox)*

the effects of people and their dogs walking on pathways, fields and beaches in the area of Irishtown, south Dublin Bay, found that foraging birds, spread across the intertidal area, largely tolerated people and dogs moving predictably along coastal paths, and these caused very little disturbance.[33] However, when dogs and people left the paths they sometimes caused the birds to fly. Dogs were implicated in three quarters of the disturbance events that caused ten or more birds to take flight.

Of those birds studied, oystercatchers spent less than 1% of their feeding time in flight as a result of disturbance, while Brent geese flew about twice as much after disturbance. In Strangford Lough, a study found that wigeon flew at greater distances from human activity than brent geese and were less likely to return to their preferred sites.[34] The effects of this extra flight on the survival of the birds are not known exactly, but it is likely that it may be significant, especially in spring, when the birds must increase their body weight rapidly to give them the energy for migration. Perhaps the only solution is for the local authorities to create no-disturbance zones at certain times of year to allow the birds some refuge, in the same way that no-shooting refuges elsewhere have been shown to benefit waterbird survival. The bird flocks are much more vulnerable when they are roosting in tight flocks at the high water mark.[35] This one of the reasons why the East Coast Trail and cycleway should not be routed along the seaward side of the railway

Kitesurfing event on
Dollymount Strand *(John Fox)*

embankment between Merrion Gates and Blackrock. This area holds a vitally important high tide roost of waders, gulls and brent geese.

John Fox has recently undertaken research into how recreational disturbance in Dublin Bay affects feeding by oystercatchers.[36] When direct disturbance occurred to individual birds, their prey capture rates, time spent searching for prey and the numbers of prey-finding activities all declined. Disturbance to individuals resulted in increased time spent running, flying, preening and remaining stationary or being vigilant. Fox also looked specifically at how these waders responded to the relatively recent sport of kitesurfing. Where disturbance did occur, particularly from kitesurfing, oystercatcher numbers were reduced. Kitesurfing was identified as a significant cause of disturbance and, when ongoing, appeared to completely displace many of the oystercatchers from the sandflats.

Seabirds

Seabirds are relatively poorly understood compared with land birds because they are out of sight for much of the year. They are creatures of both land and sea, although their time on dry land is brief compared to the proportion of their life spent in or over the ocean. For example,

Herring gulls on a coastal building *(John Fox)*

terns spend most of the year feeding at sea or migrating between the northern and southern hemispheres. They only come to land to breed for a few weeks in spring and summer and even then, they will fly out to sea to catch fish to feed their young. Their very short legs make them quite clumsy on the ground, but when they take to the air their flight is both strong and graceful.

Dublin Bay is used by seabirds throughout the year, but many of them breed elsewhere. Breeding sites for seabirds around the bay are quite limited. The cliffs of Howth Head, and Ireland's Eye hold some large colonies of seabirds. The islands around Dalkey on the south side also hold a few breeding seabirds and some artificial sites in the ports and harbours provide good nesting places for black guillemots, common and Arctic terns. While many seabirds remain in the offshore areas throughout the day, gulls spend long periods in the inner parts of Dublin Bay. They are among the most familiar of the seabird species and many live very close to cities and towns. Huge roosts of gulls occur on the sandflats of Sandymount and Merrion Strands and the Tolka Estuary. These are mostly black-headed and common gulls, but significant numbers of herring gulls and great black-backed gulls also occur. There is often a large peak of gulls on the strands in the evening as birds gather to roost, having fed elsewhere during the day. The late Oscar Merne and colleagues recorded huge peaks of nearly 40,000 black-headed gulls staging here prior to their spring migration along the east coast.[37] In Dublin Port, flocks are constantly present around the effluent discharge from the Ringsend Waste Water Treatment Works, and they can often be seen feeding in the wake of large ships. Many black-headed and common gulls feed inland, on grassland or on arable land, where they find soil invertebrates. Herring gulls are well known for their scavenging behaviour on refuse in cities and fishing ports. They have also developed a habit of nesting on the roofs of tall buildings, which they treat as substitute cliffs or islands that are mostly free of ground predators. Stand in any part of Merrion Square in the early morning in summer and you will hear the loud cries of the gulls between the chimneys high above the streets. This behaviour was first recorded in O'Connell Street in 1972 and by 2016 there were widespread nests in the city and coastal towns such as Howth.

The main colonies of cliff-breeding seabirds are on Howth Head and Ireland's Eye, to the north of Dublin Bay. Lambay Island, about 11km north of Howth, has the largest seabird colonies on this side of the Irish

Sea and is probably the breeding site of many of the seabirds that feed in Dublin Bay. A census of Howth Head in 2015 recorded the following species: kittiwake, common guillemot, razorbill, fulmar, shag and herring gull. Kittiwakes were the most numerous, with over 1,770 nests. The seabirds of Ireland's Eye were surveyed by Oscar Merne and Brian Madden in the 1980s and 1990s.[38] Eleven seabird species were breeding regularly on the island and it was of national importance for seven of these. By 2015 the most numerous seabirds were common guillemot, with 4,410 individuals, and razorbill, with 1,600.[39]

Perhaps the most impressive are the gannets, which colonised Ireland's Eye as recently as the 1980s and increased from 17 nests in 1984/85 to 547 nests in 2013.[40] This rapid growth is thought to be due to immigration (or overspill) of birds from other colonies around Ireland and Britain. They regularly feed in Dublin Bay, where they dive vertically into the water. Until the early twentieth century, gannet colonies were raided each summer for the eggs and fat-rich chicks, which could be easily harvested and salted for winter food.[41] This hunting pressure reduced the gannet populations to a perilously low level, but more recent protection has resulted in rapid population growth and the colonisation of several sites that had no gannets in recorded history.

Gannets nesting at Ireland's Eye
(John Fox)

Dublin Bay offers a very attractive feeding habitat for a variety of seabirds. A selection of these can be seen from the deck of any ferry entering or leaving Dublin Port. Many of these birds spend the majority of the year feeding at sea, which makes them quite vulnerable to pollution and threats such as offshore developments. In Dublin Bay seabirds are quite accustomed to shipping and some species follow in the wake of ships, feeding on the fish and invertebrates disturbed by the propellers. Gulls, gannets and fulmars often follow fishing vessels, scavenging fish discards and fish offal.

In 2013–14 a series of dedicated boat-based surveys of seabirds in the Dublin Port shipping channel area was carried out by Richard Nairn and Mike Trewby. The area covered was from the inner port to the outermost limit of the dredged channel at the Dublin Bay Buoy, and 28 bird species were recorded. The most frequently recorded were black-headed gull, cormorant, herring gull, common tern and common guillemot. The most abundant species throughout all the surveys was black-headed gull, with a peak of 665 in September.

The majority of these birds were roosting on and around the outfall from the Ringsend Treatment Works. A large flock of kittiwake was also

Black Guillemot nesting in a drainage pipe at Dublin Port
(Richard Nairn)

foraging in the inner port in summer but was not recorded for the rest of the year. These birds probably came from the large breeding colonies on the cliffs at Howth Head. Common and Arctic terns are common in the port from June to August (the main breeding season) but are largely absent later in the year. Black guillemots also use the shipping channel regularly during the breeding season but are relatively scarce after that. A sizeable population of these small seabirds breeds in Dublin Port, Howth and Dún Laoghaire Harbours, using old drainage pipes and other cavities in the quay walls.

Significant numbers of cormorants, shags and herring gulls use the port and shipping channel for foraging and roosting throughout the year, frequently perching on jetties and navigation lights. Common guillemots are also present throughout the year, with small flocks typically foraging throughout the bay. Most other species occur irregularly or in small numbers. A good selection of seabirds feeding at sea can also be seen from the piers of Dún Laoghaire Harbour, Poolbeg lighthouse or from the vantage point of Howth Head. Despite the regular shipping traffic, Dublin Port is a valuable feeding area for seabirds.

Kittiwakes: cliff-nesting seabirds

Kittiwakes with chicks
(Brian Burke)

Kittiwakes nest in huge, noisy colonies that can include thousands of birds. The kittiwake male returns to the same nesting site year after year. Male and female pairs may mate for more than one season. The nest is cup-shaped and made of moss, seaweed and the birds' droppings and is stuck on the top or side of a cliff or ledge. The largest kittiwake colonies

in Dublin Bay are on Howth Head between the Baily and the Nose of Howth. The female lays one to three pinkish-brown eggs. The male and female incubate the eggs and both parents care for and feed the chicks. The chicks can fly when they are about 40 days old. The kittiwake eats marine invertebrates, plankton, and fish, feeding in flocks and catching food at the surface of the water. It also dives just below the surface of the water to catch its prey – in fact, it is the only gull that dives and swims underwater.

Common terns: migratory seabirds

In summer, Dublin Bay is home to two species of breeding tern. Terns are smaller relatives of the seagull and are listed for special protection in the EU Birds Directive. The Arctic tern has one of the longest-known migration routes, having been recorded flying between the Arctic and Antarctic oceans within a single year. The tern colony in Dublin Port is one of the largest in Ireland, with up to 500 pairs of common terns and some Arctic terns. Smaller numbers of terns also breed on Dalkey Island in the southern part of the bay and a pair will occasionally even nest on the deck of a moored boat. The terns arrive from their African wintering grounds in April and leave again in September or October. In the port they breed on artificial structures such as jetties and mooring structures as well as two custom-made floating pontoons. The nests are closely spaced, with up to three or four per square metre. Adults take turns to incubate up to four speckled eggs and they regularly fly in and out of the wider bay carrying fish to feed the growing chicks. Once the

Common tern adult (left) and juvenile in Dublin Port
(John Fox)

fledglings are capable of flight, they follow the adults out to the feeding grounds where they learn to fish for themselves by plunge-diving into the shallow waters.

As the autumn progresses, the locally bred birds are joined by large flocks of terns from other parts of the Irish Sea and further afield as Dublin Bay provides reliable stocks of oil-rich fish, helping the terns to build up body condition for their long migration to the tropics. In the evenings they gather in their thousands on Sandymount Strand, and at least six tern species have been recorded here.[42]

A tern flock at Clontarf
(John Fox)

Counting these birds is particularly difficult as the swirling flocks are rarely settled and move about in the rapidly fading light. The number of terns here reached a peak of 11,700 in 2006 and 17,440 in 2016.[43] There is a high turnover of birds, as some leave within a few days, and the total number of individuals may be considerably higher. Many of these terns come from the large colony on Rockabill off the north Dublin coast, but the presence of black terns in some years suggests that some of the roosting birds have come from further afield than the Irish Sea – this species does not breed in Ireland. Common terns marked with rings from Norway and the UK were recorded in 2014 and in 2015, which shows that at least some of the birds come from outside the Dublin breeding colonies to gather here before setting out on their long migration.[44]

Seabirds on the offshore banks

The Kish and Burford banks, two shallow sandy areas that lie between Howth Head and Dalkey, are favoured by a range of seabirds for feeding, especially in the summer months. BirdWatch Ireland has carried out extensive surveys of these species and they recorded the importance of the banks for feeding terns, shag, common guillemot and a range of other common seabirds. Of particular interest is that fact that terns foraging here in summer use the Kish Lighthouse as a convenient roosting site. Terns from the Dublin Port colony probably commute out here every day to feed. Using data loggers attached to the birds' legs, BirdWatch Ireland has shown that shags nesting on Lambay Island appear to concentrate their feeding excursions on the Kish Bank, where the water is shallow enough to allow them to dive to the bottom to catch small shoaling fish.

In 1999, scientists from BirdWatch Ireland used a platform on a small vessel to carry out over 11 hours of transect counts of seabirds at the north end of the Kish Bank.[45] Counts covered both low water and high water periods as well as a rising tide. The core of this survey covered an area approximately nine degrees of latitude and 15 degrees of longitude, centred on the Kish Lighthouse. A total of 3,015 birds of 26 species were recorded around the north end of the Kish Bank in August and September 1999. Common guillemot, kittiwake and common tern were the most commonly recorded feeding species, while roseate tern, kittiwake and common tern were the predominant species seen roosting on the Kish Lighthouse. Over a thousand terns were estimated to be roosting here in September 1999. A large number of common guillemots (1,482 in September) were also recorded in the area.

Each seabird species had different distribution patterns around the Kish Bank. Cormorants and Shags were mainly found directly over the shallow water of the bank (see above), whereas large gulls appeared to be randomly scattered and occurred at approximately equal densities in the vicinity of the bank and on transects between Howth Head and the Kish Lighthouse. Kittiwakes were present both over and to the east of the bank, with reasonable numbers also towards the seabird colony on Howth Head. Terns were mostly recorded on or to the east of the northern half of the bank, and auks, principally common guillemots, were concentrated to the east of the bank. The highest densities recorded for all seabirds combined were 51–100 birds per square kilometre. Significant densities of auks (mainly common guillemots) occurred along several of the transects.

Shags roosting on the Kish Lighthouse *(John Fox)*

Research for the proposed Dublin Array wind farm on the Kish and Bray banks reported a total of 45 bird species in the area between two surveys in 2001/02 and 2010/11. Passerines and waders were migrants over the bank in late summer and autumn. The remainder of the species were true seabirds or waterbirds (divers, grebes and ducks) that use the marine waters of the Irish Sea in the non-breeding season. Species diversity was highest between July and September and lowest in midwinter, from December to the end of March. Total numbers recorded in any one survey varied from a few hundred to several thousand individuals, with the highest in July and September and lowest from October to early March.

Rarer birds on the coast

Parts of Dublin Bay are good for seeing some of the rarer seabirds and other coastal bird species. Scotsman's Bay near Sandycove, Dún Laoghaire piers and Sandymount Strand are particularly favoured by rarer gulls including Iceland, glaucous and ring-billed gulls. Mediterranean gulls, once a rare visitor to Ireland, are regularly seen now in Dublin Bay throughout the year. The piers at Poolbeg, Dún Laoghaire and Howth are also good places to see great northern diver, Slavonian grebe and Arctic skua. A small flock of sea ducks, known as common scoter, regularly winters in the south Bay.

Mediterranean gull *(John Fox)*

Land birds

Bull Island is one of the few places in Dublin where the song of the skylark in spring is louder than the traffic. The sand dunes here have a considerable population of breeding skylark and meadow pipit, both of which nest on the ground in clumps of grass. In late summer big flocks of post-breeding finches such as linnets can be seen feeding on the seeds of saltmarsh plants. Snow bunting is also a regular winter visitor to the bay and especially Bull Island. In winter the west pier in Dún Laoghaire is one of the best places to see migrant songbirds such as black redstart. Wheatears are also recorded here on spring passage. Most of these migrant birds do not stay long, but when they arrive in numbers there is a good chance of seeing a merlin hunting them in the dunes or along the shore. Kestrels are common on Bull Island, and short-eared owls join them in winter to catch their prey, mainly small rodents. Occasionally, one of these owls moves into the port to hunt rats and mice. The large flocks of feral pigeon that frequent the port are easy prey for peregrines

Short-eared owl on the Bull
Island saltmarsh
(Richard T. Mills)

and a pair of these impressive raptors nests each year on a high structure, giving them a superb vantage point over their hunting grounds.

Like the canary in the mine, birds also serve a very important role as indicators of change in the environment. If water pollution, overfishing or excessive disturbance reach unsustainable levels, the birds will be among the first organisms to respond as they are top predators in the marine and estuarine ecosystems. People have interacted with birds in Dublin Bay since earliest times and we continue to enjoy watching them as the urban area grows.

7 | Settlers on the Shore

Dublin Bay is such a familiar sight to most Irish people that we find it difficult to imagine how it might have looked before the city began. Evidence is scarce because remains of earlier settlements have been destroyed or covered up with the growth of the city but it is possible to piece together a general picture of the prehistoric bay from small clues. Around 20,000 years ago, when much seawater was trapped in thick ice sheets across northern Europe, the sea level was much lower than today and there was a low-lying stretch of land between south-east Ireland and south-west Britain. Between 20,000 and 16,000 years ago the ice sheets were melting and global sea levels had risen to replace the landbridge with an archipelago of small

This modern landscape in Clayoquot Sound, British Columbia suggests what Dublin Bay may have looked like in prehistoric times. A whale is surfacing in the foreground *(Richard Nairn)*

islands surrounded by shallow water. Between 15,000 and 14,000 years ago even these stepping stones disappeared beneath the sea as a large pulse of meltwater resulted in a rapid rise in global sea levels.[1]

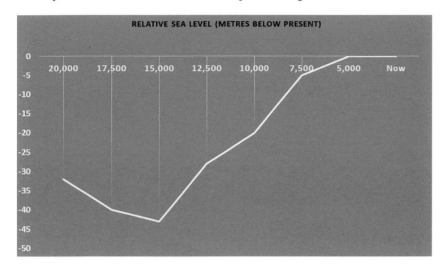

Graph showing changes in relative sea level (in metres) on the Dublin coast from 20,000 years ago to the present (after Edwards and Brooks 2008[2])

A Mesolithic landscape

Can we reconstruct the prehistoric landscape of Dublin Bay as it was when the first settlers were living on Irish coasts? Recent evidence has been uncovered showing that humans may have been active in Ireland during short periods between glaciations about 12,500 years ago. This revelation has come from an item in a museum collection – a single bone of a brown bear with cut marks, found many years ago in a cave in County Clare. The ice then advanced and Ireland was largely covered by thick glaciers again, much as Greenland is today. By 10,000 years ago the ice had retreated again, except from the north-east of Ireland, and people probably migrated northwards into the island.

The Mesolithic period is when we find the earliest evidence of human activity in the Dublin region. Fish traps on the Liffey and shell middens at Dalkey and Sutton show that people were already living a fisher-forager lifestyle on the Dublin coast. The earliest known remains of a coastal settlement in Ireland, at Mount Sandel on the estuary of the River Bann (in today's County Derry), have been dated to around 8,600 years before present (ybp).[3] If we accept this date as approximately the period when people re-appeared in Dublin after the last glaciation, the graph above suggests that the Dublin coastline was then about 10–12m below its present level.

121

The 10m depth contour on the modern Admiralty chart suggests that the coastline then ran straight across from Howth Head to Dalkey. It is probable that the modern Burford and Kish banks are more recent features that developed once the sea level rose. The available evidence suggests that the present Dublin Bay was then a flat coastal plain, at about the time the first known human settlers arrived in Ireland after the Ice Age (see artist's impression below). However, the present Dublin Bay is choked with extensive sand deposits and these may have been washed in from the rising Irish Sea in more recent millennia.

Artist's impression of Dublin Bay about 8,600 years ago (Paul Francis)

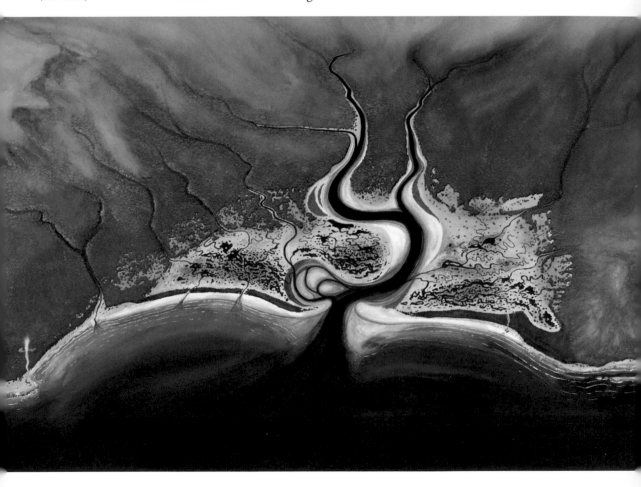

The river channel was a dynamic feature, changing its form as sand shifted around the bay. We know from maps of the seventeenth and eighteenth centuries (see Chapter 9) that, before the Liffey walls were built, there were multiple channels emerging from the river mouth.

These probably changed their positions over time – as in large estuaries such as Wexford Harbour today. Certainly, the middle part of Dublin Bay was filled with extensive sandbanks, known as the North and South Bulls. At the upper levels of the beach, where the sand dried, it was blown ashore to form sand dunes on low-lying parts of the land such as Sutton and Fairview (see Chapter 5). We know that in medieval times there was an extensive phase of dune-building around the Irish coastline during a particularly stormy climatic phase.[4] In the inner, more sheltered parts of the bay, sand dunes would have been fringed by saltmarsh with winding channels and creeks. The marshes that form the inland edge of Bull Island today are some of the best examples of saltmarsh in Ireland – but they only formed in the last 200 years.

Who were the first Dubliners?

The evidence so far uncovered suggests that the earliest settlers after the last Ice Age almost certainly set up camp on the coast, and Dublin Bay would have offered an attractive campsite with a wide shallow river estuary, dunes and shelter from storms. The site at Mount Sandel, on the estuary of the River Bann, was occupied by people who used arrowheads and axes made from flint flakes. This indicates that they lived by hunting and trapping small game and fish and had no knowledge of farming. At certain times of year they probably lived more off gathered plant foods than hunted meat. Remains of plant foods found at the site included hazelnuts, white water-lily seeds, and pear or apple seeds. Animal bones suggest that wild pig was a major prey item and there were also some mountain hare and dog or wolf bones. Farming, as a way of life, had not reached Ireland at this time.

It is likely that Dublin Bay had one or more similar settlements of fisher-foragers living in small huts made of timber poles, perhaps roofed with rushes, turfs or even seal skins. Most likely this was a boat-based community. Their transport routes would have been along the coastline, and there would have been camps at the river mouths where there were shellfish to collect, fish to trap and seal pups to hunt in the breeding season.

How would this coastal plain have appeared to the first people who landed on the shoreline? Some 8,000 years of subsequent sea level rise, deposition of sand and shifting of sediments by wave and tidal action have virtually obliterated any evidence of the habitats that Mesolithic people would have found here. However, just to the south of Dublin

Bay, the shoreline at Corke, north of Bray Harbour, provides us with some clues. The famous Irish naturalist Robert Lloyd Praeger walked this shoreline in 1896 and he takes up the story:

> One day in February last, Mr. R. Welch and I strolled along the beach northward of the new harbour at Bray, and just within the confines of the County of Dublin. At the verge of low water, where the slope of coarse shingle gives way to a more level stretch of fine sand and boulders, which is only left dry at spring tides, we noticed some stumps and boughs of trees, and on examining them, found that they were embedded in a compact layer of peat, which dipped southward at a low angle. The peat was full of branches and roots, and of cones of the Scotch Fir. On the southern side it disappeared under a bed of fine blue clay containing sea-shells; to the north, its broken edges overlay a stratum of coarse grey sand, with rounded fragments of granite. We had but cursorily examined the spot when the tide crept up again and soon hid it from view. Here evidently was a geological story to be unravelled; a long history lay buried with this old peat-bed under the mud and shingle which the sea had heaped upon it; and it was for us to read that history, if we could.[5]

Remains of submerged pine forest at Bray (Robert Welch, from Praeger 1896)

What Praeger and Welch had stumbled upon was in fact a prehistoric forest of Scots pine with the timbers embedded in peat. The trees could have grown on the site or logs may have been washed downstream and become embedded in sediments in a delta. Even the presence of peat on a submerged shoreline suggests settled terrestrial habitats at a lower sea level than that of today. As would be expected of two of Ireland's finest naturalists of their day, they made a detailed description of the site, which was published a few months later in the journal *The Irish Naturalist*. Even 120 years ago, Praeger understood that their discovery demonstrated the relative changes in land and sea levels since the last Ice Age. Much more recent technology using radiocarbon (carbon 14) dating enabled a precise date of 8,600 ybp to be estimated for the submerged timbers. This puts it into the Early Mesolithic, about the same age as the Mount Sandel settlement in Derry, and possibly early human activity on Lambay to the north of Dublin. If we assume that the submerged peat and pines at Bray represent the general vegetation of the Dublin coast at this time, it also suggests that the area now covered by at least 10m of seawater in Dublin Bay (inland of a line from the Baily Lighthouse to Dalkey Island) may also have been covered with woodland 8,600 years ago (see picture on page 21).

Ancient pine trunk on north beach, Bray *(Rob Goodbody)*

Of course, the estuary of the River Liffey would have spread across the centre of this great coastal plain (see the artist's impression on page 122). In his monumental work on the Shannon Estuary, Aidan O'Sullivan presented a reconstruction of an ancient coastal landscape.[6] This included a description of a paleo-environment in an estuarine setting which could equally apply in Dublin Bay. As the gradient of the

This modern view of an estuary in Vancouver, British Columbia, shows how Dublin Bay may have looked in Mesolithic times when the river delta spread out across sandflats *(Richard Nairn)*

present Dublin Bay, from the present seabed down to the 10m-depth contour is that of a gently shelving plain, it suggests that there would have been a series of wide vegetation zones from dry land through coastal marsh to the beach. The meandering river estuary probably changed its position through time and there would have been many lakes and pools left behind (see page 122).

In the Mesolithic period (7,000 to 4,000 years ago) early settlers would also have hunted, fished and gathered plant foods along the Liffey estuary. The estuary in those times was probably a complex network of freshwater wetlands and tidal channels, with saltmarsh and mudflat intermixed with reed swamps, fens and wet woodland. The interior of the country at this time would have been a vast wilderness of forest, heath and wetland. The trees were predominantly oak, birch and hazel on the drier acid soils, with ash and hawthorn in the limestone interior along the meandering eskers of gravel and sand. The low-lying midlands were filled with woods and wetlands, looking a little like southern Finland today.[7] These forests were impenetrable in places but rich in small game such as wild boar, hare and duck. Human hunters would have competed for this valuable prey with bears and wolves and a range of birds of prey such as eagles, buzzards and red kites. The rivers held rich stocks of salmon, sea trout and eels, but there were no coarse fish such as pike. Ospreys and white-tailed sea eagles would have hunted for fish in the extensive wetlands, just as they do today in parts of Ireland and Scotland.[8] Marsh harriers would have bred in reed swamps around the lakes and beavers probably built dams on the streams, creating even more flooding. Forest plants and animals included birds such as woodpeckers and mammals such as the red squirrel. The birds of open grassland, such as skylarks, would have been rare and swallows and house martins were probably confined to breeding in caves as there were few permanent buildings. Rabbits did not appear until the Normans arrived in the twelfth or thirteenth century and magpies were unknown.

These earliest-known Irish people may have brought some animals with them; perhaps hunting dogs or domestic animals would have come in the boats. Almost certainly there were also unintended passengers such as house mice and rats, concealed in foodstuffs. But, by and large, the wildlife that had found its way to Ireland after the last Ice Age had come by itself. When the landbridge is thought to have existed, between 20,000 and 16,000 years ago, Ireland would have been at the ice edge and any animals crossing here would have been living in Arctic-type conditions.[9]

Early Dublin occupants

Although the Viking discoveries in Dublin are best known, recent excavations at a number of city centre locations have revealed that Dublin has a much older, prehistoric past.[10] The earliest of these sites was uncovered by Melanie McQuade at Spencer Dock on the north side of the Liffey near what was then the mouth of the river. Here a previously unrecorded Mesolithic shoreline and the remains of up to five wooden fish traps were identified. The traps were formed around rows of stakes driven into the sand at low tide. These were interwoven with wooden rods to create fences that were used to funnel fish at high tide into traps formed out of wattle baskets. The traps were constructed almost exclusively of hazel, but small amounts of birch, ash and the wood from pomaceous (apple-like) fruit trees were also used.[11] Fish swimming in with the incoming tide would get caught in the traps and could then be retrieved by fishermen at low tide, when they could walk out across the sands from the shore.[12]

Mesolithic hazel basketwork from an intertidal fish trap excavated below North Wall Quay, Dublin. Each red and white bar represents 50cm. *(Melanie McQuade)*

McQuade suggests that the fish traps could have been used to catch any of the fish swimming into the estuary, including flounder, plaice, mullet and migratory species such as salmon, trout and eels; and that a fisher-forager group living nearby was gathering hazel rods and trimming them with stone axes.[13] Radiocarbon dating demonstrated

127

that these fish traps were built during the late Mesolithic period (about 6100–5700 years BC). This makes them some of the oldest fish traps yet found in Ireland and western Europe.[14] Later excavations revealed the partial remains of a middle Neolithic fish trap (3630–3370 years BC), suggesting that this was an important method of fishing over several millennia.[15, 16]

Reconstruction of an intertidal fish trap (Artwork by Simon Dick, reproduced from O'Sullivan (2001)[17])

Coastal occupation sites from the Mesolithic period, often marked by shell middens, have been identified by archaeologists at many sites around Ireland. These middens are small mounds containing seashells, ash, charcoal and bone, usually found in layers of dark soils, rich in organic matter, within beach materials. Such middens have been found at the two extremities of Dublin Bay at Dalkey Island and Sutton.[18] On Dalkey Island, the middens are located on a promontory on the northwest corner, facing the mainland. Here, in the 1950s, David Liversage undertook a series of excavations that revealed evidence of occupation in Mesolithic, Neolithic, early Bronze Age and medieval times – a period of thousands of years.[19] As well as the ubiquitous limpet shells, this site contained flint tools such as scrapers, blades, cores and hammer stones. There were also postholes underneath the shells, providing evidence of some more long-term occupation spanning the Mesolithic–Neolithic period. At another nearby site, bones of cattle, sheep, seals, fish and birds were recovered, along with flint arrowheads, hammerstones, axeheads and Neolithic pottery. Human bones were also found underneath the

Dalkey Island *(Richard Nairn)*

midden, suggesting that this was a ritual burial site. The island may have been a place used for working, hunting and for both domestic and ritual activities on a seasonal basis.

On the north side of Dublin Bay, another kitchen midden of discarded shells, up to 100m in length, was found at Sutton at the western edge of the Howth peninsula[20] and this was later dated by Frank Mitchell at 5,000 ybp.[21] The remains suggested that late Mesolithic people had also settled here and that they lived on at least 20 types of shellfish on the seashore, as well as hunting wild boar, hare, wolf and fish, as indicated by the bones discovered here. We might envisage that these sites at Dalkey and Sutton were used as camp sites in spring and summer by small bands of people, perhaps extended families or tribes, who also exploited seabird eggs and chicks as well as seal pups over the summer months on the nearby cliffs and beaches. The traditional hunting of seabirds and seals continued on the west coast islands as late as the early twentieth century.[22]

On the coast of Kerry, Ferriter's Cove on the Dingle peninsula has produced a wealth of information about the foraging habits of the people who lived here in the period 4600–4300 BC.[23] In autumn these bands of people may have moved inland, following the migrating salmon and eels to supplement a diet of wild plants, hazelnuts and wild fruits. The apparent absence of any large occupation sites on the Dublin coast tends to support the picture of seasonal use in the Mesolithic and Neolithic. The fact that some flint flakes were packed in an inverted position into a pit at Dalkey Island suggests that these sites may also have had some ritual significance to the early people.

Lambay Island, to the north of Dublin Bay, was the discovery site of two collections of unsystematically surface-collected lithics (stone tools). Analysis and mapping of this material demonstrated the presence of human activity during the later Mesolithic and it seems very likely that people were present on Lambay from the Early Mesolithic. Widespread activity across the island has also been revealed, as well as the persistent use of key places over long periods. The excavation of a Neolithic axe-quarry site on the island also shows the importance of Lambay in early Dublin and in the wider Irish Sea region.[24]

Along the north side of the River Liffey, the remains of a burnt mound, which may have been part of a *fulachta fíadh*, were identified by Abi Cryerhall beneath a considerable depth of medieval deposits. The mound consisted of a spread of burnt stone and charcoal measuring approximately 4m long, 3.7m wide and 0.15m deep. Analysis of the remains suggested the presence of alder, elm and blackthorn charcoal within the mound matrix. Radiocarbon dating indicated that the mound was Early Bronze Age in date (3,938–3,744 ybp). Burnt mounds have been found all over the Irish landscape and various uses have been suggested for them. They are typically located in wet places and have an associated trough or pit, which was allowed to fill naturally with water. Hot stones from a fire were then placed within the pit to heat the water. After the water cooled, the burnt stones would have been piled up nearby, creating the burnt mound. Traditionally it was assumed that these troughs were used for cooking food. More recently, other uses for these structures have been suggested, such as bathing, dying cloth, brewing beer and use as sweat houses.[25]

On the south side of the River Liffey, Claire Walsh uncovered additional evidence for Early Bronze Age activity at Kilmainham. This site, which consisted of a small cremation cemetery, was located on a gravel ridge overlooking the River Liffey, just to the north of the Royal Hospital. In total there were six burial pits, each of which contained cremated human bone. Three of the burials contained pottery vessels, while the remaining graves just had small 'token' deposits of burnt bone.

The bone came from an adult male who died sometime around 1928 years BC (carbon 14 dating). The other items recovered included small cups and beads. This small but important cemetery was probably the burial ground of members of an extended family who lived and died in Kilmainham nearly 4,000 years ago.[26]

More evidence of Bronze Age activity was also identified at Islandbridge, where the remains of an extensive riverside revetment, or retaining wall, were excavated by Kevin Lohan. Although heavily disturbed in places, this wooden structure was nearly 130m in length. It consisted of a post-and-wattle fence erected a small distance into the river, with a large quantity of wood dumped behind it to consolidate the ground on the landward side of the fence. Radiocarbon analysis indicated that the wooden revetment dated from the Late Bronze Age/Early Iron Age. Its exact function remains uncertain, although its location right beside the ancient fording point at Kilmainham may be significant.[27]

Closer to the city centre, Iron Age waterfront structures, including a timber-laced gravel bank with an associated hurdle path and a brushwood platform, were identified by Teresa Bolger at Ormond Quay. The excavation site was located near the confluence of the Liffey and one of its northern tributaries, the River Bradogue. This district had a series of creeks, inlets and channels right up until the seventeenth century. The structures were located at the river's edge and were radiocarbon dated to c. 2160–2060 BC.[28] There is also recent evidence of fish traps and other waterfront activity on the south side of the Liffey dating from the Iron Age.[29]

It is probably no coincidence that most of the prehistoric sites described above were found along the edge of the River Liffey; it is likely that the deep deposits of river silt layers found along the river's edge afforded greater protection from damage by the deep eighteenth- and nineteenth- century basements so characteristic of the city centre. This is lucky, as these sites are an important addition to the story of Dublin.

Viking Dublin

Although it is widely believed that the Vikings founded the town of Dublin, there were almost certainly Christian settlements already there at the time they arrived.[30] Among the best preserved evidence for the beginnings of Viking Dublin come from the extensive remains uncovered at sites such as Wood Quay and Fishamble Street, as well as the deep deposits of medieval archaeological remains that are found across much of the city centre. When the first raiding parties beached their wooden ships in Dublin Bay, they found a wide estuary with river channels winding between sand and mudflats. The Irish annals first record that a Viking fleet was present in Dublin in AD 841. New research has shown that the Liffey area of Dublin holds the largest burial complex of its type in western Europe, excluding Scandinavia. Between the late eighteenth century and 1934, at least 59 graves were discovered in the Kilmainham–Islandbridge area.[31] The huge number of artefacts found, dating from between AD 841 and 902, indicate the importance and wealth of Dublin at the time. Each of the Vikings found was buried with artefacts, so these were aristocratic burials. It shows that large numbers of warriors were coming to Dublin at this time, supporting the view that this was an offensive invasion. The bodies were buried on both sides of the Liffey and along the River Poddle. In 2003, Linzi Simpson excavated the remains of four Viking warriors in South Great George's Street: three are believed to have been buried between about AD 670 and 882 and the other some time later.[32]

The Vikings established an enclosure on the banks of the river which they could defend and use as a base from which to raid other parts of the

Reconstructed Viking ship *Sea Stallion of Glendalough* in the Irish Sea *(Richard Nairn)*

Irish coast. The exact location of this *longphort* is not known, but it was subsequently attacked by native Irishmen, and the Norse people were expelled to northern England and the Isle of Man. By AD 917 they had returned and settled in the town of *Dubhlinn* between Christ Church and Temple Bar on the banks of the Liffey. Excavations in this area have shown that the town was enclosed by an earthen bank beneath a post-and-wattle fence. Within it there were streets laid out around the hill. The outlines of at least 150 houses have been uncovered in this area, each with vegetable plots, gardens and refuse dumps. There were animal enclosures, workshops and storehouses in the town, suggesting a settled community that was farming the surrounding land. The town was a hub for craftmakers who used raw materials such as wood, leather, bone, antler, amber and metals. By the late ninth century Dublin had become an important trading centre.

Excavations at Wood Quay, Dublin city in the 1970s (courtesy of Patrick Wallace, National Museum of Ireland)

The town held a mixed population of Irish and Norse people and included farmers, traders, craftsmen and slaves. They raised cattle, pigs and goats and supplemented their diet with fish and shellfish, which would have been plentiful in the estuary. They probably used wooden fish traps similar to those from earlier periods and other estuaries around Ireland.[33] Fishing in the wider bay area is also suggested by finds of lead line-weights, wooden net-floats and stone sinkers in the excavations. Studies of the animal remains in the town of Dublin have identified a variety of fish species, some of which could only have been caught from boats. The finding of an iron harpoon head in the town suggests that the

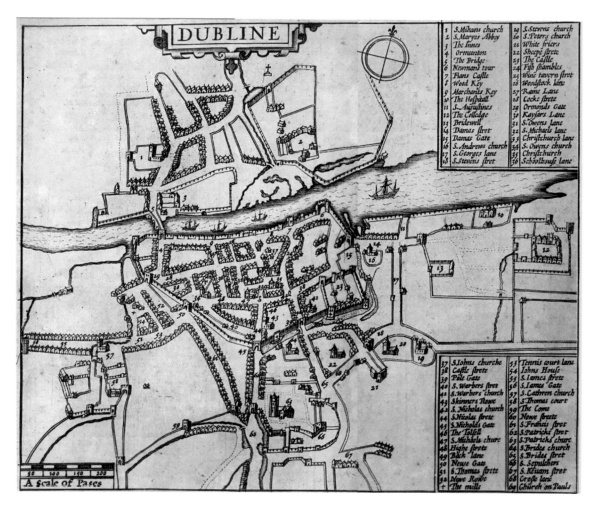

DUBLINE

1	S.Michans church	19	S.Stevens church
2	S.Maryes Abbey	20	S.Peters church
3	The Innes	21	White friers
4	Ormunton	22	Sheepe ftrete
5	The Bridge	23	The Castle
6	Newmans tour	24	Fish shambles
7	Fians Castle	25	Wine tavern ftret
8	Wood Key	26	Woodstock lane
9	Marchants Key	27	Rame Lane
10	The Hospitall	28	Cocke ftrete
11	S.Augustines	29	Ormonds Gate
12	The Colledge	30	Kaysars Lane
13	Bridewell	31	S.Owens lane
14	Damas ftret	32	S.Michaels lane
15	Damas Gate	33	Christchurch
16	S.Andrews church	34	S.Owens church
17	S.Georges lane	35	Christchurch
18	S.Stevens ftret	36	Schoolhouse lane

37	S.Iohns churche	53	Tennis court lane
38	Caftle ftrete	54	Iohns Houfe
39	Pole Gate	55	S.Iames ftrete
40	S.Warbers ftret	56	S.Iames Gate
41	S.Warbers church	57	S.Cathren church
42	Skinners Rowe	58	S.Thomas court
43	S.Nicholas church	59	The Come
44	S.Nicholas ftrete	60	Newe ftrete
45	S.Nicholds Gate	61	S.Frcncis ftret
46	The Tolfell	62	S.Patrick ftret
47	S.Michaels chur	63	S.Patricks chur
48	Highe ftrete	64	S.Brides church
49	Back lane	65	S.Brides ftret
50	Newe Gate	66	S.Sepulchers
51	S.Thomas ftrete	67	S.Kruan ftret
52	Move Rowe	68	Croffe lane
†	The mills	69	Church on Pauls

A Scale of Pases

John Speed's map of Dublin in 1610

Vikings were also hunting marine mammals, such as porpoise and seals, which are still plentiful today in Dublin Bay. The rich natural resources of this coastal area provided the ideal location for the growth of a settled population and its increasing influence in Europe.

Dublin was expanding rapidly in the late twelfth century.[34] By the end of the thirteenth century the Anglo-Norman town had outgrown the original Norse–Irish settlement in both size and sophistication. Churches dominated the urban skyline and the wooden quaysides on the Liffey were being replaced by stone revetments. Because of the dangers to larger ships from the shallow sandbars in the bay and the river, merchants no longer had access to the town. Dalkey at the southern limit of the bay was already being used as a mooring to transfer goods to smaller vessels which could then enter the river.

In 1610 a lease of some waterfront lands at the mouth of the River Poddle, east of the city, marked the start of a reclamation of islands and mudflats on the south side of the Liffey estuary that would ultimately continue all the way to Ringsend. John Speed's map of the city in 1610 shows a number of waterside walls on both north and south river banks. By the seventeenth century Dublin had become a major international trading centre, and the early maps show a rapid expansion of building around the bay (see Chapter 8).

Artist's impression of medieval Dublin on the banks of the Liffey in Dublin *(courtesy of the Friends of Medieval Dublin)*

8 | Built Landscape

The Pigeon House Hotel at Poolbeg *(Rob Goodbody)*

The modern history of Dublin Bay and the port of Dublin began in the opening years of the eighteenth century, with concerted attempts to alter the bay to suit the needs of shipping and commerce. Previous alterations had taken place along the banks of the Liffey, extending the land out into the water and enclosing the river within quays or walls. These alterations, which began in the medieval period, could be seen in great detail from the archaeological excavations at Wood Quay in the 1970s (see Chapter 7). They continued well beyond that period, however, and much of the land occupied by Dublin's quays today was reclaimed from the river. The beginning of the eighteenth century saw this trend move on to a much larger and more ambitious scale, and to encroach on the bay itself, rather than just the riverbanks.

Thomas Phillips' map of Dublin, surveyed and produced in 1685, shows in great detail the inner part of the bay as it was on the eve of the new century, and the great incursions into the bay. The map has west at the top, including the city itself, with the bay below it. Prominent on the southern shore, to the left in the map, is a great star fort. This was Phillips' proposal for the defence of the city – it was never built. The point at which the river suddenly widens out is approximately the location of today's Loop Line railway bridge, so that the whole of the future sites of Custom House Quay, George's Quay and City Quay were out in the river at that time, as was the site of the Custom House. Ringsend was a narrow spit, projecting out into the bay, running along the line of Tritonville Road and with a broad swathe of water between this spit and the city. On the Dublin side of this stretch of water the road shown to run along the shore line is today's Sandwith Street.

Phillips' map of Dublin Bay, 1685 *(Reproduced with permission of the British Library)*

On the right-hand side of this map North Strand Road can be seen running along the strand and Ballybough Bridge is shown crossing the Tolka. Further east, Castle Avenue in Clontarf, with houses along its length, leads to Clontarf Castle. Within the bay itself the greater part of the area is shown as 'strand', with the Liffey breaking into separate channels. The southernmost channel, near Ringsend point, appears to be strewn with wrecked ships, which reflects the danger the bay presented to shipping, with its shifting sands and shallow waters. Clontarf Island is prominent in the middle of this section of the Bay, and it is shown in green, suggesting that it was dry and supported some form of plant growth.

Two decades after Phillips produced his map a proposal was put forward for altering the channel of the river, and this was shown on a map produced in 1704. While the map is not easy to read, as the land is not depicted clearly, it can be seen that the channel out from the mouth of the Liffey to Ringsend and beyond is totally different from what had

Map of Dublin Bay, 1704
(Dublin Port Archive)

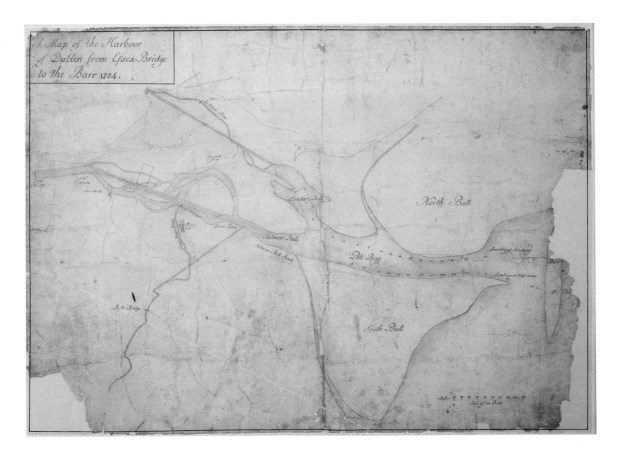

138

been there less than 20 years previously. Instead of three gently curving channels running out to Ringsend, with two beyond, there was now one very sinuous channel, with a tightly curved branch bending northwards before turning back. Whether this was based on actual surveys of the channels or on conjecture is not known. As a way of overcoming this constant shifting of the river channels and to introduce a route that was easier to navigate, it was proposed to straighten the Liffey channel and this was shown on the map. It was also proposed to form a straight channel for the Tolka, called the Ballibogh River on this map, and also to straighten the Dodder, rerouting it to run through the Ringsend spit to join the Liffey channel further east. It is not clear how seriously these proposals were considered, how they would be achieved or who proposed them, but in the end they were not implemented.

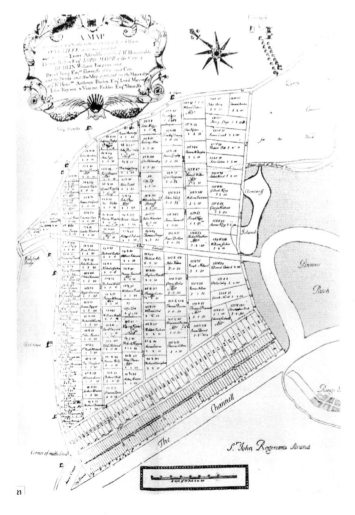

Proposal for North Lotts by
J. Macklin, 1717

Very soon after this, however, a major incursion into the bay was planned and put into action. This became the substantial area to the east of North Strand Road, all the way out to East Wall Road and partly incorporating Clontarf Island. There had been an earlier attempt to enclose this part of the bay in 1682, when the land was surveyed and divided into 152 lots, which were allocated to various people on the basis that each new landholder was to protect their new property from the sea. This was an unworkable proposition, as it fragmented the responsibility for reclaiming the land, but in any case problems arose over the allocation of land and the scheme was abandoned.

When the scheme was revisited in 1710, the method of reclaiming the land from the bay was revised. This time it was to be the city authority that enclosed the land, through the Ballast Office Committee, which looked after the port affairs, and work started in that year to carry the scheme into effect. Beginning at the edge of the Liffey, near the northern side of the present Butt Bridge, a series of wicker baskets full of stones, known as kishes, were set down in the water to form a barrier and behind this an embankment of sand, gravel and mud was piled to create an enclosure. This was the beginnings of Custom House Quay and North Wall Quay. Seven years later, in 1717, the furthest extremity of this barrier was reached and the work turned northwards onto the line of what is now East Wall Road. At this stage, the city assembly – the equivalent of today's city council – laid out the plan for the project and set up a committee to implement it. The initial plan was that this northbound barrier would run all the way to Clontarf, except for a new straight channel or canal so that the Tolka could continue through this reclaimed land to reach the Bay.[1]

To form North Wall Quay a wall was built along the river's edge, and another 18m back from the river, and the area between was infilled with dredgings from the river. The first stage of this major project was the only part to be implemented, though it involved the reclamation of a huge area, from the Tolka estuary to North Wall Quay. Within this area a grid of streets was planned, many of them named after the various offices and bodies connected with the city administration – Sheriff Street, Mayor Street, Guild Street and Commons Street. Each of the new streets was laid out by infilling the line of the street up to the new ground level. This resulted in a series of rectangular areas of unreclaimed land and it was the responsibility of each of the new landholders to infill his own plot.

A completely different method of reclaiming the land on the southern side of the Liffey was undertaken soon after the work began at North Wall. In 1712 John Mercer took on a lease of a tract of the water stretching along the southern side of the Liffey, running along George's Quay and City Quay and extending back to Townsend Street. He began the construction of a wall and quay, but the project foundered on his death in 1718. The city itself took on the task of completing this quay, continuing a section of quay that was already being constructed by the city, and hence it became known as City Quay.[2] The quay was completed in 1720.

A far more ambitious private enterprise project was begun in 1713 when Sir John Rogerson, a member of the city assembly and a former lord mayor, was granted a lease on the entire strand eastwards from City Quay to Ringsend. Unlike John Mercer, Rogerson pursued the project vigorously and set about building the quay that bears his name, and which extends for a little over a kilometre. As had been done at North Wall Quay, Rogerson began to build two walls and to fill in the space between them with dredgings from the river, for which he paid the city by the ton. The wall was completed by the early 1720s, when it was turned alongside the Dodder to reach Ringsend Bridge. Although he completed the wall, Sir John Rogerson didn't live to see the project truly come to fruition, as the infilling of the land behind the quay was slow and the uptake of the reclaimed land by tenants was disappointing at first. Nonetheless, this project was enormous in scale and began the process of reclaiming the huge area bounded by Sandwith Street, Grand Canal Street, Shelbourne Road and the Dodder.

Liffey mouth with Sir John Rogerson's Quay to the left (1730s)

141

Charles Brooking's map of Dublin, published in 1728, shows North Wall Quay and Sir John Rogerson's Quay, though with little development on the land as yet, and with a note on the area behind North Wall Quay that 'this part is walled in but as yet over flowed by the tide'. Rogerson's land on the southern side had new streets laid out at the city end, now represented by Lime Street, Erne Street, Hanover Street East, and Windmill Lane. This may have been anticipating development, however, as Rocque's map of the bay, produced in 1757, shows less development.

The construction of these two walls channelled the river, created new quays for shipping and formed the basis for the reclamation of huge areas of land. While the enclosure of the Liffey would have assisted shipping, the major problems that the port still faced were the presence of the bar that limited the depth of water, and the continuously shifting channels. In addition, the area of the bay immediately outside the river mouth was a busy anchorage, allowing ships to rest up for a time without incurring port fees or cluttering up the quays. The area was not well sheltered, however, and improvements were needed if the port was to remain viable for modern shipping.

The first major incursion into the bay solely for the purpose of improving the port for shipping, as opposed to the previous endeavours that involved land reclamation, was initiated in 1715. In January 1714/15[3] the Ballast Office Committee reported to the city assembly that 'it was the opinion of merchants and other skilful men that the south side of the channel, below Ringsend, be piled, which will raise the south bank so high, that in time it will be a great shelter for shipping which lie in the harbour.' At its meeting in April the city assembly gave its consent to this project.[4] The building of the South Wall is described in Chapter 9.

South coast

Ringsend

Weston St John Joyce wrote that 'before the Dodder was confined between artificial banks, it flowed at its own sweet will in numerous streams over a considerable tract of marsh and slobland at Ringsend, and in time of flood caused much perturbation among the inhabitants – the waters of the river and the waves of the sea rolling without let or hindrance over land now covered by terraces and dwelling houses.'

Joyce quotes Gerard Boate, who wrote in 1652 of the effects of such floods: 'Since that time a stone bridge hath been built over that brook upon the way betwixt Dublin and Ringsend: which was hardly accomplished with the brook in one of its furious risings, quite altered its channel for a good way, so as it did not pass under the bridge as before, but just before the foot of it, letting the same stand on the dry land.' Joyce continues: 'The stone bridge referred to by Boate (built between 1629 and 1637) was where Ballsbridge now stands – the only route at that time between Dublin and Ringsend, except for those who hired what was known as a "Ringsend Car", to cross the shallows then intervening between that place and the city. All the tract lying east of City Quay, Sandwith Street, Grand Canal Street and north of Lansdowne Road was then washed by the mingled waters of the Dodder and the sea and could be traversed only with danger and difficulty by pedestrians.' Sir John Rogerson's enclosing walls and quay not only impounded a substantial tract of land, but also created a western edge to the Dodder estuary.

The lowest effective river crossing had been at Ballsbridge and from there the Dodder broke up into shifting channels to form a delta. While the road running via Ballsbridge gave reasonable access to Irishtown, it was a long way round to get to Ringsend and the shortcut across Sir John Rogerson's reclaimed land and the Dodder estuary became well used. John Rocque's map (see page 144) of Dublin Bay, published in 1757, shows the situation clearly. The walls built by Sir John Rogerson

Detail from Brooking's map showing the South Lotts (1728)

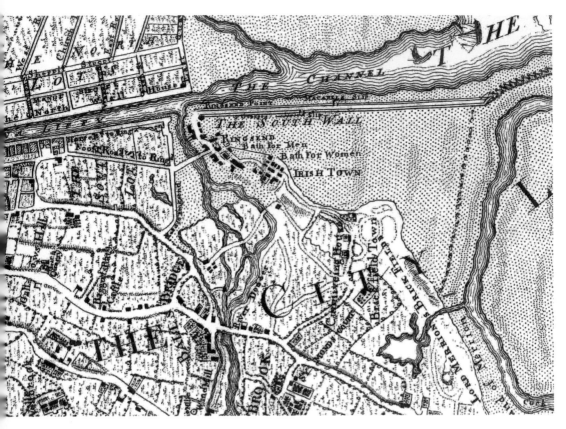

Detail of John Rocque's map of
County Dublin (1760)

are labelled 'Horse Road to Ringsend', while the shortcut was 'Foot Road to Ringsend'. This foot road ran in a straight line along Townsend Street to the street now known as Hanover Street East, where it crossed on two bridges over rope walks – long alleys where ropes were stretched during the manufacturing process. From there the foot road turned to run to Ringsend Bridge, which had been built in 1727, as the first attempt to span the Dodder directly to Ringsend village, rather than via Irishtown.[5] While this road was mostly destroyed with the construction of Grand Canal Dock in the 1790s, the bend in the road at Hanover Street East and the humpback of the bridge over one of the rope walks still remain.

The bridge that had been built to Ringsend in 1727 was destroyed in a flood in 1787, following which a precarious temporary crossing was set up with a timber beam, with a handrail, and this was recorded in a view by John James Barralet. An architectural competition was held for the design of a replacement bridge and this was erected in 1789, but was, in turn, destroyed by a flood in 1802.[6] By this time a connection between Ringsend and the city had become more important, as Ringsend had in

Ringsend Bridge in 1787, by John James Barralet
(Reproduced with permission of the British Museum)

1796 become the packet station – the landing point for ships carrying mail and passengers. It became clear that a bridge in this location had to withstand severe flooding, a tall order given the lack of any bedrock to provide a reasonable foundation. The architect of the new bridge, John Semple, devised a novel approach to the problem. Instead of an arch over the river, he built a full ellipse of stone, so that the arch that is visible above the river is matched by a similar arch below the river. This spread the weight of the bridge over a wider area and ensured that the storm water would not undermine the edges of the bridge. He also chamfered the edges of the arch to help the flow of water beneath the bridge.[7]

In 1791 the Grand Canal Company began construction of the canal to the south of Dublin to reach the Liffey near Ringsend. In the following year it was decided to construct extensive docks at the canal end. The canal and docks were completed in 1796.[8] This did not alter the mouth of the Dodder, however, as the canal company kept its docks within the area that had been enclosed by Sir John Rogerson, except for a small area beside Ringsend Bridge where land was reclaimed to build a graving dock, which was a dock where ships' hulls could be repaired by closing gates and draining the dock.

At the same time as the canal was being built, William Vavasour put forward a proposal to the Ballast Board, which was now independent of Dublin Corporation, for the enclosure of the Dodder downstream from Ballsbridge. The Ballast Board agreed to this, despite opposition from the Grand Canal Company. Vavasour constructed walls to enclose the Dodder, turning the river through a tight bend below Lansdowne Road and creating a substantial tract of reclaimed land on either side of the channel.[9] Not much development occurred on these lands during William Vavasour's lifetime and the Ordnance Survey first edition six-inch map of 1843 shows the land almost entirely undeveloped. The exception was that Bath Avenue had been laid out and a small number of buildings had been erected at the western end, one of which was called New Holland Lodge.

Early painting of the sloblands west of Ringsend. To the left are the masts of sailing ships moored in the River Liffey. A stone bridge is visible in the centre of the picture and Howth Head is on the horizon.

Sandymount

The southern coast of the bay east of Ringsend and Irishtown remained in a relatively natural state until the end of the eighteenth century, when the first changes took place, while in the nineteenth century much of this coastline was altered significantly in a very short period.

De Gomme's map of 'the Citty and Suburbs of Dublin', produced in 1673, shows Sandymount as a coastal area separated from the city proper by the wide estuary of the River Dodder. It narrowed towards the north to end in the village of Ringsend, which was isolated on a narrow spit and presumably surrounded by water at high tide. It is quite likely that this spit was topped by sand dunes and that the estuary of the River Dodder, to the east, was filled with saltmarsh, as it was quite sheltered from any wave action. A similar low dune feature is present today at Rosslare Point in Wexford Harbour, which protects the now reclaimed estuary of the South Slob.

The Sandymount area came into the hands of the Fitzwilliam family in the early fifteenth century and this included Ringsend, Irishtown, Sandymount and all the land as far as Booterstown and Stillorgan.[10] At the time the land was described as the great pasture by the sea, or the rabbit warren, and in the seventeenth century places in the area were referred to as the upper and lower marsh, the court of the sallies, the ridge of the brambles, the little field and the furze park.[11] This paints a picture of low-lying land with a sandy soil, suitable for rabbit burrows, but prone to waterlogging. These two would appear to be incompatible, though the name Sandymount is said to refer to a small hill of sand, known as Scallet Hill or Scalded Hill, which is now the site of the church of Our Lady Star of the Sea, and this hill would have been less waterlogged and more suited to a rabbit warren.[12] In 1731 the Earl of Fitzwilliam opened up brickfields in this area and a village known as Bricktown grew up to house the workers in the brick fields and the kilns.[13] Through the rest of the eighteenth century the area would have been subjected to the constant smell of brick kilns, while parts of the land were flooded where the material for the brick had been quarried.

A major intervention into the coastline at Sandymount occurred in the early 1790s when the Earl of Fitzwilliam constructed a sea wall along much of this length of coast to protect the land from flooding from the sea.[14] This allowed for the laying out of Strand Road alongside the wall and houses were later built along this street, facing the coast, though this did not happen immediately – as late as 1843, when the first edition Ordnance Survey six-inch map was published, there was still relatively little development along Strand Road. The work put into the construction of this sea defence is under-appreciated, though it is a substantial feature. It runs for about 2km from Seafort Avenue almost to Merrion Gates and is more than just a wall, as it is backed up by a rampart – Strand Road is at a significant height above the sea and this is all artificially raised ground. The Ordnance Survey's 1:2500 maps of 1909 have spot heights along the centre of the principal roads that show that Strand Road is generally 6–6.5m above sea level, while the levels on the roads leading off, such as Gilford Road, St John's Road and Sydney Parade Avenue, drop to 4.3m or lower. In effect, Strand Road is a dyke that keeps the sea at bay and this allowed for the infilling of the waterlogged brick pits so that the land could be developed to provide fine houses.

Merrion and Booterstown

At Merrion Gates the ground reaches close to sea level, necessitating the provision of a raised concrete ramp at the access to the beach to keep the tide out. By the 1830s a house had been built on the coastward side of this wall near to Merrion Gates, while immediately opposite the railway level crossing there were baths known as Merrion Baths. The area between these two was reclaimed from the sea in about 1860, with the construction of a sloped wall up from the strand, becoming vertical at the top. The ground behind this sea wall was infilled to bring it to road level and houses were built on the resulting reclaimed land.

Beyond Merrion Gates, the original ground level rose up from sea level, climbing gradually until it reached the village of Booterstown, 8m above sea level. Along the road to Blackrock the ground remained at this level for a time before beginning to climb again at Williamstown, reaching 16m above sea level at the bottom of Mount Merrion Avenue. These levels are still evident today, but they would have been more visible until the mid-nineteenth century, as the Rock Road ran along the coast from Merrion Gates to Williamstown and the tide washed the base of low cliffs along this stretch of road.

Weston St John Joyce quotes Brewer (*Beauties of Ireland* 1826) as follows:

> [T]he road to Blackrock is evidently the pleasantest, most frequented, and level. At Booterstown the fields are disposed in a style of judicious husbandry, the villas are neat and commodious ... The elevation of the road contributes greatly to the pleasure of the traveller. The vast expanse of the prospect, opening on the wide expanse of the ocean, the steep, indented shore, the strand stretching three miles to the lighthouse, the fertile, verdant banks, everywhere fringed with wood and hanging gardens.

This idyllic image was much changed by the time Joyce wrote in 1912:

> This delightful picture became completely altered by the construction of the railway in 1832–1834, and the old sea-wall over which, prior to that time, the storm driven waves had often swept onto the road, thenceforth became the boundary of a foul-smelling saltmarsh, the exhalations from which in time drove everyone out of the neighbourhood except for those whose circumstances obliged them to live there.

View of the coast at Booterstown with the new railway crossing the open sea, c.1845, from *Kirkwood's Dublin & Kingstown Railway Companion* (Reproduced with permission of the National Library of Ireland)

Booterstown Marsh

The building of the Dublin and Kingstown railway in 1834 cut off a significant area of shoreline from daily incursions of the tide. Between Merrion Gates and Salthill this left a sizeable area for reclamation and conversion to other uses. In the 1830s, the resulting tidal lagoon covered more than 28 hectares. In the following decades much of the area was infilled with rubble and domestic refuse, part of it now forming Blackrock Park. Most of the rest of this 'new land' remained in private ownership, leaving only Booterstown Marsh still subject to flooding by seawater at high tide. By 1876 the marsh at Booterstown was in agricultural use, made possible by the use of water control systems. A large gate valve was installed at the Williamstown outlet to the sea, which was closed on the rising tide and opened on the ebb tide. Some landfill soil raised the level of the marsh and it was irrigated with fresh water from local streams. During both world wars the marsh was used as allotments, but with increasing prosperity these fell idle and in the 1950s the area was used as pasture. Old cultivation ridges can still be seen on the surface of the marsh. The water control systems were also neglected, allowing salt water to flow back into the system. The marsh was acquired by An Taisce in 1971 to protect it from development; it was designated as a bird sanctuary and it is now managed by that organisation (see Chapter 4).

A map prepared by Charles Vignoles, engineer to the railway company, shows the original coastline and indicates the degree to which the railway ran across the open water, while cutting into various promontories.[15]

Vignoles' plan for the Dublin and Kingstown Railway, 1834 (Reproduced with permission of the National Library of Ireland)

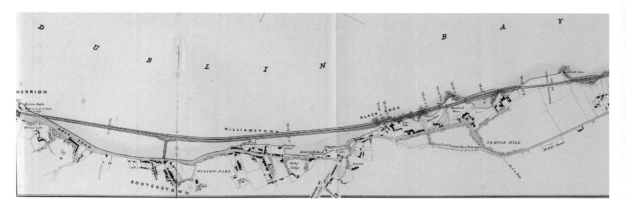

Blackrock

The rise in the road level between Williamstown and Mount Merrion Avenue is significant, but is probably not noticed by the average road user. It is much more evident to those who use Blackrock Park. The section of the park opposite Mount Merrion Avenue is relatively small and rises to a summit in the middle, with a pavilion at the high point. Beyond this area steep flights of steps descend to the lower level, which can also be approached via a ramped pathway. By either route the descent is dramatic and runs down the original cliff face to the point where the sea formerly met the land. Sharp as the change in level may be, it appears to have been cut down to some degree during the landscaping of the park in the nineteenth century.

This higher ground level at Blackrock is the result of a geological boundary. The city of Dublin is built on low-lying ground, with limestone beneath. The limestone bedrock continues out of the city southwards to Blackrock, where it meets Leinster granite. The Dublin limestone is of a type known as calp, which has a high mud content and is generally of quite poor quality. It is much less resistant to erosion than the granite, hence the lower ground level in the city. The two types of rock are visible at Blackrock both in their original positions and as the constituent stones in older boundary walls. An outcrop of limestone is visible in Blackrock Park, near the lake. The park wraps around the boundary of an eighteenth-century house known as Lisaniskea or *Lios an Uisce*, which has a stone wall marking the boundary to the park. Against this wall is an area of limestone projecting through the grass.

This limestone provided the name of the town, which originally referred to a rock outcrop on the shore. While it is a dirty mid-grey in colour when dry, the local limestone is black when wet. As most of the rock along the shore line here is the golden granite, an outcrop of black rock would have been notable. The village of Blackrock was originally called Newtown and its core was in the part of Main Street that forms the western end of Newtown Avenue. There was a castle at the eastern end of Newtown Avenue, which was probably a late medieval tower house dating from the fifteenth century. It was owned by the Byrne family and was known as Newtown Castle. Weston St John Joyce relates that Blackrock 'was variously called Newtown-at-the-Black-Rock, Newtown on the Strand by the Black Rock, Newtown Castle Byrne, or simply Newtown, so that "Blackrock" is simply an abbreviation of its ancient title'.[16]

The location of this black outcrop of limestone is uncertain. Joyce quotes an account of a visitor to the area in 1825: 'I looked out in various directions for the Black Rock, expecting to see some stupendous mass … but could find nothing more than a dark coloured limestone crag, just peeping above the surface near the water's edge.'[17] Joyce concludes that the original rock had already (by 1825) nearly disappeared. He places the rock as 'under the Park-keeper's lodge, formerly the Peafield baths'. These baths stood alongside the present Rock Road, on the Williamstown side of *Lios an Uisce*, and all that is left on the site now is a small square building, built of limestone rubble, standing in the park, but with its door and windows blocked up. Perhaps this building was constructed with the last remnants of the Black Rock, though this is very close to the remaining outcrop of limestone mentioned previously.

Even before Joyce published his book, that location for the rock had been disputed by Patrick J. O'Reilly, who pointed to old maps, such as

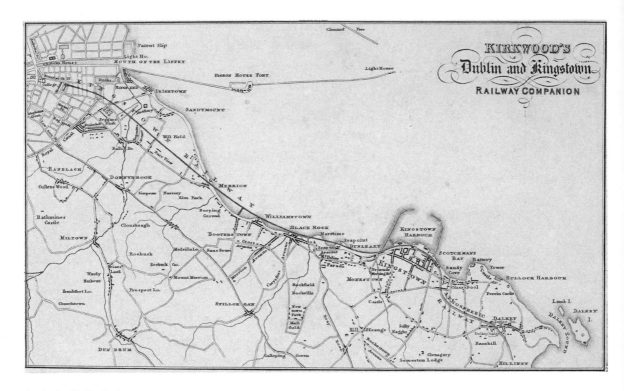

South side of Dublin Bay from Kirkwood's railway map, *c.* 1840s *(Reproduced with permission of the National Library of Ireland)*

that by Bernard Scalé, published in 1773, which showed the rock to be away from the shore, to the north of Blackrock Cross.[18] This rock is still there, though it is small and only visible at low tide, so it is scarcely a major landmark. Scalé's maps of Dublin were based on the earlier maps by John Rocque, whose map of County Dublin shows 'The Black Rock from whence the Town takes its name' as being offshore from the present station.[19] Rocque's more detailed map of Dublin Bay, dated 1757, shows the whole coastline from Merrion to Blackrock as being littered with rocks, particularly in the vicinity of Blackrock Park. Given that these would all have been limestone, they would all have been black, raising many uncertainties as to the location of the original Black Rock – though Rocque's depiction may have been no more than a mapmaker filling in blank spaces.

Seapoint to Salthill

Between Blackrock and Seapoint the original coastline was rocky, formed by a promontory of granite projecting into the sea. This is largely still extant, though it is less prominent than it was originally, as the railway line crossed another small bay close to Seapoint. This has since been infilled

View of the railway at Seapoint, c.1845 (Reproduced with permission of the National Library of Ireland)

and reclaimed and is now a sports pitch at Tobernea Terrace. A view along the railway in the mid-nineteenth century showed this as still an open body of water with Seapoint House, a hotel, rising above it.

In 1890 this enclosed body of water was to contribute to a tragedy caused by the discharge of sewage into the sea at a point where the railway reduced the degree to which the water was changed with each tide. A family of five girls who lived in Seapoint Avenue collected mussels from this enclosed area of the sea and took them home to eat. Almost immediately after eating them the girls, their mother and a servant girl fell ill, and the mother and four of the daughters died.[20]

Beyond Seapoint, the shoreline was marked by cliffs as far as Salthill. These appear to have been cliffs of glacial till or similar material, rather than granite, judging by their appearance in a painting by James Arthur O'Connor. The decision of the Dublin and Kingstown Railway Company to knock the cliffs down for purely aesthetic reasons would seem to support this assumption. It was reported in 1834 that the railway ran through 'a portion of deep cutting, through granite rocks, with a handsome bridge of granite, to the Martello tower at Seapoint, from whence to Salthill the Railroad runs at the bottom of Monkstown cliffs, with an ample promenade at the sea side, and divided from the new foot

153

path by a neat iron railing. All the rugged cliffs have been levelled down, and formed into pleasing slopes, which the taste of the owner of the adjacent cottages will soon cover with flowers and shrubs.'[21]

James Arthur O'Connor's view is from the beach at Seapoint, looking towards the old village of Dunleary. The village itself is hidden behind the overhanging cliff, but the pier may be seen, with the Dunleary Martello tower at its landward end. These were the cliffs that the railway company regraded and handed over to the adjacent occupiers to tend as gardens, with the intention of having a more attractive view for passengers using the railway. By the time the railway opened in 1834 the scene had changed dramatically and the land fell more gently from the houses at the top of the cliffs to the railway line and the shore at the base. This was recorded by Andrew Nicholl in one of a series of images he published to mark the opening of the railway. It is probable that the material from these cliffs was used by the railway company as a filling in the embankments and causeways along the line of the railway.

Eight years after the railway opened, William Makepeace Thackeray stayed the night in the railway company's hotel at Salthill, while touring Ireland for the purpose of writing a travel book. He left an intriguing account of a walk in the vicinity of the hotel:

> Strolling about in the neighbourhood before dinner, we went down to the seashore, and to some caves which had lately been discovered there; and two Irish ladies, who were standing at the entrance of one of them, permitted me to take the following portraits, which were pronounced to be pretty accurate.

Re-enactment of cannon fire from the Martello tower at Seapoint *(Rob Goodbody)*

What is intriguing about this is the nature of the caves. If this was a granite cliff it would not be expected that caves would form in the rock, nor would they occur in cliffs of glacial material. The description is not sufficiently detailed to identify the location of the cliffs, to know whether they were at Dunleary or in the other direction towards Seapoint. The comment that they had 'lately been discovered' suggests the possibility that they had been found during the construction of the railway. There is anecdotal evidence of a cave in the cliff at the back of the old harbour, on

Thackeray's sketch of the caves near Salthill

the site now occupied by offices and apartments, and another that was formerly in the grounds of Boland's bakery on Cumberland Street, at the top of the cliff, now occupied by Dún Laoghaire Further Education College.[22] It is possible that these were old mine workings, though there is no known record of mines here, and it is not clear what mineral could have been worked. Lead was found in the granite in Blackrock in the eighteenth century, but it was not worked.[23] Lead occurred in the granite at numerous locations from Dalkey to Glenmalure, though in all those instances the lead was found where the granite was in contact with the adjacent mica schist, which does not occur at Dún Laoghaire.

Dún Laoghaire and its harbour

The village of Dunleary, which has been in existence since medieval times, was established alongside a small creek where a stream entered the bay. This creek offered shelter in the otherwise inhospitable waters of Dublin Bay, and this gave the impetus for the establishment of a small fishery. A pier was provided at some time in the distant past, offering further shelter for boats. The little harbour was of sufficient size to be the landing place for some passenger boats and coal boats seeking to avoid the problems with the bar at the mouth of the Liffey.

The small harbour received a significant boost when the decision was made to provide it with a substantial new pier and this was built to the designs of General Charles Vallancey. Parliament allocated the first funds for this project in 1759 and the pier was completed in 1767.[24] This pier is now known as the Coal Pier, in the inner harbour at Dún Laoghaire, though it is now wider than its original form. Vallancey's pier is the one seen in James Arthur O'Connor's view from Seapoint (see page 154). The construction of this pier substantially increased the enclosed area of the harbour and would have allowed bigger fishing boats and bigger coal and passenger ships to use Dunleary.

A much greater change to the shoreline at the harbour occurred in 1821 when work commenced on the building of the West Pier. The dangers to ships in Dublin Bay arising from easterly and north-easterly storms was exacerbated by the difficulties of entering the mouth of the Liffey due to the bar and the shallow waters it created. The substantial number of wrecks in the bay, and along the east coast in the vicinity, had led to calls for some form of shelter or asylum for ships in these circumstances. The double tragedy of the ships the *Rochdale* and the *Prince of Wales* in November 1807 (described in Chapter 10) led to renewed attempts, and the prime mover was a Dublin-based shipbroker of Norwegian extraction named Richard Toutcher.[25] He believed that a pier was needed near Dunleary, not to create a harbour, but to provide shelter from the easterly and north-easterly storms until it was safe to proceed to the port of destination. His efforts led to the passing of the necessary Acts of parliament and work started on the new pier in 1817. This was the pier now known as the East Pier, as it was not envisaged initially that a second pier would be built.

The original concept for the pier at Dunleary would not have affected the shore to any significant extent, other than at the point where the pier reached land. It was not intended that there would be a port here and, in fact, there was no town here at the time. To the east of the old fishing village of Dunleary the land was of poor quality, rocky and covered with gorse and brambles, and there were few buildings between Dunleary and Glasthule. The commencement of the construction of the pier changed this, as many of the workers building the harbour would have brought their families, leading to the need for services such as grocers, tailors, shoemakers and suchlike. While the population of the village of Dunleary before the harbour works began in 1816 is unknown, there were about 60 houses, suggesting a population of about 300 persons. Five years later, in 1821, the first census recorded that there were now more than 1,500 people living in the town of Dunleary.[26]

In the same year the census was taken, a new Act of parliament provided for the construction of the West Pier, to create a fully enclosed harbour. This had dramatic effects on the old harbour of Dunleary as the new pier was to project from the rocky coastline adjacent to the village. To bring the substantial quantities of stone required to build this pier a new railway line was laid down, running from Dalkey, past the works at the East Pier, to reach the old harbour near Vallancey's Coal Pier. From there it ran around the margin of the creek to the western side, where the pier would be built. This railway necessitated the construction of a new platform along the base of the cliffs, avoiding sharp turns, and this turned the natural rocky margin of the harbour into a regularly curved artificial embankment. As part of this exercise, the remnants of the medieval pier were broken up so that the stone could be used in constructing the embankment.[27]

Modern view of the East Pier, Dún Laoghaire *(Richard Nairn)*

158

There is a drawing in the National Library of Ireland that shows the scene during construction of the West Pier. Towards the right the tower of the Church of Ireland Monkstown parish church is seen prior to its enlargement between 1829 and 1831.[28] The hill to right of centre is Salthill, while that at the left-hand margin is The Hill, Monkstown, which at that time had a substantial house at its crest.

Also in 1821, the construction site for the new pier had a significant visitor. Immediately following his coronation, the new king, George IV, embarked on a visit to Ireland, the first visit by a reigning monarch in peacetime since medieval times – James II and William III had visited, but only to fight each other. The king had landed at Howth, but wanted to leave through Dunleary. This was for sound reasons. The original plan had been to fund the construction of the pier through a levy on ships using the port of Dublin, though this was always going to require tight budgeting. Once the decision was made to build a second pier there was no way that local funding would cover the cost and hence a substantial amount of the finance had to come from central taxation funds. As a result, it ceased to be a local project and became a royal harbour; and King George was eager to see his new harbour. Three lasting effects of this visit were the erection of a commemorative obelisk, which commemorates the harbour commissioners more than it does the king; the naming, by the king, of the harbour as 'The Royal Harbour of King George IV'; and the naming of the nascent town 'Kingstown'.

This royal imprimatur may have influenced the growth of the town, as it is difficult otherwise to explain why its population began to burgeon. During the 1820s the already enlarged town of Dunleary expanded its population to 5,735, or 380 per cent of its 1821 population.[29] This growth continued through the nineteenth century, creating a substantial town. Two factors now existed to encourage the formation of a port based in the new harbour. The increase in population, resulting in a town of significant size, was one. A more important factor was simply the existence of a large enclosed body of water. Ships began to shelter under the lee of the new pier even as it was being built, not only in stormy weather, and the harbour commissioners provided moorings and charged harbour dues. The harbour was also favoured by the Royal Navy, as ships could be stationed in its sheltered waters, away from the crowded conditions of the port of Dublin, while the lack of dependence on the tides meant that naval vessels could arrive and depart at will.

While Kingstown never became a naval port, it remained a base for naval vessels throughout the nineteenth century.

A third significant factor emerged early in the history of the harbour when the relatively new mail packet port of Howth began to silt up. This made it difficult to use for the mail ships, which needed to be able to sail according to timetables and not according to the tides. This was exacerbated with the introduction of paddle steamers in 1820, as they were of deeper draught and often ran aground in the harbour, particularly as there was rock on the harbour bed. The problem became so significant by the mid-1820s that the post office began to experiment with running mail ships connecting Kingstown with Liverpool and Holyhead. The post office moved to Kingstown permanently in 1834, making this the new principal passenger port for the Dublin area.[30]

With the emergence of the harbour at Kingstown as a favoured port for ships to moor and for mails and passengers, new facilities were needed that would result in significant alterations to the coastline between the piers. The construction of the harbour now involved more than just the two piers. A temporary post office jetty was constructed and later a wharf, known as Victoria Wharf, subsequently renamed St Michael's Wharf, was built opposite the end of Marine Road – itself a creation by the harbour commissioners. This wharf was completed in 1837, the year the young Queen Victoria came to the throne, and also the year that the railway was extended from the old village of Dunleary to the new station at Kingstown, right beside the new wharf. Next to Victoria Wharf a small harbour for boats was built, accommodating the smaller craft using the harbour, such as the tenders from the larger ships moored in the open water. Later a new pier was erected within the harbour, parallel to the old Coal Pier, and known as Trader's Wharf. This catered for boats with a deeper draught than could use the Coal Pier and was then adapted to take railway track so that minerals could be imported, such as lead from the Isle of Man to be smelted at the lead works at Ballycorus. The final major work to be erected as part of the new harbour was Carlisle Pier, which was completed in 1859 and which became the new location for the mail ships, complete with a rail connection.[31]

Further alterations were made to the coastline within the harbour with the erection of two yacht clubs in 1843 and 1850, with their forecourts and boat slips, and the addition of a third club in 1870.[32] The waterfront was altered by the construction of roads to serve all these facilities and there is now little left of the original rocky foreshore.

Scotsman's Bay

The origins of the name Scotsman's Bay are obscure. One popular explanation, that it is named after the Scottish engineer John Rennie, who designed the harbour, is not correct – the name appears, as Scotchmans Bay, on John Rocque's map of Dublin Bay, published in 1757. It is possible that a Scottish ship, or a ship called the *Scotsman*, was wrecked in the bay and remained as a hulk long enough to give the name to the bay. Scotsman's Bay is rocky. Even though the shoreline has been moved at least 35m out into the sea, and up to 70m in places, there are still many rocks visible in the tide. This is the reason why the East Pier is located where it is. The designer, John Rennie, chose the location as being as far east as possible to ensure that there was a good depth of water, while not venturing into Scotsman's Bay, so that the seabed beneath the harbour would be sandy, rather than rocky. Old Ordnance Survey maps show the extensive areas of rocks that projected out from the shore and were uncovered at low tide. These had been quarried, as described below.

This coast became populated in the early nineteenth century. The Smith family, who ran the quarries that provided the stone for building

Scotsman's Bay and its rocky shoreline *(Rob Goodbody)*

161

the harbour, laid out Newtownsmith, and Martello Terrace and Windsor Terrace followed. Beyond Newtownsmith, the houses ran down to the sea, but there was no road along the shore. Then in 1921–22 the urban district council laid out a new road along the shore and connected it to Glasthule by the aptly named Link Road.[33] The works carved through the gardens of houses and necessitated the demolition of a substantial house named Romanesca.

In 1936 Dún Laoghaire Borough Council decided to build a new sea wall along the coast and advertised for tenders for the work.[34] This substantial mass concrete wall runs along the shore from the former Dún Laoghaire Baths, along the front of Windsor Terrace, Martello Terrace, Newtownsmith and Marine Parade, as far as Marine Avenue, and encloses a substantial area now given over to a park, with a car park and with a walkway along the shore at the base of the wall. This substantial undertaking altered a significant length of the coastline to the east of Dún Laoghaire as far as Glasthule.

Sandycove Point

While the most prominent historical survivors at Sandycove Point are the military fortifications – the Martello tower and its attendant gun battery – a greater impact on the coastline resulted from quarrying. The Great South Wall and the North Bull Wall were both constructed of granite, the former in the eighteenth century and the latter in the nineteenth. In both cases, the stone came from the quarries belonging to the Ballast Board in the Bullock and Sandycove area. Those at Bullock were largely on dry land, while the quarries at Sandycove were on the shore. In both cases the quarried stone was loaded onto barges at the shoreline, or at Bullock Harbour, and was floated across the bay to the construction site.

The entire coastline of Scotsman's Bay was quarried and must have resulted in significant alterations to the coastline. In the photograph on page 161, taken from the top of the Martello tower at Sandycove, the extensive area of rock along the shoreline is the result of quarrying activity that removed the granite from above sea level, leaving an area of rock that has been heavily shattered by blasting and which is covered at high tide. An area almost clear of rock is seen running towards the left in the photograph, towards the old Sandycove Baths, and this appears to have been deliberately cleared, probably to provide a place for barges to be floated in prior to the construction of Sandycove Harbour. A little

to the west of this the remnants of a stone pier may be seen at low tide. This is an enigma, as it is in a rocky area that is not suitable for bringing in barges, while it is also absent from all maps of the area. This area was probably quarried as part of the construction of the Great South Wall in the eighteenth century.

The quarries around Sandycove Point are extensive and have totally altered the original coastline. The use of this area for quarrying may go back to the eighteenth century, though this is not certain. The Ballast Board leased land in this area for quarrying in 1804 and it is probable that the present bathing place known as the Forty Foot was originally blasted out of the rock to form an inlet for the barges that transported the stone. The bathing place is certainly not natural, being a very straight deep cutting into the granite. All around the point the rock formations appear to have been altered to a significant extent and the works carried out by the Sandycove Bathing Association following its foundation in 1880 have altered it further, with steps cut into the rock, pathways and so on.[35]

Forty Foot Hole, probable loading bay for granite barges *(Rob Goodbody)*

The quarrying has cut the land down to sea level, leaving the jagged rocks as a level platform, bounded at the shoreline by a sheer granite cliff. This is similar to the quarried rock along the shore of Scotsman's Bay. This is not a form that granite takes at the coast and is entirely artificial. The quarry workers blasted the stone down to a level beyond which it was impractical to go, given the periodic inundation of the tides. The rocks on the shore are heavily shattered by blasting and many remnants of drill holes can be seen, where the quarry drilling teams laboriously hammered their chisels by hand into the hard rock, ready to take the blasting powder that would bring out the stone. The white beach at the foot of the cliff comprises angular fragments of granite – again a feature that would not normally be found on a beach that had been pounded by the seas over the millennia. The stones are the fragments left over from the blasting. It is probable that this quarry also provided the stone for the Martello tower and the adjacent gun battery.

The harbour at Sandycove is a popular bathing place on summer days, with its sandy beach and its sheltered, shallow waters – at least at high tide. This probably the location of the original Sandy Cove, though the coastline has been altered so much by quarrying, parks and road

Sandycove Harbour
(Rob Goodbody)

construction that it is difficult to be certain. What is known is that the present harbour was built by the Board of Ordnance, probably soon after taking the lease in 1804, as a place for bringing in barges for bringing out the granite from the quarries. From 1803 there was a lifeboat stationed at Sandycove, seemingly the first lifeboat station in Ireland.[36] The timing of the lease of 1804 indicates that unless the Ballast Board had a previous lease at Sandycove, the stone could not have been taken from here to the South Wall, which was built in the eighteenth century. The North Bull Wall dates from the 1820s and Sandycove Harbour could well have provided stone for its construction.

Bullock to Dalkey

Beyond Sandycove Point evidence of further quarrying activity may be seen along the eastern coast of Sandycove and running all the way to Bullock Harbour. Significant changes to the coastline occur at Bullock

Bullock Harbour, with the shoreline quarry beyond *(Rob Goodbody)*

Coliemore Harbour, with
quarried rock face at left
(Rob Goodbody)

and Coliemore Harbours. Bullock Harbour is medieval in origin and
the monks based at Monkstown had a fishery based at Bullock. The
present harbour is a later construction, however, built by the Ballast
Board to house the local fishing boats and to provide a loading place
for the barges that took the granite to Dublin for the construction of the
South Wall and the North Bull Wall.

Coliemore Harbour is also of significant age, though just how old
it is is uncertain. Dalkey is a medieval town and it is known that goods
were landed at Dalkey and transported to Dublin. The castles in the
village were used by merchants for the safe storage of goods. Where these
goods were landed is unknown, however. It is often assumed that it was
at Coliemore Harbour, but this is not certain. The present Coliemore
Harbour was built in 1868 for the Ballast Board to the designs of the
board's engineer, Bindon Blood Stoney. The contractor was the well-
known local quarry owner and contractor John Cunningham.[37] The
harbour is significantly larger than the previous harbour on the site
and its creation involved extensive blasting to enlarge the area and to
provide the stone for the very high piers. The sloping area to the side of
the slip is bedrock, cut back into this shape, while the eastern side of the
harbour is a sheer face of granite resulting from blasting.

166

Northern coast of Dublin Bay

The northern coast of the bay has seen many changes over time, particularly in the nineteenth and twentieth centuries. However, a significant stretch of the coast, along the southern side of the Howth peninsula, has seen little change, while the number of projects that have resulted in changes along the rest of the coast is relatively small, in comparison with the southern coast.

Before the reclamation of land between North Wall and the Tolka estuary, the North Strand Road was known as North Strand and was literally that – with land on one side of the road and the sea on the other. The road led out to Ballybough and on reaching the Tolka estuary it turned westwards, following the margin of the bay, to Ballybough Bridge. The area of Ballybough between North Strand Road and Ballybough Road was known as Mud Island. Ballybough is an ancient settlement and the name means Poor Town, so it was traditionally an area that was less than salubrious. Mud Island was the poorer part of Ballybough and was said to have been settled by refugees of the MacDonnell family that had been dispossessed in the Ulster Plantation.[38] It seems likely that in the past this low-lying land was at least partly cut off at certain stages of the tides, though the first detailed maps of the area, those of de Gomme in 1673 and Phillips in 1685, do not show this area as an island. Later maps, such as those of Rocque, Thomas Campbell and John Taylor, do not show it as having water on the southern or western sides.

The North Strand Road became a turnpike road in 1786, when an Act of parliament was passed to establish trustees to improve and maintain the road from Dublin to Malahide. Six more Acts of parliament followed in quick succession as the legislation was fine-tuned – in 1789, 1791, 1792, 1793 and 1798.[39] The 1792 Act recognised that the turn off the North Strand Road to Ballybough Bridge, followed by another turn along Fairview Strand to reach the shore of the bay, was not efficient and it proposed the construction of a new bridge – 'it will be necessary to build, erect, and make a new bridge and causeway, eastward of Ballybough Bridge'.[40] The Act was sponsored in the Commons by the Hon. Richard Annesley, Sir John Blaquiere and Sir William Gleadowe Newcomen and brought to the House of Lords by Richard Annesley, hence the name given to the bridge. The bridge was built by William Pemberton and completed in 1797.[41] This was replaced by the present bridge, which is much wider, in 1928.[42]

The 1792 Act noted that no owner had been identified for the triangle of land at the margin of the Tolka estuary that would be enclosed from the bay by this bridge and it effectively gave the turnpike trustees the authority to reclaim the land. This did not happen, however, and it was more than a century before this triangle, between Fairview Strand, Annesley Bridge Road and the Tolka, was developed. The 1907 Ordnance Survey map shows Addison Road fully developed, as was half of Cadogan Road and the western side of Annesley Bridge Road; the street directory for 1908 lists none of these three streets, while in 1909 they appear to be fully developed.[43]

At that stage, in the Edwardian period, Annesley Bridge Road and Fairview were built on the western/north-western side, while open to the strand on the opposite side. There were mudflats here at low tide, though it was not quite the open sea, the tides only reaching this area through three arches beneath the Great Northern Railway viaduct. This railway line started out as the Dublin and Drogheda Railway and was first mooted in 1836, when the engineer William Cubitt produced a report on a potential line between Drogheda and Dublin, opting for a coastal line. The contractor William Dargan was engaged to build the line and work commenced in 1838, but was halted while a rethink on the route was undertaken. By 1840 the coastal route was confirmed. Dargan recommenced construction, and had the line ready for trial runs by 1844.[44] The engineer for the line was John MacNeil, who brought some innovative techniques to the task, including wrought-iron bridges at the Royal Canal and Rogerstown Estuary. His bridge over Clontarf Road crosses at an angle of about 36° off a right angle, necessitating the use of rifle vaulting, where the courses of stone under the bridge twist from one side of the bridge to the other, rather than running in horizontal courses. It is known as the Skew Bridge, as it crosses the road at an angle. The first use of rifle vaulting had been in Ireland in the 1780s on the County of Kildare Canal between Naas and Sallins.[45] The first railway bridge in Ireland to use the technique was the triple-arched bridge at Grand Canal Dock, built in 1833–34. MacNeil built twin arches at Clontarf Road, one to carry the road and the other the sea, though both now take the road.

In essence, the railway made little difference to the coastline. It emerged onto the open sea at East Wall Road and crossed on a high embankment, pierced by three arches, before disappearing away from the bay again at Clontarf Road. The arches to let the tide in and out at Fairview were larger than those on the Dublin and Kingstown Railway

Skew railway bridge at Clontarf Road (*Rob Goodbody*)

at Blackrock and Booterstown, so the water quality did not suffer, at least in theory, and the area remained part of the bay, albeit cut off, for the rest of the nineteenth century. In practice, things were not quite so pleasant, not because of the railway, but because of a sewer laid by Drumcondra township. Raw sewage was discharged into the Tolka upstream from Ballybough Bridge at the ebb tide, but did not all exit through the railway arches. The sewer was originally supposed to have taken the effluent further down the Tolka to East Wall Road, beyond the railway, but this part was not constructed. As a result, the mudflats opposite Fairview were offensive. The City Engineer, Parke Neville, proposed a solution in 1873, to use the slob land as the city dump, thus getting rid of the open water and killing two birds with one stone. This plan proceeded, but not until 1907, after the Local Government Act of 1898 had brought Clontarf, with Fairview, into the jurisdiction of the city. During the period 1907 to 1930 the city's refuse was deposited in the area between the railway and Fairview and this included the rubble arising from the destruction of buildings during the 1916 Rising and the civil war.[46]

The coast of Clontarf remained relatively unchanged until the twentieth century – if we define 'coast' as the shoreline, rather than the

169

construction of houses along the northern side of the road. Thomas Phillips's map of Dublin, produced in 1685, shows a road running along the shore from Fairview as far as where Vernon Avenue is today, and this remained the case, though the road surface would have been improved. The significant interventions into the shoreline related to certain economic activities, including fishing, shellfish production and mining. There were two villages at Clontarf in the eighteenth and nineteenth centuries – one based around Clontarf Castle and the old church, in Castle Avenue; and the other, known as Clontarf Sheds, almost a kilometre away where Vernon Avenue joins the coast today. The latter settlement was a fishing village, with fishing boats and shellfish industries. To the south-east of Clontarf Sheds there was an extensive oyster bed, shown on Rocque's map of the bay published in 1757.

The sheds of Clontarf with fishing boats on Dublin Bay
(Cormac F. Lowth collection)

The ground landlords of Clontarf were the Vernon family and over the years they had a number of legal disputes with Dublin Corporation over rights to the bay, including protracted litigation in the early eighteenth century in relation to rights over shellfish.[47] John Rutty, in his *Natural History of the County Dublin* observed that there were good cockles on the North Bull, about Clontarf, and that these were eaten abundantly by the poor as food and by the rich as sauce, while the best mussels in the county were to be found at Clontarf.[48]

Mining and quarrying also led to litigation. The coast had been used for these purposes over a long period and the sixteenth-century mason Sir Peter Lewys had quarried limestone on the shore at Clontarf when he was carrying out works at Christ Church Cathedral. This had the advantage of ease of transport, as stone would be lifted straight into

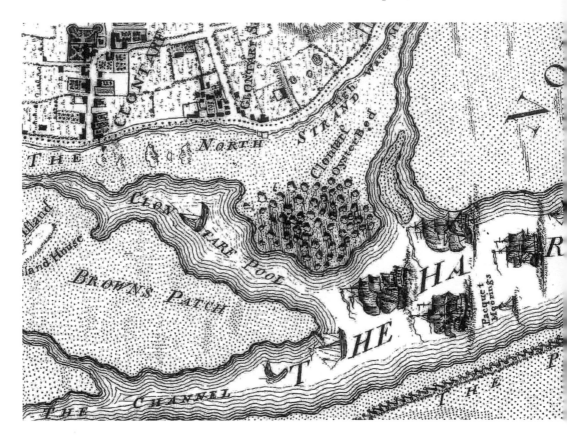

Detail of Rocque's map of 1757 showing oyster beds at Clontarf

boats and floated up the Liffey to Wood Quay; however, a significant disadvantage was that the works were drowned with every incoming tide.[49] In the 1720s the Vernons were in dispute with Dublin Corporation, which had granted a plot of land on the North Strand for quarrying.[50]

It was probably as a result of the limestone quarrying that veins of lead ore were discovered at Clontarf, as it was found in a number of limestone quarries around the city, such as at Dolphin's Barn, Robswalls and Baggot Street. The mines had been identified here at an early date, however, being known during the Tudor period; and Colonel Edward Vernon secured a grant of the lead mine from Charles II in 1661.[51] Mining certainly took place in the mid-eighteenth century, as recorded by Rutty:[52]

On the North Strand, almost opposite to an old Quarry near Clontarf Town, are two or three veins of Lead Ore, one whereof, at the distance of about 80 yards from the shore, was wrought upon in the year 1768 by some Miners, who raised there upwards of 14 Tons of Ore, which afforded them good wages. On the surface appeared a kind of yellowish Ochre, they would not sink deeper than about 30 feet, nor could they make large openings, as their Pits were filled every Tide with the Sea water, which they were obliged to pump and lade out, so that they could not work at raising the Ore more than two or three hours every Tide. This Ore produced, when smelted, about twelve hundred [weight] Lead in each Ton of Ore, and some Silver was found in the Lead upon assaying it, but not worth refining.

A Lead Course near Crab-Lough, was formerly wrought upon by Capt. Vernon, whose estate it was, but he desisted working it, as it did not answer his expectations.

The first edition Ordnance Survey six-inch map, published in 1843, marks a small circle on the strand just to the east of Castle Avenue and opposite a quarry; the circle is labelled 'Hole made in search of Lead'. This is unlikely to be the 1768 shaft and is more likely to be an early nineteenth-century excavation. Richard Griffith noted in 1828 that the lead vein 'at Clontarf is comparatively of recent discovery, and has been worked and abandoned several times since February, 1809, when the first shaft was sunk. This mine is situated on the north coast of Dublin Bay, near the village called the Sheds of Clontarf; and before the present embankment was formed, the vein might be seen at low water, traversing the Calp [limestone] strata and running into the sea.'[53] He adds that the first shaft, the only one of importance, was sunk to a depth of 16 yards (about 14.5m) and that a considerable body of ore was raised in the last working of the mine, but the sides of the shaft collapsed and the works were discontinued. Lead was encountered on the shore again in 1908 during the works to provide main drainage, which 'showed that the lead ore was by no means worked out'.[54]

Colm Lennon cites F.W.R. Knowles, author of *Old Clontarf*, as stating that an abandoned shaft remained on the seafront in the early twentieth century, while another stood on the foreshore, topped by walls about 20 feet thick. When the promenade was being developed in the 1950s the shaft was filled in, the tower was cut down to sea-wall height and made into the base of the circular shelter beside Clontarf Baths.[55] The thickness of the walls appears to be a misinterpretation, as the shelter is about 20 feet, or 6m, across; this is seen in the photograph opposite.

Shelter on top of former mine-shaft on promenade at Clontarf
(Rob Goodbody)

The circular shape of this shelter is precisely on the spot where a circle of the same size was shown on the Ordnance Survey's 1:2500 map, published in 1907, just before the sewer was laid along the seafront. This certainly lends credence to the proposition that this is the top of the mineshaft. The sketch below shows the mineshaft in its original state in 1879. The construction of the tower would have been carried out as a means of excluding the tide from the shaft to make it easier to work

A sketch of the mineshaft on the shore at Clontarf, 1879
(George Ivor Nairn)

Cork Exhibition. 1934.

the lead vein. The circular base of the shelter is constructed of local calp limestone, though heavily repaired with mass concrete.

The shelter was built as part of the laying out of the promenade along the shoreline of Clontarf, totally altering the nature of the coast. The impetus for building the promenade arose from the frequent flooding events that had occurred along Clontarf Road in the nineteenth century and it was first proposed in 1911. Dublin Corporation had the greater priority of providing housing to eliminate the city's slum problem and it was 1931 before this scheme progressed, receiving the sanction of the minister for local government in December of that year. The first task was to enclose the area and this was achieved with the construction of a substantial sea wall 2.6km in length, commencing in June 1932 and finishing in 1934. Over the next three decades the area between the wall and Clontarf Road was filled in with material that included the ash from the Dublin Gas Company's gas works.[56] Other material was dredged from the bay.[57] The various concrete shelters that grace the promenade were built in the 1950s.

The coastline had not changed much before the twentieth century, as may be seen on Thomas Phillips' remarkably detailed 1685 map of Dublin. In the extract shown below, Mud Island is seen at the left-hand margin, then the Tolka estuary, the shoreline at Fairview, with Malahide Road and Howth Road joining the coast road. To the right of centre

Detail of Phillips' map of 1685 showing Fairview and Clontarf (Reproduced with permission of the British Library)

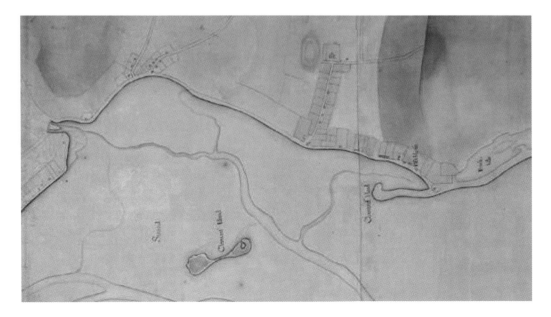

Castle Avenue runs northwards, with houses built along it and with Clontarf Castle straight ahead at the turn of the road. Further eastwards again is the Vernon Avenue area, known as the Sheds of Clontarf, with one of the buildings labelled 'Fish House'. Here two features appear that are not familiar to the modern viewer. A substantial spit projects out from shore and a little to the east of it is a lake. The text on this lake reads 'Brick Kill' – presumably brick kiln, suggesting that the lake may not be a natural feature, but a flooded pit from which brick clay has been quarried. The lake and 'Brick kilns' are depicted on Bowes' map of 1728.

The spit continues to be seen in some form or other through the eighteenth century, initially as a spit on maps such as Stokes in 1725, Bowes in 1728 and Gibson in 1756. Rocque in 1757 shows it as a sandbank marked 'Furlongs' and it appears in this guise in a few later maps. Francis Giles shows it as a spit on one of his 1819 maps and as a sandbank marked 'Furlong' on another. The first edition Ordnance Survey map shows a sandbank at right angles to the shore with a footpath marked running southwards along it to the end, which is marked 'The Point'. By 1907, the Ordnance Survey's 1:2500 map shows areas of sand and shingle along the shore, without any specific shape, though the label 'The Point' is still marked, some 500m offshore.

In 1818 this part of Clontarf was described as follows:[58]

This village is now the great resort of bathers from the north side of the city. Its rere is intersected by rural alleys, called green lanes, which are laid out with neat villas for the accommodation of company in the summer months. From the shore a wooden wharf ran to a considerable distance into the sea, at the extremity of which was a platform with seats, for the accommodation of company; it was an attractive spot, and where on a summer's evening, the sea breeze was enjoyed with peculiar pleasure. [This was called Weekes's Wharf, from the benevolent individual who erected it. It was intended to allow ships to procure water, which was piped under the platform]. Some time since Clontarf was a celebrated fishing town, and this part was called the sheds, from the number of wooden edifices erected there for the purpose of drying fish.

This area of the coastline was changed with the construction of the promenade, which runs eastwards as far as the Bull Wall. Beyond the Bull Wall the changes to the coast are less dramatic. Significant alterations took place in the vicinity of Watermill Road when the causeway was built to Bull Island in 1964, while beyond it the present cycleway towards Sutton is laid out on reclaimed land.

The opening of a tram route from Dublin to Clontarf in 1873 had not changed the coastline, as the trams used the existing road.[59] However, when the route was extended to Howth in 1900 by the Clontarf and Hill of Howth Tramroad Company Ltd, the existing roadway along the coast was inadequate and was widened to accommodate the two lines of tram track, necessitating cutting back into the slopes. Part of the line ran through the St Anne's estate and was carried out under an agreement with Lord Ardilaun.[60] The trams ceased to operate on this line in 1941, while the steep bank along some parts of James Larkin Road are a reminder of the modifications to the coast that were carried out by the tram company.

The area along the coast of Kilbarrack and Baldoyle has changed little, other than the modest alterations to the coastline when the Howth Road was built. There had been a road leading to Howth since time immemorial, but the erection of the harbour at Howth between 1807 and 1816 as the port for the mail ships led to a major upgrading of the road. Up to that time the road was dangerous, with the sea running over it at high tide in places; no mail coach could safely travel it during the day and it could not be used at all during the night.[61] In 1823 a grant was provided to upgrade Howth Road, which allowed for the reconstruction of the entire length of the road, including the construction of a 2.4km wall along the coast of Baldoyle and Kilbarrack to protect the road from the sea.[62] The work on the road was completed in 1826. Distances along it are marked by milestones of cut granite bearing cast-iron plaques that record the number of miles to Howth and to Dublin. The old Irish miles were abolished in that same year and the Howth Road milestones were the first in Ireland to record distances in statute miles. These are similar in style to the milestones along the A5 through England and Wales, which was considered to be part of the same road, connecting London with Dublin, and the roads on both sides of the Irish Sea were designed by the eminent engineer Thomas Telford.

There had been a small harbour at Howth for centuries, though it was too small to be used for purposes other than small fishing boats. In 1800 the possibility of building a harbour at Howth was put forward as a means of providing shelter for ships in storms, with a canal connection

through Sutton and on to Dublin.[63] A second suggestion put forward the potential of Howth as the location for a harbour for mail ships and this was a particular need given the Act of Union and the transfer of power from Dublin to Westminster, when rapid postal communications became vital for the Dublin administration. Work began on the harbour at Howth in 1807, though without the canal, and shortly afterwards John Rennie was taken on as engineer for the project following a dispute with the original engineer. Rennie redesigned the harbour and introduced a railway to bring stone, on wagons hauled by horses from quarries at Kilrock, to the east of Howth.[64] Balscaddan Road now runs along the line of this railway. On completion the harbour became the mail packet station for Dublin, but with the advent of larger steam ships Howth Harbour soon became too small and the mails were transferred to Kingstown (Dún Laoghaire). Instead, Howth Harbour became the fishing port that it remains today.

Fishing luggers in Howth Harbour
(Cormac F. Lowth collection)

177

Martello towers

Standing prominently near the shoreline in several places around Dublin Bay are Martello towers, some of them with gun batteries. Although they were invariably mentioned by writers who visited the Dublin area in the nineteenth century, they did not alter the coast to any great extent. Nonetheless, they are part of the character of the Dublin coastline and are part of the furniture of the bay in the public mind.[65]

From 1792 Britain and Ireland, along with Austria and Prussia, were at war with France and a number of attempts were made to land French troops in Ireland to assist popular rebellion. While these invasions did not succeed, the threat remained until peace arrived with the Treaty of Amiens in 1802. By that time, Ireland had become part of the United Kingdom and military decisions were made in London to a greater degree. The treaty broke down in 1803 and military powers decided that

Martello tower at Red Rock near Sutton *(John Fox)*

there was a significant chance that Napoleon's forces would attempt a landing near Dublin to take the city. The response was to plan a line of defence along the coast, not to prevent an invasion, but to discourage it and, if it took place, to delay the attack long enough for the army to turn out in force to repel it.

The defences were to be Martello towers, based on a small tower in Corsica, at Cape Mortella, which in 1794 had managed to hold off an attack by the Royal Navy for two days, sinking one of the naval vessels, despite being manned by only 33 men and three guns. Dublin was not the first location to receive Martello towers: two had been built in South Africa and three in Nova Scotia in the 1790s; and one each in Trinidad and Sri Lanka in 1801. The biggest group prior to those in Dublin were in Minorca, where 12 Martello towers were built between 1798 and 1802. It was these that inspired the design of the Dublin towers.

Twenty-eight sites were selected along the coastline between Balbriggan and Bray and 26 Martello towers were built in a very short period in 1804–5, eight of them with gun batteries; two further gun batteries were built without Martello towers. In Dublin Bay eight Martello towers were built along the coast between Dalkey Island and the city, four of which had gun batteries, while on the northern shore of the bay the only Martello tower was at Sutton. The surviving Martello towers around the bay are at Red Rock at Sutton and, on the southern coast, at Dalkey Island, Bartra Rock at Bullock, Sandycove, Seapoint, Williamstown and Sandymount, while another lies just outside the bay at Howth and others to the south along Killiney Bay and to the north along the coast of Fingal. The gun batteries at Dalkey Island and Sandycove also survive. The two Martello towers that are now missing on the southern side of the bay were at Glasthule, which stood on a site that is now within the People's Park in Dún Laoghaire, and which was demolished in 1849 to facilitate quarrying; and at Dunleary, near the site of the bridge over the DART line near the coal harbour, which was demolished during the construction of the railway in 1836–37. The gun battery stood on the site now occupied by the Irish Lights building and the former coastguard station.

The Martello towers are all similar, but not identical. The tower at Sutton is built with rubble stone that is rendered on the outside, while the roof vault is of brick. Those along the southern shore benefited from the availability of granite and were built with cut stone, both externally and internally, and the gun batteries are also beautifully built with cut granite.

The length of time that these towers and gun batteries were occupied by the military varied. The one at Howth was the first to be decommissioned north of the bay, when it came to be used as a telegraph station in 1852. The tower at Sutton was relinquished by the Royal Artillery in 1881. On the southern side, most of the surviving towers were decommissioned in the 1870s and 1880s, though the Sandycove tower was only vacated by the military in 1897. This one was subsequently leased by Oliver St John Gogarty, whose friend James Joyce stayed in the tower for a few days in September 1904, subsequently using the tower, and his experiences in it, as the basis for the first chapter of *Ulysses*. The Sandycove tower is now the James Joyce Museum and Tower.

9 | Historical Maps

There are many maps that show Dublin Bay – probably several hundred – but most contain little detail and do not enlighten us much as to how the bay looked in the past. They include atlas maps and maps covering large areas, such as the whole of Leinster or even the whole of County Dublin. The majority of maps date from after about 1800 and detailed maps before that date are rare, though they can be very informative. Many of the well-known historic maps of Dublin city do not show the bay, as they confine themselves to the built-up area of the city; as the city gradually expanded towards the east these maps began to show more and more in that direction. A case in point is the maps that were bound into the street directories of the city from 1760 onwards, of which there are more than a hundred. The earliest of these only showed the east of the city as far as North Strand and Merrion Street, but by the 1830s they had extended downriver to show Ringsend and East Wall, with Fairview managing to squeeze into the corner at top right. The major exception to this trend was John Rocque, whose maps will be discussed later.

Maps may be divided into three types and the type will determine how rare they are. First, there are manuscript maps. Then there are printed maps, which can be subdivided into published and unpublished. Manuscript maps are one-offs, as each is drawn by hand and is unique. In practice, however, there is often more than one copy, either a rough first copy followed by the final neat version, or, in some cases, a second or third (almost) identical good copy, laboriously copied by hand. Of the printed maps, the published versions could be in a book, such as a street directory or a government report, or sold as a separate item. Unpublished printed maps were less common in the past, but they did exist. Because of the labour involved in preparing copies of manuscript maps, not to mention the chances of error in the copying, a map could be engraved and printed for private use, such as for a board meeting. The Ordnance Survey sometimes produced maps that were not published – and still does so today.

Many of the maps of Dublin Bay were printed and published; a few were printed and not published. Some of the most colourful and interesting of the maps of the bay are the manuscripts prepared for the various authorities that successively took responsibility for the care of Dublin Port.

There is another way in which maps of Dublin Bay can categorised – by purpose. First, there are maps produced for general purposes – these include Ordnance Survey maps or the county maps produced by private publishers. Second, there are navigation charts, which can reveal a great deal of information about the presence of channels, sandbanks, wrecks and other things that sailors need to know. Finally, there are the maps that show proposed alterations, such as new piers or quays or even the realignment of a channel; these are often manuscript maps, as they were only intended for the eyes of those who would carry out the alterations; they were not for publication. A fourth category, less pertinent here, is the thematic map, which might show data such as pollution levels in the water or the distribution of feeding grounds of particular bird species.

Given the paucity of paintings, engravings, watercolours and other views of the bay from the period when the port was expanding and the bay undergoing change, the best way to illustrate the developments over time and the changes in Dublin Bay is through a succession of maps.

Seventeenth century

There are no good maps of the bay earlier than the late seventeenth century. As it happens, people made no major changes to the bay before this time, the alterations being confined to the city and the river, as we saw in Chapter 8. If we are to try to define the natural area of the bay prior to human intervention, the probable interface between the river estuary and the bay would occur near the Custom House or Butt Bridge, and nothing significant had occurred downstream from that point by the 1670s nor, in fact, into the 1700s. We are fortunate that the three main maps from the seventeenth century are of a very high standard and are very detailed.

The first of these is a manuscript map prepared in 1673 by Bernard de Gomme, who was investigating the potential for improving security by constructing a star fort as a citadel. Given that the most likely direction from which an attack would come would be the sea, de Gomme's proposal was for a substantial fort at Ringsend. At the time Ringsend was a narrow spit projecting into the bay between the Dodder estuary

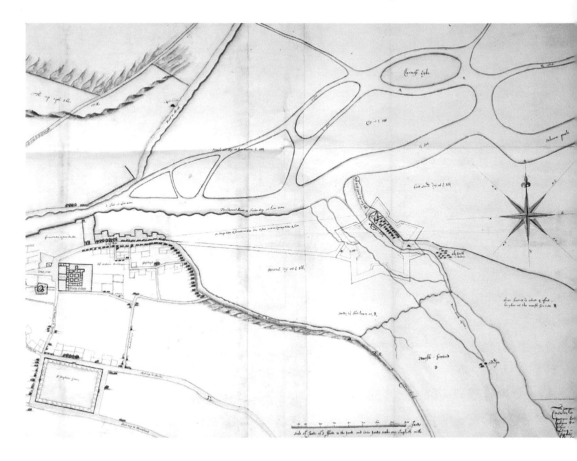

Detail of Bernard de Gomme's map of 1673 *(Reproduced with permission of the British Library)*

and the open sea. The map shows the inner part of the bay, extending out as far as the North Strand and Sandymount and depicting the various channels running from the mouth of the Liffey. On the northern side of the bay, North Strand Road runs along the shoreline, with few buildings, while on the southern side Townsend Street has houses on both sides, while Sandwith Street runs along the edge of the Bay and is only built up on one side. The village of Ringsend is shown, with a substantial building at its northern end. This appears to be a fort and may have been the one that the city authorities ordered to be built in June 1582.[1] The ground landlord, Colonel Fitzwilliam, was given permission to demolish it in 1655, though it appears that he did not take it down until some years later, as it appears on maps for another 30 years or so.[2]

Twelve years after Bernard de Gomme prepared his map, another military engineer was detailed to survey Dublin to assess its defences. Captain Thomas Phillips was sent to Ireland by James II to survey Irish towns and forts[3] and produced a substantial map of the Dublin city area.

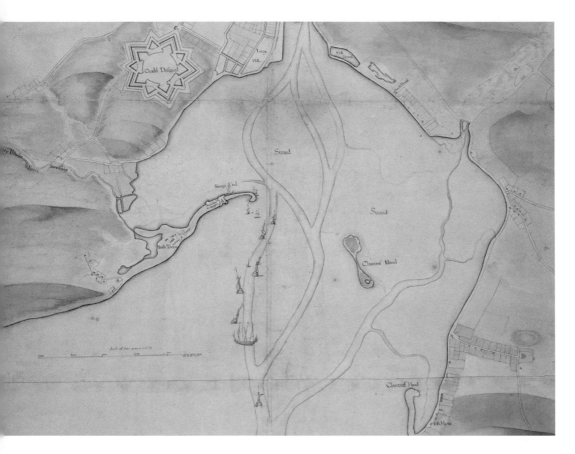

Like de Gomme's map before it, Phillips' map includes a plan of the city itself as well as a sizeable section of the bay. In this case, a greater area of the bay is included and it is shown in greater detail. The fort is still visible on the Ringsend peninsula and another peninsula can be seen across the bay at Clontarf, near where the bottom of Vernon Avenue stands today. The channels in the bay are clearly marked, the main channel having shipping sailing in it and, more dramatically, a number of wrecks. Phillips considered that Ringsend was not the right place for a citadel, probably because it would be too easily cut off from land, and he located it where Merrion Square was later to appear.

A few years later the first chart of Dublin Bay was published in *Great Britain's Coasting Pilot*, published in 1693, though the survey was carried out in 1686.[4] This map uses a much smaller scale than the previous two and covers a larger area, running north to Portmarnock and south beyond Dalkey. The detail is lacking, only including enough to help a sailor to navigate, though the fort is still depicted at Ringsend.

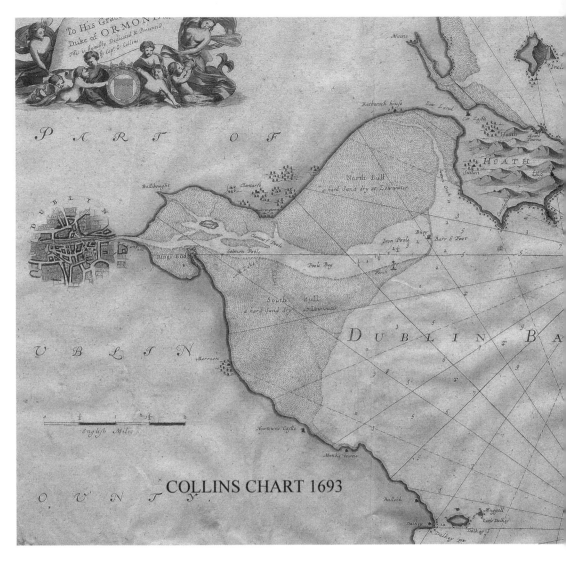

To His Grace
Duke of ORMOND
This is Humbly Dedicated & Presented
by Capt C. Collins

P A R T   O F

Balibought

DUBLIN

Clantarfe

North Bull
a hard Sand dry at Lowwater

Katbarock house
Low Land

Co. Cassle

HOATH

Sutton

Rings End

Salmon Poole

Poole Boy

Iron Poole

Bury
Barr & Foot

South Bull
a hard Sand dry at Lowwater

D U B L I N   B A

D U B L I N

Merrion

Newtowns Castle

English Miles

Monks towne

COLLINS CHART 1693

C O U N T Y

Bullock

Dalkey

Dalkey Br

Collins' map of Dublin Bay, 1693

Alarmingly, the configuration of the channels in the bay on Collins' map is quite different from those shown by Phillips and it can only be hoped that Collins was right, given that ships' captains were relying on his map to access the port.

It was also around this time that the first map of County Dublin was published. William Petty had carried out a major survey of most of Ireland in the 1650s (the Down Survey), and in 1685 he published an atlas based on his findings.[5] The atlas included a map of Ireland and maps of the four provinces and 32 counties. The scale is small, there is little detail and the map contributes nothing to our study of Dublin Bay.

Early eighteenth-century land reclamation

After that initial flurry of activity, the production of major maps such as these slowed for a time. The end of the war between William of Orange and James II had brought about a lasting peace and pressure to fortify the city eased. The new impetus for map-making came from proposals for new works, many of which were ambitious, to say the least. Up to this time there was a dispute as to who had responsibility for the shoreline along the river and the harbour. Dublin Corporation claimed that its charter from King John had given it the relevant powers, while the Lord High Admiral claimed jurisdiction over the seas. The deadlock was broken in 1707 when the city agreed to grant the Lord High Admiral a hundred yards of sailcloth each year, and in return he allowed the corporation to carry out new works on the shoreline. Arising from this agreement an Act of parliament was passed establishing an office to be known as the Ballast Office, which would be under the control of the city authorities, and which would take charge of the river, the port and the harbour. The act came into force in 1708 and the corporation appointed a committee to manage the Ballast Office.[6]

Apart from day-to-day maintenance, repairing the Liffey quays and maintaining the shipping channel, the biggest problem the port of Dublin had was the bay itself. The sediments on the seabed tended to shift and the channels shifted with them, making it difficult to navigate. A more serious problem was a sandbar that ran across the mouth of the Liffey, over which there was little depth of water at low tide. These interrelated problems would exercise the minds of the Ballast Office and the ships' captains for another century and a half and would result in some dramatic interventions into the bay.

Even before the agreement was reached over the responsibility for the bay a dramatic proposal was drawn up to make substantial alterations. A manuscript map, held in the archives of Dublin Port Company, bears the simple title 'A Map of the Harbour of Dublin from Essex Bridge to the Barr 1704'. There is no indication of who drew the map or at whose behest.

The inner part of the bay is shown, with the shoreline from today's Fairview to Merrion Gates, and with the river channels. The village of Ringsend is shown prominently; the fort is no longer present. The dramatic element in the map is the set of proposals to realign the three river channels into straight lines. A new straight channel for the Liffey would be cut from near Butt Bridge to a point somewhere near the roundabout leading from Sandymount towards the East Link Bridge –

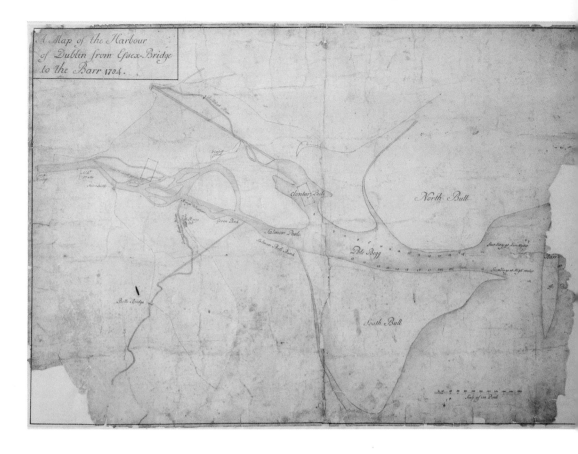

A Map of the Harbour
of Dublin from Essex-Bridge
to the Barr 1704.

a distance of about 3km. The Tolka would get a new straight channel leading south-eastwards past an island called Clontarf Island, the total length of the cutting being about 2.5km. The proposed realignment of the Dodder was to be shorter, taking it less than 1.5km north-eastwards, though this would require a cut through the isthmus of Ringsend, in fact through Irishtown. Whoever proposed this draconian feat of engineering is unknown, but it is not heard of again.

Proposals for realignment of the river channels, 1704 (*Dublin Port Archive*)

The confirmation of the city's powers to control the shores led to other proposals that were also ambitious in engineering terms, but with a focus on income rather than improving the port. As seen in the previous chapter, land had been reclaimed from the Liffey from Viking times and this continued until the present Liffey walls and quays were completed in the mid-nineteenth century. However, in the early eighteenth century the city set its eyes on the bay. The work was to be carried out in two separate schemes: the northern side of the channel was to be managed by the city itself; the southern side would be in private hands.

On the southern side of the Liffey the quays ended at Hawkins Quay, now part of Burgh Quay. An attempt had been made by a man named Philip Croft, in the late seventeenth century, to enclose the next part of the shore, but this was unsuccessful and in 1712 the city assembly – the body of elected members of Dublin Corporation – granted a lease to John Mercer. He built walls alongside the river channel, around the low tide mark, and infilled between the walls to form a quay. By 1715 he had enclosed a strip of the shoreline and named it George's Quay, presumably after the monarch, George I. John Mercer went no further than this, though, and the city took over the next strip of the shore and built sea walls to enclose it – hence the name City Quay.[7]

That Philip Croft had failed to enclose the land he had leased and John Mercer ran out of steam after enclosing about 250m of the shoreline is put into perspective by the achievement of Sir John Rogerson. He leased a section of the shore from where Creighton Street now meets the river and Ringsend Bridge and proposed to enclose it. In view of the enormity of the task, he converted his simple lease into a Fee Farm Grant, which would give him greater control and longer-term certainty to enable the fulfilment of a substantial and long-term project.[8] Work began by 1716 to build the quay walls and by the early 1720s it had reached the Dodder and turned around to meet Ringsend Bridge – a total length of about 1,500m. By contrast, the city took four years to build the quay walls along the 400m of City Quay. Sir John Rogerson saw the walls completed, but died in 1724 before any significant development had taken place.[9]

The land enclosed by Sir John Rogerson's walls was substantial. The old shoreline had run along Sandwith Street and Grand Canal Street, so the entire area to the east of Sandwith Street as far as the Dodder was enclosed, between Grand Canal Street and the river. It was a long time before it was all back-filled and developed and as late as 1792 the wall was breached in a storm and the South Lotts were flooded, with people plying boats over the area, including the Duke of Leinster, who sailed through the breach in the wall and landed, apparently, at Merrion Square.[10] The nearest he would have been able to approach would have been the bottom of Holles Street, which was at the shoreline – which explains the slope of the street.

While the enclosure of the southern shores was largely in the hands of Sir John Rogerson, the city adopted a different approach on the northern side of the channel. There had been an attempt in the 1680s to lease this area to tenants, who would be obliged to enclose it and reclaim it, but this did not work. In 1710 the newly established Ballast Board began to enclose the northern boundary of the river with a new wall and this reached its eastward limit in 1717, when the construction works turned northwards along what is now East Wall Road.[11] In 1717 the Ballast Office committee presented a report to the city assembly in which it set down its proposals for the land to the north of the new river wall (see the map on page 139). This envisaged the continuation of the eastern wall northwards to the Tolka estuary, where it would turn westwards to Ballybough Bridge, now Luke Kelly Bridge. On the northern side of the Tolka, referred to in the report as Ballybough River, a similar enclosure was to take place, with the Tolka running in a canal 24m wide, while the land to the north was enclosed almost as far as Castle Avenue. The resulting land was to be laid out in streets and plots, with the plots being leased to tenants who would provide the fill to reclaim the land.[12] Only the southern section of this work was ever completed, though this was a substantial work in itself and the layout of the land today, including streets such as Mayor Street, Sheriff Street and Guild Street, are recognisable on the map prepared at the time.

Tackling the bar problem

The biggest problem to face the port of Dublin over the centuries was the bank, or bar, that ran north–south across the middle of the bay, creating a shallow area at the entrance to the Liffey channel. At best, this was an inconvenience, as it meant that ships had to wait for high water before they could enter or leave the port. At worst, it was a positive danger. Ships could easily run aground on the bar, though the risk was reduced significantly by using pilots who knew the channels well and would guide ships in and out. Worse than the danger of running aground was the danger of a ship being caught in the bay by a storm and being unable to run for shelter because the bar prevented access to safer waters. Over the centuries many ships were wrecked in the bay after being caught in such an exposed position; the worst storms were the easterlies and north-easterlies, which blew straight into the bay. In such a storm it would be difficult for a ship to sail out of the bay, even if there had been a safe shelter nearby – which there was not.

This problem increased over time as ships evolved, becoming larger, heavier and requiring deeper draught. The caravel was the ocean-going ship that was developed in Portugal in the fifteenth century and used by explorers such as Magellan, Dias and da Gama. These ships had a displacement ranging from around 50 tonnes to 150 tonnes. In the sixteenth century the galleon was developed and remained the dominant large ship until the late eighteenth century; most were below 500 tons, though they could be larger. Later in the eighteenth century the brig became the dominant large transport ship, though some larger vessels – simply known as ships – also traded through Dublin. Many of the vessels using the port were smaller than these and hence had less of a problem with the shallow waters over the bar. Even in 1804 the Ballast Board suggested that the port could operate effectively with ships of just 200–300 tons.[13]

In 1719 Captain Greenville Collins proposed that a canal be constructed around the margin of the bay to bypass the bar and allow ships to enter the port at any time. This canal was to have its entrance near the shore at Sutton, utilising the existing channel at Sutton Creek, from where it would run close to the shore past Baldoyle, Kilbarrack, Raheny, Clontarf, after which it would cross towards Ringsend and joining the Liffey channel. The reason for the circuitous route would have been to minimise the amount of drifting sediments that might silt up the canal, and this would be helped further by the construction of a pier. Gabriel Stokes, a well-known Dublin surveyor, produced a number of maps of the bay in the 1720s for the Ballast Board and in the accompanying illustration (facing page) he shows the bay with the canal near the coast and the wall or pier to protect the canal.

The south wall

Shortly before Greenville Collins produced his proposal for a canal, the Ballast Board had prepared its own solution to the problem of safe anchorage within the channel and had submitted it for the approval of the city assembly. As we saw in Chapter 8, the board concluded that raising the bank of the south side of the channel below Ringsend would provide shelter for shipping. The board had begun to source the materials that would be needed, including piles – posts to be driven into the seabed – and kishes, which were woven baskets that would contain stones to form a barrier, similar to those used today in coastal defences – though the kishes for the south wall would be on a somewhat larger scale.

The Ballast Board's next report to the city assembly was on 29 April 1715, when the costings of the project were presented. This included 200

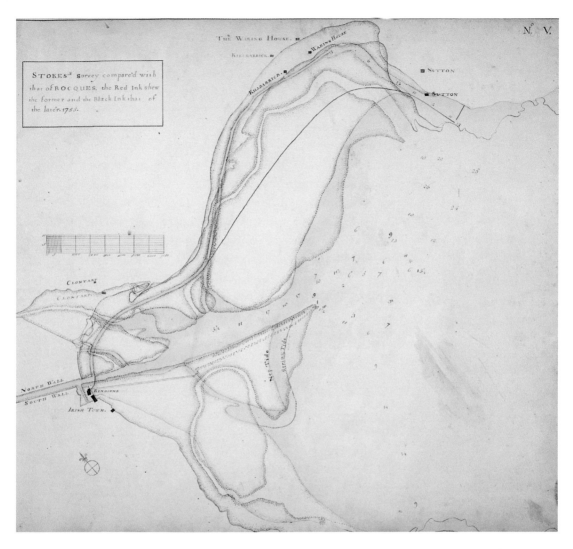

STOKES' survey compared with that of ROCQUES, the Red Ink shew the former and the Black Ink that of the later. 1755.

tonnes of oak timber, 150mm by 225mm and from 3m to 4.5m long; 1,200 straight oak poles 100mm by 150mm across and 3–4.3m long; and a thousand kishes. The city assembly authorised the Ballast Board to proceed with the project and this was the beginning of the project that was to become the Great South Wall.[14]

Work began in the following year and was fairly easy at first, as the piles could be driven into the sands in relatively shallow water. Piles were initially driven by a piledriver brought from the Netherlands, though a similar machine was built in Dublin, no doubt copying the Dutch piledriver, which allowed the Ballast Board to dispense with the services of the Dutch crew and save that expense. Working from the highest

Stokes' map of the bay, showing Collins' ship canal (*Dublin Port Archive*)

191

point of the sands adjacent to the channel, the piling continued in both directions into ever-deeper water until in 1721 it became impossible to drive piles at the depths of water that were encountered. From this time onward the method of construction changed; now substantial frames the size of modern shipping containers were prefabricated at Ringsend and floated to the site, where they were loaded with stones and sunk to the bottom.[15]

On its completion this structure ran over a distance of approximately 2.7km between the present-day sites of Pigeon House Harbour and the Poolbeg Lighthouse. It was known as the Piles, despite not all being constructed of piles, and is shown on maps of Dublin Bay of the period, including Gabriel Stokes' map reproduced on page 191.

The dual purpose of the Piles was to provide a sheltered anchorage for shipping and to prevent the drift of sands from the South Bull into the channel. While there were problems with the effectiveness of the Piles, they certainly made an improvement. However, they were isolated in the bay and did not connect to land, so various solutions were put

Map of the bay by Stokes, with Wills' proposals for a wall *(Dublin Port Archive)*

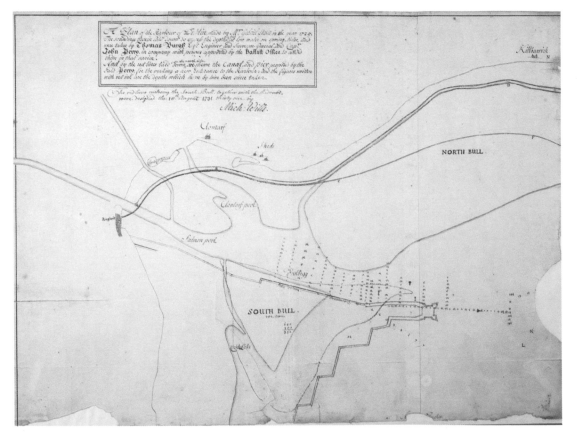

forward to join the Piles to Ringsend, which would be difficult, as the water was deeper between Pigeon House and Ringsend than it was to the east of Pigeon House, where the Piles had been driven. In 1731 a new proposal was put forward by Michael Wills, which would involve building a wall southwards from the Poolbeg end of the Piles to reach the shore at Sandymount.

The wall as planned by Wills would zigzag across the bay near the South Bull to reach the shore and would also run further into the bay from Poolbeg, with a redoubt or fort at the eastern end, to act as an advance defence of the city. The construction of a wall was begun that same year, though it appears that it was not the wall proposed by Wills, which would have had to contend with some deep waters. It is unclear how far the project advanced, but John Rocque's map of County Dublin, published in 1760, shows some form of structure running from Pigeon House to Sandymount; it is shown more as if it were a line of boulders rather than a wall. Strangely, Rocque's map of Dublin Bay, produced three years earlier, does not show this feature.

The Piles continued to give trouble and in January 1746/47 the Ballast Office reported that the works had been damaged by the weather, while one of its boats had sunk. Over the next couple of years each report related that repair works were continuing, suggesting that the Piles were deteriorating.[16] This is not surprising, as timber is susceptible to attack by the shipworm when in salt water, as a result of which timber bridges in estuaries have a lifespan of only ten to 20 years.[17]

A more major phase in the works emerged in April 1748, when the Ballast Office reported to the city assembly its intention to build a double wall from the western end of the Piles to Ringsend and that they had entered into a contract with Benjamin Pemberton to carry out the work.[18] A double wall is two walls running parallel with each other, the space between infilled with material such as stones or sand. The city assembly agreed and the works began. The resulting wall was shown as being complete on Rocque's map of the Bay, published in 1757. It survives today, though largely unappreciated, as it lies beneath York Road and Pigeon House Road, as far as the old Pigeon House Harbour.

Rocque's 1757 map shows that the wall and the Piles are not aligned, so there is an angle between them. The back story to how they were built explains this apparent anomaly, as the Piles were driven into the sand originally as a stand-alone barrier to protect the anchorage and there was no reason why they should align with Ringsend Point. The location

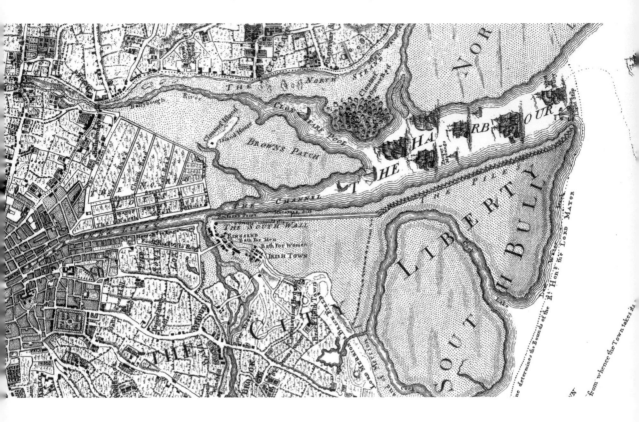

Detail of Rocque's map of 1757 showing South Wall and the Piles. The number of sailing ships shown in the Liffey confirms the importance of the port at this time.

of both wall and Piles was affected more by the need to facilitate the channel than any aesthetic desire to make them run in a straight line.

In April 1759 the Ballast Office reported to the city assembly that yet more damage had occurred to the Piles. On the other hand, the new wall from Ringsend to the Piles was nearly finished. They then informed the assembly that they 'were of opinion that when the said wall is finished to Ringsend, it would be proper to carry it down eastward to the end of the piles'. The city assembly gave them the authority to proceed, and in such a simple, understated way, the go-ahead was given to construct the massive sea wall, 2.7km long, stretching from the Pigeon House to Poolbeg.[19] The project was substantial and difficult, involving building in the water, and it was not until the mid-1790s that the wall was complete. Captain William Bligh (see page 200) was reputed to have been involved in the construction of the South Wall, but Sean de Courcy points out that Bligh did not visit Dublin until after the wall was complete. However, it was Bligh who suggested that the seaward section of the wall be raised in height, as it is clear from examining the wall that the topmost section was added later.[20]

Placing piles at the edge of the river channel would have had safety implications and these remained when the piles were augmented by a substantial stone wall. The Ballast Office was aware of the danger and could see that a lighthouse was needed. With considerable foresight and initiative they made sure that the new wall provided for this eventuality. In July 1762 they reported to the city assembly, 'we have the pleasure to acquaint your honours, that we have began the foundation of the east abutment, at the end of the piles, for the intended new wall with success, (which may also serve for a foundation for a light house, if hereafter it should be thought proper to build one)'.[21] By 1764 the lighthouse was under construction and it was completed in 1767, the first light being lit in September. This innovative lighthouse used candle power, previous lighthouses having merely had braziers of coal burning to indicate their position at night.[22]

Shipping at the entrance to Dublin Port in the early nineteenth century, by William Sadler (1782–1839) *(courtesy of Adams Dublin)*

195

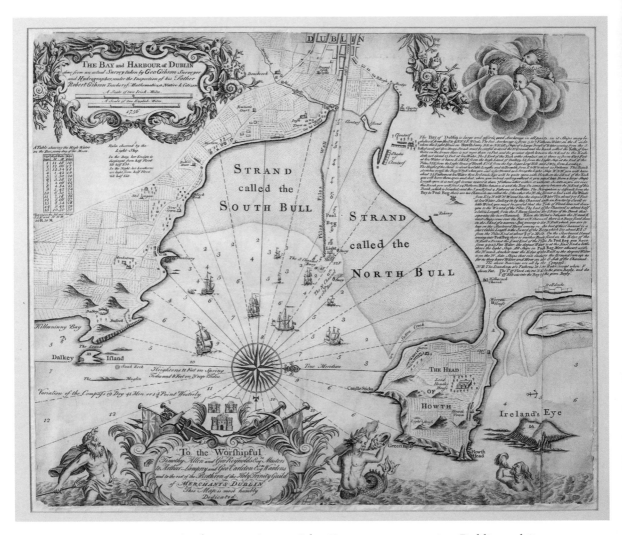

Gibson's chart of the bay, 1756

At the same time as John Rocque was surveying Dublin and its environs, George Gibson was producing a chart of Dublin Bay, which he published in 1756. This was before work started on the wall at Poolbeg and the chart shows the Piles still in place, while the wall to Ringsend is present. Notable on the chart is a lightship located at Poolbeg, at the end of the Piles, which had been placed in this position in 1735.[23]

In 1762, George Semple produced a set of maps which he presented to the Ballast Office. These were largely compiled from previous surveys of the bay, showing differences between surveys, which would have been partly due to inaccuracies in surveying, but more significantly would have reflected changes in the river channels, sandbanks, etc. in the bay over time. Some proposals for improvements to the bay were included.

In a note accompanying the maps, Semple said that he had 'given the sundry shiftings and changes of the sands'. From his examination of the way in which the sands and the channels had shifted, he concluded that 'all which doth most evidently demonstrate the happy effects of erecting the new pier', while offering 'two different designs for completing the same and further improvements necessary'.

In the example reproduced here, Semple's proposal appears quite radical. He is not only proposing to continue the wall right out to Poolbeg, but to build a similar wall on the northern side of the channel, continuing both of these walls towards the opposite shores at Sutton and Booterstown and reclaiming 2,444 plantation acres north of the

Map by George Semple, 1755
(Dublin Port Archive)

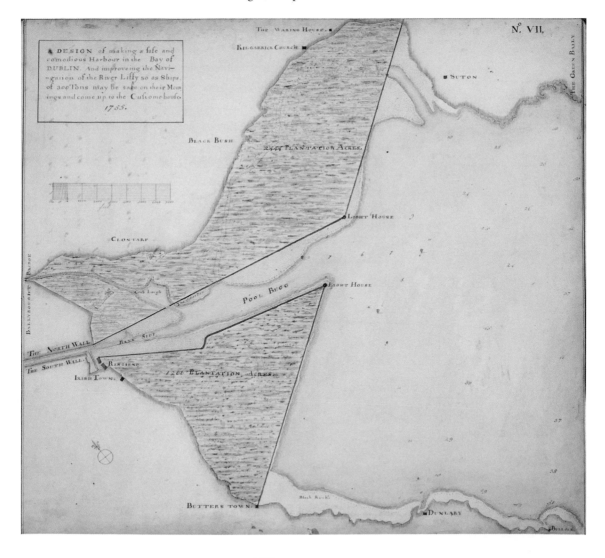

river and 1,266 plantation acres south of the river. These would equate to 1,600 hectares on the North Bull and 830 hectares on the South Bull.

It appears that Semple had not been engaged by the Ballast Office to prepare these maps, or any other work, and they are more akin to a portfolio, which he hoped would win him employment on the designs of new works proposed by the Ballast Office. As it appears that he was never engaged by the Ballast Office, his efforts were in vain.[24]

The construction of the South Wall seems to have engaged the energies of the Ballast Office in the late eighteenth century, as little other work was proposed by way of improvements to the Bay at the time. They were, of course, carrying on the normal duties of a port authority, ensuring that the day-to-day running of Dublin port was as smooth as possible, with channels kept clear, quay walls repaired and so forth.

In 1786, parliament introduced a bill proposing to replace Dublin Corporation's Ballast Office committee with a new, more independent body, to be known as the Corporation for Preserving and Improving the Port of Dublin, though it was generally known as the Ballast Board.[25] This body was given responsibility for a greater part of the bay than its

A tall ship in the Irish Sea approaching Dublin *(Richard Nairn)*

predecessor, including the management of Dunleary Harbour and the maintenance of lights as far as Dalkey.

The new Ballast Board decided that the existing arrangement for passenger ships was not adequate. These ships sailed into the channel and dropped anchor in the sheltered anchorage near the Piles and South Wall, from where passengers were ferried ashore by local boatmen. To improve facilities a small harbour was constructed midway along the South Wall. At that time there was a blockhouse on the wall that was operated by John Pidgeon, one of the Board's employees, who provided accommodation for travellers.[26] It is worth noting that accommodation was essential, as all ships were powered by sail at this time and were dependent on the right weather conditions before they could sail. As a result passengers sometimes had to wait days, or even weeks. In 1793 the Ballast Board decided that Pidgeon's blockhouse was not adequate accommodation and a hotel was built at the harbour. The harbour was taken over by the military in 1798 and Pigeon House Fort was built, which remained a military station for more than a century.

A surviving wall of the Pigeon House Fort with the harbour in the background. *(Richard Nairn)*

In 1800 the parliament in College Green passed an Act that gave, on a temporary basis, responsibility for the improvement of Dublin Port to the Directors General of Inland Navigation. This body had been in existence for some years and was concerned with canals and river navigation. The directors looked for advice from various experts. Sir Thomas Hyde Page presented a 53-page report with wide-ranging proposals, including providing a safe anchorage in Dalkey Sound, building a new pier at Sandycove Point and connecting Sandycove with the city by means of a ship canal.[27]

The North Bull Wall, harbours and ship canals

While Hyde Page was preparing his report, the board engaged Captain William Bligh of the Royal Navy to survey the harbour. Apart from his exploits on the *Bounty* in the south Pacific, Bligh seems to be best remembered in Dublin as the man who proposed the North Bull Wall as a means of ridding the port of the notorious bar. In fact, he is not the one responsible. He did carry out a very detailed and accurate survey of the bay, which included a review of all the previous surveys, which he found to be inaccurate.[28] His major proposal was a wall on the northern side of the channel – but not in the form the North Bull Wall takes today.

Portrait of Captain William Bligh of the Royal Navy *(by Alexander Huey courtesy of the National Library of Australia)*

Bligh pointed out that the depth of water over the bar was greater than the depth at the quay walls, and hence a greater priority was to improve that situation. His proposal was to extend the existing North Wall eastwards into the bay to cut off drifting sands from the river channel, much as the South Wall had done. By confining the channel the current would also scour the channel and keep it clear. Finally, he suggested an intensive programme of dredging, employing 350 men for the purpose. The suggestion that a wall should be built from Clontarf, rather than as an extension of the North Wall Quay, was put forward by two members of the Ballast Board, Leland Crosthwaite and George Macquay.[29] This idea had, in fact, been put forward in 1786 by William Chapman, the engineer who had proposed in the previous year that the Grand Canal should be run around the southern margin of the city to join the Liffey at Ringsend.[30]

The year after Bligh's printed report and chart of the bay were published, the eminent Scottish engineer John Rennie was engaged to carry out a report on the harbour and Dublin Bay to investigate, among other things, the proposal for a pier from Clontarf. This was Rennie's first engagement in the Dublin area, though he went on to have a distinguished

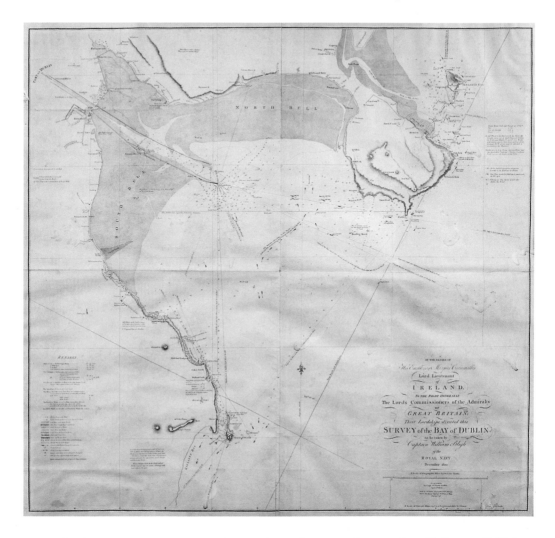

Bligh's survey of Dublin Bay, 1801, showing proposed north wall *(Dublin Port Archive)*

record, taking over as engineer on the Royal Canal in 1803, for Howth Harbour in 1809 and Dunleary Harbour in 1815, as well as working on the docks near the Custom House. Rennie's recommendation to the Inland Navigation Commissioners was threefold. First, he supported the suggestion that a wall be constructed from Clontarf towards Poolbeg, his proposal being to leave a gap of 165m at the Clontarf end. His second proposal was to create a tidal reservoir on the South Bull with an opening into the channel at Ringsend; and his third was to provide jetties at Clontarf. He suggested that it might be necessary to extend the ends of the proposed northern wall and the South Wall eastwards.[31] The thinking behind his first two proposals was to provide two very large bodies of water that would be tidal and that would fill and empty with the tides running through a narrow entrance at Poolbeg. The result would be a strong current at the bar that would scour it away. A further report was submitted by Captain Daniel Corneille, an engineer, who proposed a different alignment of the wall from Clontarf; it would run over a longer distance and would have a curve.

The Inland Navigation Commissioners sat on these reports for 16 years before acting on them, even though the bar continued to be an inconvenience to shipping and lives continued to be lost. John Rennie also considered Hyde Page's proposals for harbours of refuge at Dalkey Sound, Sandycove and Dunleary. He considered Dalkey Sound to be totally unsuited as a shelter for larger square-rigged vessels, though it would suffice for small craft as a shelter against east winds. He proposed to build a pier between Dalkey Island and Lamb Island to increase the shelter available. He also disagreed with Hyde Page's proposal for a harbour at Sandycove, preferring one at Dunleary. His Dunleary proposal was not the one that would be built some years later, but a smaller pier, near the site of Traders Wharf. The basis for the suggested harbours at Sandycove and Dunleary was that they would act as entry

Chart by Francis Giles showing proposed North Bull Wall
(Dublin Port Archive)

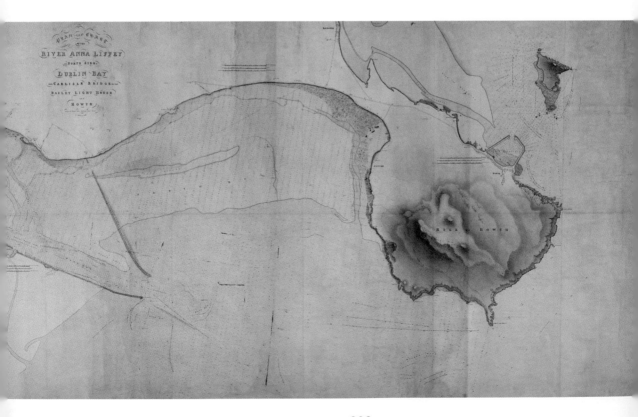

points to ship canals to enable ships to travel in safety to a dock near the Dodder. Rennie's objection to the Sandycove option was mainly based on the cost, due to the difficulties of building a canal into Scotsman's Bay. Rennie agreed that on the northern coast the waters around Ireland's Eye provided a reasonable anchorage and he proposed enhancing it. There was also a proposal for a canal to connect this anchorage, through Sutton, to docks near the Custom House, though Rennie did not consider this to be as good a choice as Dunleary.[32]

In the end, it was not the Commissioners for Inland Navigation that proceeded with the North Bull Wall but the port authority itself – the Ballast Board. In 1818 they engaged a surveyor, Francis Giles, who did a lot of work with John Rennie, and Giles prepared three maps at different scales showing detailed soundings in the channel, the river and the bay, while also showing the proposed wall. Giles worked closely with George Halpin, the engineer to the Ballast Board. Work commenced on the construction of the wall in 1819 and was completed about five years later.[33]

The delay in implementing the scheme for the North Bull Wall was unfortunate and appears to have been due to lack of funds for such a major operation. The exchequer, both in Dublin and in London, was hugely strained by the cost of the Napoleonic Wars and a series of unpopular taxes had been introduced in Ireland to help balance the books, including a window tax and taxes on servants, carriages and horses.[34] It was only with the sale of Pigeon House Harbour to the military authorities that funds became available.[35]

In the interval between Rennie's recommendation and the implementation of the wall project, a new impetus appeared that drove an alternative solution to the problem of the bar. This arose from a double tragedy in November 1807, when two ships carrying recruits destined for the wars with Napoleon left Pigeon House Harbour and immediately ran into a major storm. After 36 hours the ships were still in the bay and still in trouble; and both were wrecked – one at the base of the Martello tower at Seapoint and the other a little closer to Blackrock. Virtually everyone on board perished, about 380 people in all (see page 232). This resulted in a campaign to have a new pier built at Dunleary to provide shelter for ships caught in storms and to allow them to ride at anchor in comparative safety until the storm blew over. This campaign was led by a Norwegian-born ship broker named Richard Toutcher, who was based at Sir John Rogerson's Quay. His campaign ultimately succeeded and John Rennie was engaged as the engineer to design the new pier. This was not the pier that Rennie had suggested in 1800, which was merely the entrance to a proposed ship canal with some anchorage, but a major breakwater to provide safe anchorage for a large number of ships. Shortly before construction began Rennie suggested that a second pier and a fully enclosed harbour would be a more effective approach, and this is what was built.[36] The massive harbour, enclosing a hundred hectares of sea, was completed in the early 1840s and changed the southern side of the bay.

It may be worth reflecting that the Commissioners Appointed to Inquire into Tidal Harbours in the 1840s were not impressed by the delay in building the North Bull Wall, commenting that 'it does not

Rennie's plan for the two piers at Dunleary (Reproduced with permission of National Archives, Kew)

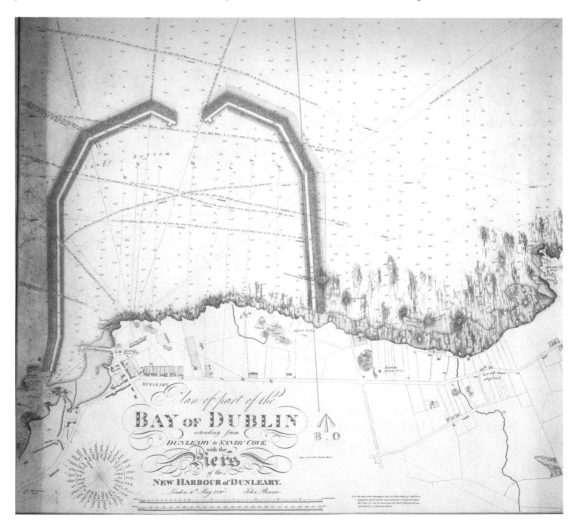

appear, nor is it easy to understand, why this proposal thus supported was not acted upon at the time; the pressing necessity for something being done was made manifest to all by the wreck or damage within the Bay or harbour of not less than 124 vessels in the six years from 1797 to 1803. After a lapse of 17 years the Clontarf wall was adopted, and it has proved even more beneficial to the bar than had been anticipated.'[37] One wonders whether, if this scheme had gone ahead in 1803 rather than 1819, there would have been such a strong case for a harbour at Dún Laoghaire, and perhaps it might never have been built.

10 | Maritime Heritage

In earlier chapters we have seen how the landscape around Dublin Bay changed as the city spread out around the sea coast. The tidal area was also changing as sections of it disappeared under city streets, and the wild shores were largely replaced by an engineered coastline. Some of the original features have now completely vanished.

Clontarf Island

Clontarf Island was once a familiar part of north Dublin Bay. In 1818 it was described as:

Clontarf Island in 1878 *(sketch by Alexander Williams first published in* The Irish Naturalist*)*

> Formerly of greater magnitude, and having still to be seen the ruins of a house, to which the citizens resorted to recreate themselves. It seems to have been formed by the sand brought from the South Bull, sweeping around the east wall of the Lots. Since this sand has been intercepted by the South Wall, the island

has gradually decreased, and is now nearly washed away by the torrents of the river Tolkay [*sic*]. [1]

A painting of the island by Alexander Williams accompanied his paper on the bird life in Dublin Bay.[2] During his long life (1846–1930), Williams observed quite substantial changes in the bay, but his detailed description of Clontarf Island is exceptional by the standards of his time:

> One of the most remarkable changes that has taken place is the total disappearance of what used to be a very romantic feature in the landscape, the Island of Clontarf. Thirty years ago this place was a conspicuous object and of considerable dimensions, measuring about 400 yards long, and about 40 yards wide, and 16 feet in height. It was situated close to the road which bounds the City on the east, and which extends from the Alexandra Basin, North Wall, as far as the River Tolka at Annesley Bridge, Fairview. It was a busy and populous place, and between the island and the well-known East Wall bathing slip a deep and swift current ran at ebbing tide that sometimes proved fatal to swimmers. The highest part of the island was composed of coarse banks of yellow clay, full of pebbles and layers of sea-shells, and those banks bore a thick covering of grass, which with a profusion of sea-pink made the place look gay and bright. Here the fishermen used to spread their nets on poles to dry, and various kinds of craft were hauled up on the grassy banks out of the reach of the tide during the winter. There were two picturesque wooden cabins where the men lived all the year, and a large covered bathing-shed stood close to the big swimming-pond, which was enclosed by wooden stakes and tree stumps. During the long warm summer evenings there was plenty of animation as the boats full of bathers were ferried across from the city side, and the grassy banks were a favourite resting place for tired artisans.

Williams went on to describe the disappearance of Clontarf Island:

> The demand that sprang up for the materials to make concrete led to the sale of the island, and long strings of carts and horses conveyed away the gravel, of which it was composed, at low water to the Clontarf shore, and at high water iron and wooden

barges came sailing round from the Liffey and anchored, and when the tide fell, leaving them high and dry, were filled with gravel of all sizes, and sailed away with their cargoes when the sea returned. This work was carried on for so many years that, almost imperceptibly and apparently unnoticed, the whole place became flattened down and brought level with the surrounding mud at low water, and even at the present time barges may daily be seen slowly carrying out the process of destruction, and scraping away anything that may still remain to show the site of the Island.

The last vestiges of Clontarf Island went into the landfill that created Fairview Park in the twentieth century.

Bull Island

The North Bull was the original name given to the shallow sandbanks north of the Liffey mouth, between Clontarf and Sutton. Following the building of the Great South Wall there were noticeable changes in the sandbanks to the north of the river. In 1801, Richard Broughton, secretary to the Ballast Board, in a letter addressed to the Directors General of Inland Navigation in Ireland, commented that, 'the north bull … has increased very much, both in extent and height, during the progress of the works on the south side, and more especially since their completion.'[3] This was partly due to the scouring of sand from the mouth of the Liffey since the building of the Great South Wall. This sand was swept north by the circulation in the bay. The previous January, Captain William Bligh had presented the Directors General with a map on which the dry part of the North Bull was marked as a very small patch. In their own submission to Lord Lieutenant Cornwallis in 1804, the Directors General supported the proposal of the Ballast Board and referred to 'the degree of accumulation which had already appeared on the north bull since the building of the south pier, so great that a considerable stripe of it remains dry at high water and has on it a growth of marine plants'. This was the small oval patch that Bligh had mapped three years earlier – it had by now become 'a considerable stripe'. In 1818, the Ballast Board engaged an English engineer, Francis Giles, to prepare a plan for a wall to extend from the Clontarf shore to the north spit of the Pool Beg. In the map that Giles prepared, the island had grown into a spear-shaped spit of land about 5km long. This feature was marked on his map as the

'Sand Island', but Giles later referred to it as 'the Green or Bull Island'. So, in a remarkably short time – about 18 years – a substantial new sand dune system had started to develop from sand that was washed ashore on what is now Dollymount Strand (see page 202).

It is interesting to speculate whether the onshore movement of sand to the North Bull could have been assisted by some exceptional storms in the early years of the nineteenth century. A meteorologist, Richard Kirwan, published a series of papers on state of the weather in Dublin in the *Transactions of the Royal Irish Academy* about this time.[4] For example, he recorded that there were 13 storms in 1802, 17 in 1803 and 23 in 1804. By 1805 Kirwan was recording the wind speed and he gives a breakdown of the number of extreme events recorded in that year as storm, great storm or tempest. This suggests that a period of extremely high winds around this time may have helped move the sand from the beach to begin building the sand dunes of the Bull Island.

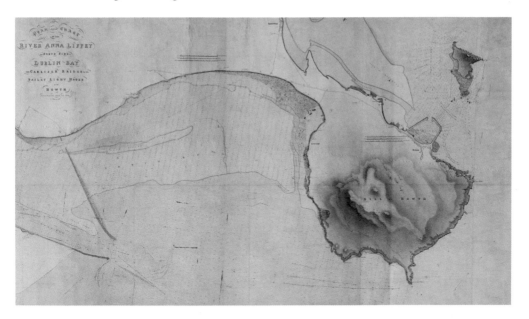

Detail of Giles's chart of the north bay showing the beginning of Bull Island in 1818

With the building of the North Bull Wall, the bar across the Liffey mouth, then only 2m deep at low tide, began to decrease in size. By 1822 the channel had deepened to 2.6m and by 1856 it was 4m deep. This coincided with the increase in width, length and height of the sand dunes at the Bull Island. The island was now connected to the shoreline and the walk across the wooden bridge became a popular amenity. By 1873 the original wooden structure was beginning to decay, but its

proposed demolition was greeted with outrage by the public and the board was persuaded to repair and rebuild the bridge instead.

Alexander Williams described his first-hand observations of these changes in the later part of the nineteenth century:

Coastguard buildings at the North Bull Bridge 1879. These buildings and bridge still exist. *(sketch by George Ivor Nairn)*

> Whilst the sea has been making such havoc with the coast line at the south side of the entrance to the Liffey, it is satisfactory to see that there has been a steady increase and addition to the dry land taking place near the extremity of the North Bull opposite to Sutton. In the seventies [1870s] there existed here a tract of land composed of sand-hills covered thickly with vegetation called the 'Green Island,' which was separated from the main part of the North Bull at high water by a wide portion of sea. The old Clontarf fishermen used to relate how during a heavy

easterly gale a coasting vessel was driven across this submerged part on to the shore of the inner channel near the ruined church at Kilbarrack. For many years there has been a gradual and almost imperceptible accumulation of sand and shingle taking place, and the intervening space has been in the course of time completely filled up, so that now one can walk to what used to be the island, over a wide district reclaimed by nature from the sea, carpeted thickly with vegetation, and raised several feet above the reach of the highest tides.[5]

South Bull

The South Bull is the old name given to the area now known as Sandymount and Merrion Strands. At their widest point these sandflats are several kilometres wide from low-tide mark to the upper edge of the shore at Strand Road. The South Bull has changed dynamically over the period of recorded history.

In 1908 Alexander Williams wrote: 'On the south side we have had a serious encroachment of the sea between the Pigeon House Fort and the Poolbeg Lighthouse. An important range of sandhills of some height and rich in verdure existed some years ago along the edge of the sea in line with the lifeboat house, and protected the White or Shelly Bank from the waves'[6] (see picture opposite). Shelly Banks is still the name given to the area of Sandymount Strand that lies immediately south of the iconic twin chimneys of the Poolbeg Power Station. Williams commented on the Shelly Banks sand dunes:

> They also served as a background to the artillery targets and were high enough to prevent the shells going out to sea when the Royal Horse Artillery were practising with the guns on Irishtown Strand. On public holidays numbers of people used to spend the day on the sandhills, picnicking and indulging in various sports. The larger portion of this fine range [of sandhills] has completely disappeared owing to the incursions of the sea, leaving only a small green island away out on the Shelly Bank, and now, during very high tides in stormy weather, the waves are driven over the intervening space. The lifeboat house, now unroofed and useless, stands a long way seaward and the coast has to be protected by wooden piling and immense quantities of loose limestone blocks placed along the shore to break the force of the waves and prevent

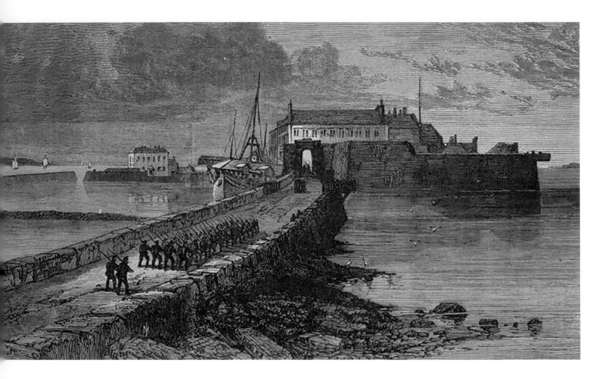

Pigeon House Fort and
Sandymount Strand *(courtesy of
the National Library of Ireland)*

further encroachment or damage to the South Wall, whilst the remains of the old targets may be seen 100 yards seawards of the new high tide mark.[7]

On 5 October 1907, the Dublin Naturalists' Field Club held an excursion to the Shelly Banks, situated at the South Bull, and at that time a considerable area of low sand dunes, with a fair though naturally restricted flora, remained, though much decreased in size. One of the club's members, W.F. Gunn, wrote in the *Irish Naturalist* in 1912:

Wishing again to examine the 'bank' I proceeded there on September 21, but was surprised to find that it is now non-existent, having been completely washed away. The only evidence of its former existence is a slight elevation of the sand over a small portion of the site. In the map accompanying the vegetation of the district lying South of Dublin, by Pethybridge and Praeger, dated 1905, it appears as a strip about three quarter of a mile in length, and it may be worth recording its disappearance. It illustrates the changes which are gradually though constantly taking place along the County Dublin shores.[8]

Shelly Bank dunes today
(John Fox)

Foraging on the shore

Cockles and mussels

Most people who visit Dublin hear the story of Molly Malone – immortalised in the song 'Cockles and Mussels' – 'In Dublin's fair city, where the girls are so pretty, I first set my eyes on sweet Molly Malone'. A fictional character, Molly was reputed to be a prostitute by night and a street seller by day – 'As she wheeled her wheelbarrow Through streets broad and narrow, Crying cockles and mussels, alive alive-o'. The produce that she sold was indeed live shellfish collected by the poor people of the city from the wide sandy bay.

Collecting shellfish from Dublin Bay was a common practice over many centuries and most of them were eaten uncooked and ... alive! Cockles, mussels and probably other shellfish, such as razorshells and periwinkles, all represented a cheap, protein-rich source of food for the growing number of poor of the city. The importance of this practice is recorded in local place names, including the Cockle Lake, a deep channel on Sandymount Strand, and the Cockle Bed near Clontarf.

In the early twentieth century it was estimated that 70,000 to 80,000 quarts of cockles (between 2,000 and 3,000 million shells) were

Cockles, tellins and a large otter shell on the beach at Sandymount Strand (John Fox)

213

Statue of Molly Malone in its original location outside No. 1 Grafton Street *(Richard Nairn)*

consumed annually in the city of Dublin.[9] Threepence a quart (about three cents for just over one litre) was a typical price for cockles bought on Dublin's streets or in the public houses in 1900.[10] In 1772 John Rutty, a medical doctor and naturalist, wrote that cockle broth 'purges' and 'strengthens the limbs of weakly children'. Mussel was considered more risky and 'frequently occasions great disorders'.[11]

Up to 70 people were engaged in collecting cockles on Dublin shores over a century ago. These were raked in shallow water rather than on the dry sand, so it was cold and difficult work, but for some people it probably meant the difference between survival and extreme poverty. Detailed records of cockle landings were kept by coastguards for the period 1893–1913 throughout Ireland, but there was almost certainly a large and unrecorded harvest in addition to the official records.[12] They record between 80 and 104 tonnes landed annually in Dublin in this period.[13] T.J. Browne, who undertook an enquiry for the Local Government Board in 1904, estimated that some 80 tonnes of cockles

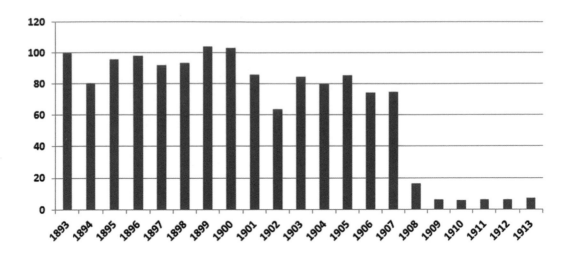

Cockle landings (tonnes) in Dublin 1893–1913 *(after West et al.[15])*

per year were eaten on the streets of Dublin, three quarters of them raw.[14] From 1900 on, the landings declined slightly, but in the six years before the First World War, the annual harvest of cockles was dramatically reduced to about 6 tonnes. So why did this dramatic change occur?

The Fever Hospital and House of Recovery opened in Cork Street, in the south inner city, in May 1804. The hospital was located in a poor, densely populated part of the Liberties district.[16] Dublin had six typhus epidemics in the eighteenth century and the hospital was extended in 1817–19 to help cope with a national epidemic. During 1847 nearly 12,000 cases of typhoid were recorded at the hospital during a period of about ten months, although 'amongst the poor at their own houses, vast numbers remained there, who either could not be accommodated in hospital, or who never thought of applying'.

'She died of a fever, and no one could save her.' Ironically, the reference to death from (typhoid) fever in the song 'Cockles and Mussels' was almost certainly related to the consumption of the very shellfish that Molly Malone was selling from her barrow. While much of the human waste in the city was removed by cart with the ashes from coal fires, by the end of the eighteenth century some of Dublin's sewage found its way, untreated, into the River Liffey and Dublin Bay, often through open sewers and local streams. By the early twentieth century this was a major problem. Browne reported in 1904 that Dublin cockle beds were grossly polluted and he attributed the high incidence of typhoid in the city to the consumption of contaminated cockles. His colleague E.J. McWeeney found in the same year that up to 60 per cent of the Dublin Bay cockles he examined contained bacterial indicators of sewage.[17] In 1890, five members of one family in Blackrock died from eating contaminated mussels (see Chapter 8).[18] The coliform bacteria that human sewage contains would have been a significant feature around the river mouths and in the bay. Filter-feeding shellfish, such as cockles and mussels, are today known to concentrate such pollutants in their flesh and it is quite likely that this could have led to serious food poisoning and even death from 'the fever'.

A ban on fishing the polluted waters led to the collapse of the shellfish harvesting here. 'Now her ghost wheels her barrow, Through streets broad and narrow, Crying cockles and mussels alive, alive-o.'

Oysters

Oysters were popular among the people of Dublin until the early nineteenth century. John Rocque's well-known map of Dublin Bay, published in 1757, clearly shows a large oyster bed in north Dublin Bay, just off Clontarf (see page 171). This was not unusual in the eighteenth century as almost every bay and estuary around Ireland had natural beds of the native oyster that were often taxed to raise money for the Church or other local authorities.[19] Freemen of Dublin city had the right to dredge oysters freely within the bar of Dublin Bay, in the Liffey estuary. At this time, the main oyster bed was at Poolbeg, where sailing ships moored to wait for the rising tide that would take them over the bar.

In 1595, the corporation ordered the restoration to the Clontarf oyster bed of all gravel and stones brought up by the dredges 'for the better preserving of the pool'. By 1700, the corporation had leased the oyster beds out at a yearly rent of £5 with the condition that the lessee 'within twelve months replenish the beds with a sufficient quantity of oysters from Arklow and Glasgurrig and leave the beds well stocked on expiration of the lease'. The fact that it was necessary to bring in oysters from elsewhere was a clear indication that, even in the seventeenth century, the stocks in Dublin Bay were becoming severely depleted. John Rutty noted in 1772 that there were natural oyster beds near the piles at Poolbeg and that pearls could be found in these. There were also some oysters at Howth and in Dalkey Sound, with others further north at Ireland's Eye, Malahide and beyond. Artificial oyster beds were to be found at Crab Lough at Clontarf and near Sutton. Both of these artificial beds had been transplanted from Arklow and the oysters were very small, measuring little more than 50mm. Renewal of these beds had to be carried out frequently, as the oysters were consumed faster than they grew.[20]

Rutty's account shows that by the eighteenth century the Dublin oyster beds were largely exhausted and Dr Browne reported in 1903 that introduced species, chiefly from America, were laid in Sutton Creek in north Dublin Bay.[21] Sometimes these layings also included oysters from other parts of Ireland and from as far afield as Britain, France and Portugal. In the early nineteenth century there was no slackening in the exploitation of oyster beds and the popularity of these shellfish may have been due in part to their reputed aphrodisiac qualities. By the early twentieth century there were no oysters in the bay due to overfishing and probably also water pollution. A Clare landowner, Burton Bindon, opened a hostelry in Dublin known as the Redbank Oyster Dive, so called after the Red Bank oyster bed in Galway Bay. It later moved to fashionable D'Olier Street, where it was referred to in James Joyce's *Ulysses*. The oysters were known colloquially as 'Burton Bindons' or simply 'Redbanks' in mid-nineteenth century Dublin, and this is how Joyce's hero, Leopold Bloom, refers to them. The city centre restaurant remained in business until 1968.

Seine fishers on Dollymount Strand with Howth Head in the background 1879 (sketch by *George Ivor Nairn*)

Fish and fishermen

Dublin Bay was once a rich fishing ground, but today stocks are significantly depleted and no commercial fisheries survive. For millennia, local people used primitive nets laid seasonally in the estuaries of the Liffey and Tolka to catch migratory fish such as salmon and trout as they entered the fresh water to spawn. The remains of wooden fish traps have been found beneath the city where the land was subsequently reclaimed from the estuary (see Chapter 7). With better equipment, fishermen put to sea in small wooden boats with lines and nets to catch either bottom-dwelling fish such as plaice or shoaling fish such as herring and mackerel. By the seventeenth century a fleet of herring boats operated from Clontarf and a thriving local fish processing industry developed at the Sheds on the seafront (see Chapter 8). This was a collection of fishermen's huts and shanties that were used to store fishing gear and boats and to process fish. Some of these were probably lived in too. In the late eighteenth century and well into the nineteenth, Dublin Bay had abundant herring and mackerel stocks and these were caught by draft netting. This entailed a boat taking a net out in a big circle from the shore and then pulling it ashore. This was done from small boats because, then as now, Clontarf shoreline dries out on low tides.

This was encouraged by Dublin Corporation, which spent considerable sums improving buildings, slipways and landing facilities. So important was fishing to Ringsend that it became known to locals as 'Raytown' due to the large quantities of rays that were landed here and consumed by the poorer sections of the population. The rays would have been given in baskets or boxes to the street hawkers to sell, along with any other unmarketable fish.

In the parliamentary session of 1773–74 an Act was passed banning trawling in Dublin Bay because 'the practice of trawling, as now carried on in the bay of Dublin, tends to injure the fishery thereof'.[22] The act stated that 'trawling in said bay has been practised frequently by many of his Majesty's revenue officers'. The penalty for fishermen if caught trawling was £10 and the seizure of the boat, nets and equipment, while revenue officers would be fined £20. This was a temporary provision until 1778, though it was later extended to 1790.[23]

Up to the eighteenth century fishing with nets from small boats was limited by the size of the net that could be lifted by hand. By the end of the eighteenth century, the introduction of the beam trawl had changed the nature of fishing in the waters off Britain and Ireland. The

Draft net fishing at the Poolbeg lighthouse *(Cormac F. Lowth collection)*

net was attached to a large wooden beam, which was lowered over the side and towed behind the sailing boat, trawling everything on the seabed. Each boat had a winch, which enabled three men and a boy to lift nets that would take eight or ten men to lift on the smaller Irish vessels of the time. This new trawling technique was developed mainly in the south Devon port of Brixham, where the existing small fishery expanded rapidly, and these trawlers began to venture further away from their home ports on the English Channel. Encouraged by the high prices of fish, the Dublin Fishery Company was formed in 1818 to operate a fleet of trawlers that could supply fresh fish to the Dublin market. The company purchased seven fishing smacks, mainly from Devon, also signing up English skippers and crews. These trawlers first fished in Dublin Bay in 1819.[24]

The trawlers were substantial wooden vessels over 50 feet (15m) in length and they were largely based at the fishing village of Ringsend on the south side of the Liffey. The efficiency of these vessels and their crews in exploiting fish populations was initially resented by the local Irish fishermen who had much less effective equipment. One of the Brixham trawlers, the *Transit*, was so successful that some local men boarded her on the fishing grounds and cut away her sails, rigging and fishing gear to prevent her crew from competing with them. However, many of the English crews settled in Dublin, intermarried with the local population and became part of the community. Some of these English family names still persist in Ringsend today, for example, Rackley, Elliot, Pullen and Dent.

The introduction of the new trawlers with their superior gear brought a much greater range of deep-water fish, such as sole and turbot, to the Dublin fish market. The fishing grounds worked by the Dublin trawlers ranged the length of the Irish Sea, from the Mourne coast of County Down to Dungarvan Bay in the south, and eastwards to the deep waters off the Isle of Man. In 1835, a government inquiry was held into the state of fisheries in Ireland. At a hearing in Kingstown (now Dún Laoghaire) the number and size of fishing vessels in Dublin Bay at the time was detailed. It was reported that 'about thirty fishing cutters are fitted out in Dublin and Kingstown to fish on the English system. They average forty tons burden but have a greater capacity than the Irish wherries employed at Balbriggan and Skerries. The largest beam trawl used is forty feet, the shortest thirty-six feet.' The witnesses at the enquiry also reported that there were a further 40 boats, averaging 3 to 5 tons each, engaged in line fishing in Dublin Bay. 'Long lines or spillards are used by all the boats with white hooks and lug bait'. It was noted in passing that 'the lug bait is diminishing on the shores of the Bay'.

Sailing trawler at the mouth of the Liffey in the nineteenth century *(Alexander Williams)* from *Leinster* by Gwynne published *c.* 1900

One vivid account of a trip from Ringsend on one of the sailing trawlers was published in the 1880s. The writer had been invited to join the trip, one of his long-held ambitions. The boat was a substantial wooden sailing craft, 40 tons in weight, 54 feet (16.5m) from stern to stem, and almost 18 feet (5.5m) across the beam.

> The crew consisted of a skipper, two men, and Jack, the boy. There was little wind starting and we were a long time getting down the Liffey; in fact only drifting. The skipper had proposed sailing to Wexford, but when we had drifted about ten miles southward off the Muglins [Dalkey], the wind came from the south-south-west, and he bore up for the Kish Bank instead. We shot the trawl at 6 o'clock p.m., and trawled till midnight on the flood tide. The evening was most beautiful, hardly any breeze; a bright moonlight; not cold. We amused ourselves shooting gulls; but, like the boys and the frogs in the fable, what was amusement to us was death to the gulls. At midnight we hauled in the trawl, getting a small mullagoon [angler fish], a turbot, and a pair of soles, some dabs and plaice – in all about half a hamper.

After several days of trawling in Dublin Bay and surrounding waters the crew had to run for cover with a north-east gale blowing. By now the catch was substantial:

> The produce of the trawling-net, when turned out on the deck, is certainly a curious and interesting sight: comprising skate, ray, brett [brill], turbot, conger eel, John Dory, gurnard, red and gray, cod, haddock, soles, plaice, herrings, mackerel, flounders, squids (small cuttle fish), and piles of queer things about which naturalists get enthusiastic, such as sea-mice, star-fish, sea urchins, comatulae [feather stars], brittle stars, seaweeds of beautiful colours and forms, beroae [?], &c. All these, of no use to the trawler's crew, they call 'curioes'. One haul, of course, does not obtain all these fish. Some, such as herring, mackerel, and sturgeon, are seldom caught. Sometimes a small porpoise is taken. The conger eels are large – up to seven or eight feet long. Turbot are bled by an incision on the underside of the tail, and they bleed very freely. This keeps them firm. They are left under the boat on deck, and must be shaded from the moonlight

which would injure them – at least so the men say. The fish are not packed in hampers until the vessel is going into port to land them, as they would spoil sooner by so doing.[25]

The advent of steam power in the early years of the twentieth century brought great changes. By 1911 only nine sailing trawlers at Ringsend were engaged in old-fashioned beam trawling, while eight sailing trawlers and nine steam trawlers were using a more modern type of net. Loans were being offered for the purchase of new motorised drift net boats and the installation of motor power in existing vessels. The First World War took a serious toll on the crews and many of the sailing trawlers tied up at Ringsend and never fished again.[26]

The range of fish species caught in Dublin Bay in the nineteenth century was remarkable. The large size of some of the specimens shows that there were substantial stocks here at that time. Some idea of the striking scale of the fish that were caught can be gained from the sea fish on display today in Dublin's Natural History Museum. These are actually casts that were donated to the museum in the 1860s by the board of Trinity College Dublin, just a few streets away.

Cast of a plaice landed in Dublin Bay in the nineteenth century, on display in the Natural History Museum. The scale bar at the bottom of the picture is 80cm in length. (*John Fox*)

Salting fish at the pier in Howth *(from* Robert L. Chapman's Ireland *compiled by Christian Corlett, The Collins Press, 2008)*

Fish were one of the principal elements of the modest diet of eighteenth-century Dubliners, and they were consumed in large quantities.[27] This was due to the relative cheapness of fish and to the religious observance of the majority of the population which dictated that no meat should be eaten on Fridays.

The variety of seafood and freshwater fish available was remarkable and included herring, hake, haddock, whiting, turbot, trout, eel and salmon. As for shellfish, it has been claimed that city dwellers seemed to favour bivalve molluscs like oysters, cockles and mussels, while country folk favoured gastropods like winkles, although the reasons for this preference are unclear. The more prosperous members of society, who ate seafood from choice rather than necessity, consumed other shellfish such as crab, shrimp, lobster and scallops. The strand at Irishtown was renowned for the large quantities of shrimps caught there until the great frost of 1740 destroyed them, and the shrimp fishery there never recovered. The artist Hugh Douglas Hamilton sketched itinerant hawkers and sellers of the late eighteenth century in his *Cries of Dublin*. These illustrations include, along with many food pedlars, vendors in the fish and shellfish trade, particularly oyster and herring sellers.

Howth was the main harbour for the fleets of herring drifters and luggers that annually followed the herring shoals around the British Isles. In addition to local boats, fleets would come from Scotland, the

Fish sellers on the pier at Howth, early nineteenth century

Isle of Man and Cornwall. Local girls were recruited to gut, clean and salt the herrings before packing them into barrels. There was also a migratory female population that followed the boats to do this work. There was similar, but more limited, activity in Kingstown. The berthage alongside here was very limited, with the 'Coal Harbour' mostly being taken up with sailing and steam colliers. As early as the 1850s fish were being transported by rail to the Dublin market from places as far away as Dingle in County Kerry, but fish were never carried on the Dublin-to-Kingstown line. Fish caught locally around Ringsend from the shore or from small boats would have gone to the Dublin market or have been sold to hawkers.

Herrings were an important part of the Irish diet as they could be eaten fresh or preserved for the winter months. They featured strongly on fast days, so much so that, following Lent, butchers led 'Herring Funerals' to celebrate their customers' return to meat, where a herring was beaten through the town on Easter Sunday and thrown into the water, and a quarter of lamb dressed with ribbons was hung up in its place.[28] During great runs of herring the fish was sold cheaply, and many women preserved their own in barrels.

From 1819, the supply of fresh fish to the Dublin fish market increased dramatically with the formation of the Dublin Fishery Company and the arrival of the English sailing trawlers. Severe competition drove the

price of fish down to one penny per lb in 1820. The company was wound up in 1830 but achieved a lot in its time, including the discovery of new fishing grounds in the Irish Sea. The introduction of the technique of trawling from Brixham to Ringsend led to the sale in the Dublin market of large numbers of sole and turbot from the deep waters.[29] Draft net fishing continued at the mouth of the Liffey until well into the twentieth century. A Pathé newsreel showed local people hauling a draft net and lifting a salmon on the Liffey shore near the Great South Wall. As well as salmon they caught sea trout, mullet and flounder. In the summer they used a net with a smaller mesh to catch 'whitebait' – the fry of herring and mackerel. This type of fishing, known in Ringsend as 'rough fishing', was practised a lot on the 'Dog Bank', a sandy bank near where the Poolbeg Yacht and Boat Club is now located.

Ringsend draft net fishermen photographed in 1934 (Cormac F. Lowth collection)

Hobblers

Of course, some inshore fishermen continued to operate from wooden rowing boats. Clinker-built skiff-type boats were once among the most numerous working boats along the east coast. However, in Dublin Bay today the number still fishing is down to single figures. In 1874,

Hobblers towing a ship to its berth on Sir John Rogerson's Quay *(courtesy of the RSAI)*

historian E.W. Holdsworth noted that 'The smaller boats employed for the line-fishery are of the same style as the Norway yawl, sharp at both ends.' Hobblers were freelance pilots, and competition was strong to be first to board the approaching sailing ships or later steamships. Often two hobbling boats would race to the incoming ship and the first to hook the vessel with a catching pole would win the prize. The successful hobbler would then pilot the ship into harbour, for which he was paid £2. He would tow the ship into its berth and might also be awarded the work of discharging the ship in the port.[30]

The skiffs worked between Lambay and Wicklow Head and they required considerable skill by the oarsmen. It was dangerous work, and many hobblers were lost at sea. Sometimes whole families were drowned, since brothers often made up the crews. The Hughes brothers were killed when their boat was sliced in half by the schooner that they

Schooners at a regatta in Kingstown Harbour, late nineteenth century *(courtesy National Maritime Museum of Ireland)*

were attending. In 1936 Dublin Port and Docks Board introduced ships' brokers and shipping agents and hobbling was banned. Most of the skiffs found along the east coast today are engaged in racing (see Chapter 11). Skiff racing has its origins in the occupation of hobbling.

Sailing heritage

The large gathering of white sails out on the water at weekends has been a familiar sight in Dublin Bay since the 1850s. In the first half of the nineteenth century, yacht racing was reserved for the wealthy because the big racing cutters needed professional crews, often recruited from among local fishermen who had the necessary expertise with sailing boats and the local knowledge of tides and winds. But the emerging sport required rules and organisers. The crucial role of Dublin Bay in the history of yacht racing has been documented by Hal Sisk, who has shown

that the bay gave Dublin some significant advantages over other yachting
centres in the British Empire.[31] It was in specifically *amateur* sailing
that Kingstown led the world, through the Royal Alfred Yacht Club,
and writing the rules of the worldwide sport. The great new harbour at
Kingstown, with its rail link to the city centre, was a key development
in the 1830s. The suburbs that grew around Dalkey to Blackrock were
among the most affluent in the country and Dún Laoghaire was the
location for two yacht clubs, the Royal St George[32] and the Royal Irish,
built in 1842–3 and 1847–50 respectively. These are among the oldest
purpose-built yacht club houses in the world.

The first amateur yacht races took place in Dublin Bay in 1854–56.
The following year, the Royal Alfred Yacht Club was formed and began
to organise regular racing with written rules and annual regattas. Large
cutters, up to 50 feet (15m) in length, raced across the bay, many with
the old gaff-rigged sails that had been such a familiar sight in the bay for
centuries. In 1887 the world's oldest one-design class of yacht, the Water
Wag, was launched. These were small 13-foot (4m) wooden dinghies
with a crew of two and they carried a large spinnaker sail set on a pole

in front of the mast. The advent of one-design yachts revolutionised sailing as it removed the advantage of different classes of boats and put the emphasis on the skill of the skipper and crew. Apart from the Water Wags, Dublin Bay Sailing Club was prominent in providing racing for small craft. The elitism of the first half of the nineteenth century was balanced from the 1850s onwards by the emergence of middle-class sailors with some leisure time, a universal trend which happened to occur first among the sailors of the Dublin Bay Water Wags, which still race every week in the bay.

Lighthouses

The lights that mark the entrances to Dublin Bay and its harbours have been beacons for generations of mariners and have saved many ships and sailors from disaster on rocks or sandbanks. The hill of Howth on the north side of the bay is visible from many parts of the Irish Sea and this was the location of one of the earliest navigation lights in Ireland.[33] The earliest formal lighthouse, a cottage-type building with a coal-burning beacon on top of a square tower, was established here in 1668. By 1790, it

The Baily Lighthouse today
(John Fox)

had been replaced by a more modern lighthouse with a lantern powered by six oil lamps. However, the location of this light was not satisfactory as it was often obscured by low cloud, mist or fog, leading to regular complaints from shipowners in the Port of Dublin. A new lighthouse was built in 1814 on the promontory known as the Baily, which is below the main cliffs. The granite tower was topped by a large lantern powered by 24 oil lamps and reflectors. The magnificent 10-tonne Baily Optic installed in 1902, and now in the National Maritime Museum, is the same one mentioned by James Joyce in *Ulysses* in 1904.

Ships passing the Baily Lighthouse must then make for the mouth of the Liffey, which today is marked by the iconic red Poolbeg Lighthouse. Initially, a floating light was moored at the end of the piles at Poolbeg and, as described in Chapter 9, the Ballast Board made provision for a lighthouse when they began the construction of the Great South Wall in 1762. Construction of the lighthouse – the first to be lit by candles, rather than coal braziers – began in 1764 and it was completed in 1768. In 1786 the Ballast Board experimented with oil lamps and the result was so successful that Poolbeg became one of the first lighthouses in these islands to be lit by oil.[34] The Poolbeg Lighthouse was raised in height and its original gallery was removed in 1813.[35] The lighthouse was completely rebuilt in 1820. The Poolbeg light was originally painted white but was changed to its present red livery to conform with the international convention for 'port' on the left side for vessels entering the harbour.

The first navigational light at Dún Laoghaire was operated from the original small harbour close to the base of the present West Pier. During the construction of the present substantial Dún Laoghaire Harbour a temporary light was located on the East Pier and was moved as the pier grew longer. When construction of the harbour walls was completed the entrance was marked by two new lighthouses, the East Pier light in 1847 and the West Pier light in 1852. By the end of 1896 both lights had been much improved and the lighthouses were decorated with fairy lights for the visit of King Edward VII and Queen Alexandra in 1907. Ships approaching Kingstown Harbour from the south had to navigate past the prominent Dalkey Island, but many vessels foundered on the Muglins rocks that lie to the east of the main island. By 1880 a conical white stone pillar was built on the Muglins but it was not until 1906 that this became a lighted beacon.

Off the entrance to Dublin Bay, one of the greatest hazards for shipping is the long, narrow Kish Bank. This was not marked until

Poolbeg Lighthouse in an easterly storm *(John Fox)*

1811, when an old Dutch ship was moored here with three lights and a loud gong that could be sounded by the crew in fog. The twice-daily passage of the Dún Laoghaire-to-Holyhead packet ship was marked with the firing of two shots from an 18-pounder gun by the crew of the lightship and this was acknowledged by the ship with a single shot when the ship had safely passed the bank. Attempts in the 1840s to build a permanent light on the Kish Bank were abandoned when the piles here were destroyed in a gale. The bank continued to be marked by a moored lightship until the 1960s, when a substantial concrete lighthouse was built in Dún Laoghaire Harbour and floated out to be sunk on the Kish Bank. This was manned by lighthouse keepers until 1992, when it was finally automated.

Wrecks and rescues

In the days before lighthouses and accurate maritime charts, sailors, fishermen and ships' captains had to rely on the accumulated experience of older seamen to find the position of channels and submerged rocks. Some sailing vessels were unlucky to reach the bay in easterly storms when they would have been driven onto the lee shore.

There are approximately 600 recorded shipwreck events associated with the wider Dublin Bay area and the approaches to the port; about

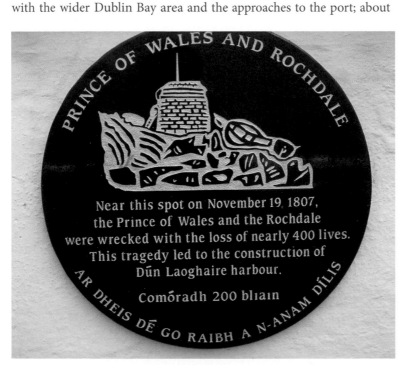

Memorial to casualties of the sinking of the *Rochdale* and *Prince of Wales* in 1807 (*Rob Goodbody*)

half of these are associated with Dublin Bar.[36] These events have been catalogued based on historical data since around 1750,[37] the single greatest concentration of documented shipwreck incidents in Ireland. The sheer number is undoubtedly due to the high levels of marine traffic in and out of Dublin Port over the centuries. The inventory does not record where wreckage lies, as the records generally only deal with the vessel before it sank. The number of known wreck sites is much smaller. Locations of actual wrecks or pieces of wreckage are based on fishermen's records of snag points and divers' records of sites located underwater. Some of the best-known wreck sites are those that have been investigated by sub-aqua divers.

In the early years of the nineteenth century Napoleon had a strong fleet of warships and the United Kingdom (including Ireland) was at war with France. In November 1807 a convoy of five sailing ships, carrying mainly army officers and their families, set out from the Pigeon House Harbour at Ringsend. As the ships left the Liffey mouth they met an easterly gale, which later increased to storm force. In one of the coldest winters of the period, the ships were hidden by sleet and snow. One ship, the *Rochdale,* tried unsuccessfully to anchor off Dalkey but was

The sinking of the *Queen Victoria* at the Baily Lighthouse, 1853 *(courtesy of National Maritime Museum, Greenwich)*

driven northwards past the small harbour at Dunleary and grounded with great force at Seapoint near where the Martello tower now stands. The ship was holed and all 265 people on board died. A second ship, the *Prince of Wales*, tried to reach the harbour at Howth but her sails were lost in the storm; the ship was driven ashore near Blackrock and 120 people lost their lives among the wreckage.[38]

On a fine February day in 1853, the paddle steamer *Queen Victoria* left Liverpool for Dublin. As she was approaching the mouth of Dublin Bay, the ship met a heavy snowstorm and thick fog. Visibility was so poor that the steamer struck the rocks just north of the Baily light on Howth Head. Panic ensued, and about eight people managed to scramble ashore. The captain ordered the engines to be put into reverse to try to run the vessel up on the North Bull. It was a fatal decision – the ship began to sink. Some passengers clambered into a starboard-quarter lifeboat. It snapped from its davits due to the overload, dropping like a stone into the sea, and drowning all on board. The port lifeboat was found to be leaking, but a young boy is said to have used his finger to plug the gap. That lifeboat managed to reach shore, with brave oarsmen returning to save another five people clinging to the ship's masts. Another 40 people were picked up by the crew of the steamer *Roscommon*. Accounts vary on the final toll, but it is believed that around 80 lives were lost, including the ship's captain. The official government inquiry found the captain to have been negligent, but it also criticised the Dublin Port Authority for its failure to place a fog-bell on Howth Head. This finding contributed to the establishment of the Commissioners of Irish Lights 14 years later.[39]

On 8 February 1861 a northerly gale blew up in Dublin Bay. The following day a heavy snowstorm struck and, with the storm still raging, a number of ships were wrecked around the bay, on the Burford Bank and neighbouring coastlines.[40] Among these were the schooners *Neptune* and *Industry*, which were both driven onto the piers at Kingstown. The Royal Navy ship HMS *Ajax* was stationed at this time in the harbour, where she was moored close to the East Pier. Her master, Captain John McNeil Boyd from County Derry, immediately ordered a rescue party onto the pier.

By this time both the *Neptune* and the *Industry* were being smashed to pieces on rocks at the base of the pier, so Captain Boyd immediately ordered a rocket to be fired to take a line to one of the ships, but this was blown back by the force of the gale. Boyd and some of the naval party then scrambled down the rocky slope of the pier towards the crew of the *Neptune*, who were now all in the water and attempting to struggle ashore. Many more men from *Ajax* and some civilians had joined the rescue party. Attempting to rescue some of the victims who were already in the water, Captain Boyd and five of the rescuers were washed into the sea by giant waves. Only one man was saved from the *Neptune*, while all but one of the crew of the *Industry* reached safety. A total of ten lives were lost in addition to six from *Ajax*. Captain Boyd's body was not found until much later. A permanent memorial to this brave man still stands on the East Pier in Dún Laoghaire.

Among the best known of the wartime casualties was the RMS *Leinster*, which was torpedoed by a German submarine near the Kish Lighthouse in 1918 with the loss of 501 lives. The ship was one of four steamers, known as the 'provinces', owned by the City of Dublin Steam Packet Company. Over 400 of the 771 on board were soldiers; 22 post

The sinking of RMS Leinster in 1918 *(courtesy of Philip Lecane)*

office staff were sorting mail on the bow's port side when a torpedo struck that part of the hull. The ship turned, in a bid to make it back to Dún Laoghaire, but a final torpedo hit the starboard side. Many were killed in the explosion, and the ship listed to port and sank, bow first, in just 15 minutes. Some of those who made it to the lifeboats perished in heavy seas. Three ships in the area helped to pick up some of the 270 survivors. The Shipwreck Inventory includes underwater photos and images of the wreck which show the ship partly buried in sand 5 miles east of the Kish.[41]

Modern navigational aids, weather forecasting and rescue services such as the Royal National Lifeboat Institution and the Irish Coast Guard have made Dublin Bay a safer place for seafarers, and maritime accidents are rare today. But the sea can be unpredictable and those using small boats should always wear buoyancy aids such as lifejackets. All the ways in which we use Dublin Bay – both past and present – are explored in Chapter 11.

11 | Using the Bay

Since the earliest settlers landed on the shores of a primeval land, Dublin Bay has provided people with a home as well as a source of food and shelter. For most people today it is primarily an area for recreation, both active pursuits such as sailing or angling and passive relaxation and enjoyment of the beautiful landscape. However, we tend to forget that the bay is also the main channel for most of the trade in and out of Ireland, and for most of the treated waste water from the city, and the location of one of our main power sources. For these reasons alone, the management of Dublin Bay is not only critical to the national economy but vital to the health and wellbeing of the largest concentration of people in Ireland. However, plans for the bay have not always been realised.

How it might have been

Among the fanciful seventeenth- and eighteenth-century schemes for Dublin Bay were the building of a citadel overlooking the south bay and a canal from Sutton running right along the shore of Clontarf to allow shipping to bypass the shallow Liffey estuary. Neither of these schemes was pursued but, by the nineteenth century, reclamation of the inner bay was proceeding apace as the North and South Lotts were converted from saltmarsh and mudflat to dry land. The same process continued in the early twentieth century as the port progressively stretched out into the bay in leaps and bounds (see Chapter 9). On the east side of Ringsend, large volumes of the city's refuse and building rubble were dumped on the foreshore, along with dredgings and substantial quantities of fuel ash from the power stations, to create the area known today as the Poolbeg peninsula.

Early plans for Bull Island

Bull Island, which began to form in the early nineteenth century from the sand that previously lay in the bar at the mouth of the Liffey, rapidly became a leisure resort for Dubliners. As the bar gradually reduced in size and height, the island continued to grow in extent, from the Bull Wall towards Howth Head. By 1868 Dublin Corporation had plans to use Bull Island as the main dump for the city's sewage, which by this time had become a major health hazard. They proposed to build a wall around the island, to transport human excreta down the Liffey on barges and cover the island with this unpleasant material. Fortunately, influential landowners in the Clontarf area were powerful enough to have the idea dropped. In addition to picnics and swimming, the island was frequently used for shooting practice, and in 1880 an international rifle match between Ireland and the USA was held there, with an audience numbering several thousand. In 1889, the Royal Dublin Golf Club. then located at Sutton, sought and received permission from Colonel Vernon and the Dublin Port and Docks Board to lay out a golf course and construct a clubhouse at the city end of the island.

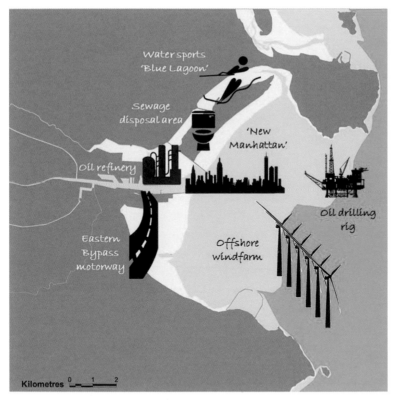

How it might have been. Some proposals for Dublin Bay that have not happened.

Sometime in the early twentieth century, a track suitable for walking and handcarts was created across the Bull Island lagoon running from a slipway at the point where the Howth Road meets the coast to the northern part of the island. Usable only at low tide, this 150m track allowed access to the island for leisure and beachcombing. Local people regularly scavenged timber, coal and other items lost overboard from ships entering and leaving Dublin Port and washed up on Dollymount Strand.

At the start of the First World War in September 1914, the army took over the whole island for military training. It was used primarily as a firing range but also for trench warfare practice. The Royal Dublin Golf Club clubhouse was used as officers' quarters and considerable damage was done to the building and to the island environment as a whole. After the war, three local people started to dig golf holes at the northern end of the island and, following discussions with the Royal Dublin, and with Lady Ardilaun, formed a new golf club, named St Anne's, in honour of the Guinness estate. The first drive-in, at what was then a nine-hole course, took place in 1921.

There were some hare-brained schemes about at this time too. One that received a lot of attention was the 'Blue Lagoon' – a plan in 1929 to create a barrage at either end of Bull Island, forming a flooded water body. This scheme proposed dams and sluices at the Bull Bridge and Sutton Strand end of the island, thereby forming a permanent lake. This lagoon was to be used for water sports and as a tourist destination. However, with the untreated sewage of the time entering the bay, it was more likely that this would have become a heavily polluted 'green lagoon' filled with massive algal growth. The island itself was to be used as a giant pleasure park modelled on Coney Island in New York.

In 1944, the two golf clubs were informed that the Irish Tourist Board had taken control of Bull Island and were preparing for its development as a tourist resort. The Royal Dublin Golf Club received notice to be ready to leave their clubhouse, as the site happened to be within the area of a proposed amusement park, aimed at creating a Blackpool-type development. In 1945, maps of the island with the proposed plans were published showing among other things, the locations of a cinema, a dance hall and a restaurant near the Bull Wall. Concerned groups, such as the Dublin Naturalists' Field Club and the golf clubs, argued that Bull Island was already a recreational ground and a nature reserve, unique in its proximity to the city, and should not be turned into an artificial playground of doubtful utility.

At the time of publication in 1977 of the book *North Bull Island, Dublin Bay*,[1] controversy was still raging about building of a causeway in the 1960s to link the island to the mainland and the proposal by Dublin Corporation to use this to dump refuse on the island itself. One of the principal concerns of conservationists was that the causeway was causing silting of the lagoons, encouraging the introduced cordgrass to spread, thus reducing the habitat available for migratory birds. This issue was examined in detail at the time by David Jeffrey, who concluded that the overall influence of the causeway was benign. He predicted that the sedimentation in this area would eventually lead to the development of a high saltmarsh fringe adjacent to the causeway and on the *Salicornia* bed. He foresaw that another 50 hectares of saltmarsh would develop in the next 50 to 100 years, adding to the roosting area available for birds.[2] In 1971 Dublin Corporation began to use the causeway to dump refuse on the saltmarsh. This caused a major controversy and An Taisce then initiated High Court proceedings on the grounds that the corporation was in breach of its own development plan.[3] This rumbled on until 1975, when the matter was settled out of court.

Schemes for the port and docks

In 1936, following the Great Depression, Irish National Refineries proposed the construction of an oil refinery in the port. At this time the Irish economy was seriously isolated as a result of independence from Britain. Agriculture, which was the largest employer, was mostly driven by horse power and human muscle. Nevertheless, oil was becoming an increasingly important fuel for road transport and for the limited industrial development of the time. The site chosen for the refinery was between the Alexandra Road and the Liffey, to the east of Ocean Pier. A licence was granted by the government and about 21 hectares of land reclaimed from the bay was leased by the port to the refinery. However, the outbreak of war in 1939 soon put paid to this proposal as both the oil and the necessary finance for the works became unavailable.

In 1972, Dublin Port and Docks Board again proposed building an oil refinery in Dublin Bay. This time the site was on the south side of the river near the Pigeon House with a new area of land to be reclaimed from Sandymount Strand. Not surprisingly, the residents of Sandymount and Irishtown were in the vanguard of opposition to this proposal because of the presence of a potentially polluting industry on their doorstep and because Sandymount Strand was highly valued for recreational purposes. The plan was vigorously opposed by environmentalists, including Seán Loftus, a lifelong campaigner for Dublin Bay, who changed his name by deed poll to Seán Dublin Bay Rockall Loftus. The proposal was eventually turned down by the minister for local government. Loftus also led opposition to the 2002 and subsequent applications by Dublin Port Company to fill in 52 acres (21 hectares) of shoreline at the eastern end of the port.

In 2008 a proposal was publicised to store millions of tonnes of carbon dioxide (CO_2) and natural gas in undersea caverns beneath the Kish Bank, off Dublin Bay, under a project being planned by an Irish–Malaysian joint venture. The Department of Energy awarded the company a three-year licensing option over eight blocks in the Kish Bank basin, which also covered oil and gas exploration. It was hoped that the project would contribute to reducing Ireland's carbon footprint as well as increasing its natural gas storage capacity, both identified by the government as strategic national objectives, but this proposal was never advanced.

Sandymount Strand

The extensive intertidal sands between the port and Blackrock had long attracted the attentions of those who wanted to expand the city eastwards. In the first half of the twentieth century large quantities of refuse and solid waste were dumped by Dublin Corporation on the foreshore between Ringsend and the Pigeon House, leading to extensive reclamation of the intertidal area at Irishtown. The ESB power station at Poolbeg was producing huge volumes of coal ash, which had to be disposed of, and this too was dumped on the northern end of Sandymount Strand in what is now called Irishtown Nature Reserve.

By the early 1990s, Dublin Corporation roads engineers were planning a proposed ring road around the city. In 2000, at the beginning of the 'Celtic Tiger' era, Frank McDonald, environment correspondent of *The Irish Times*, wrote that 'traffic chaos had become part and parcel of Dublin life', describing it as a process of 'self-strangulation'.[4] Plans had already been laid out for the western part of this road, running from the airport to Sandyford, and for a tunnel linking the motorway with Dublin Port; and work was under way on the West Link bridge across the Liffey Valley. However, the most difficult problem for the engineers was to complete the ring of the city by linking the port with the Sandyford area.

As early as 1971, an eastern bypass for Dublin was recommended in the Dublin Transportation Study. This proposal was rejected by the city council in 1980 as it would have involved demolishing a significant

number of houses and the development of a commuter route through
the south city. The densely populated residential areas of Sandymount,
Booterstown and Merrion lay in the path of this south-eastern section
of the motorway, so attention turned to building it across Sandymount
Strand. A feasibility study and environmental impact statement,
commissioned by the corporation, suggested that some of the route
could be tunnelled beneath the residential areas, but various options
were considered for the strand, including tunnelling, 'cut and cover'
and an elevated motorway on an embankment that would have cut
Sandymount off from the sea. This was hugely unpopular and in 1992 the
Fianna Fáil–Labour government announced that the project had been
abandoned – although this decision had more to do with a forthcoming
general election than with good planning.

In 1995, the new National Roads Authority (NRA) revived the plan
for an eastern bypass (now called the port access and eastern relief route).
By now, the focus had changed to a bored tunnel beneath the city from
Whitehall to the Port and a further tunnel beneath Sandymount Strand.
Labelled by some opposing politicians as 'the serpent that refuses to die',
the scheme was again inserted in the City Development Plan in 1999,
despite having been officially abandoned by the government in 1992.

Dumping on the foreshore
at Sandymount in the 1960s
(*Dublin Port Company archive*)

A public enquiry into the port tunnel on the north side of the Liffey was under way and the concept of a full orbital ring road for Dublin was attractive to the council officials and the NRA. The Port Tunnel was officially opened in 2006 and, although no further progress has been made with the southern leg across Sandymount Strand, this scheme, first mooted nearly 50 years ago, is still officially an aspiration of the authorities.

Dún Laoghaire Baths in a semi-derelict state *c.* 2000
(Rob Goodbody)

In 1843 the Royal Victorian Baths were built beside Scotsman's Bay. They were very successful and Dún Laoghaire became one of the best and most popular places in Ireland to bathe. The bathing options included sea and fresh water, hot and cold baths. Children had their own pond and paddling pools and there were medical baths. These included sulphur, seaweed, Russian and hot seawater, and hot towels were provided if required. Between 1905 and 1911 the baths were completely rebuilt by Kingstown Town Council on the site of the former gun battery, slightly to the east of the Royal Victoria Baths, and these opened to the public in 1907.[5] The original baths were later demolished. The new baths continued in use up to the 1980s, when they were closed by the council. They were reopened as the Rainbow Rapids, with water

242

slides running down into the pool. In 1997 the outdoor baths were closed when a proposal was made to develop a water park complex on the site, but this proposal was dropped after a huge public outcry, and the abandoned baths had become derelict by the early 2000s. In 2005, councillors rejected a €140 million plan which included an eight-storey building with 180 apartments over retail units and restaurants, an indoor swimming and leisure complex, and a maritime park on 5 acres of infilled seashore. The plan was revised in 2012 to a more modest €2.5 million refurbishment which would not include a swimming pool, and this is currently being pursued by the county council.

During the Celtic Tiger years of the early 2000s the newly created Dublin Docklands Development Authority (DDDA) was producing ambitious plans for creating a new urban heartland in the old city docks area between the Custom House and the modern Dublin Port. High-rise office blocks, apartments and hotels were appearing on the south side around Grand Canal Dock, and on the north side the new Convention Centre with its angled glass atrium became a landmark for this brave new world. Further east, the authority had set its sights on the Poolbeg

One political party's impression of Dublin Port as a 'new Manhattan'

PROGRESSIVE DEMOCRATS
an páirtí daonlathach

A New Heart for Dublin

peninsula, home of the ESB Poolbeg power station and the huge sewage treatment works at Ringsend. Parts of this area were also owned and managed by Dublin Port Company. In a period when money appeared to be no object, the DDDA began to develop grandiose plans for high-rise apartments, public spaces and even artificial beaches on the south side of the peninsula facing Sandymount. Of course, the economic crash of 2008 put a stop to these unrealistic ideas and the peninsula remains dominated by utilities such as the port, power stations, sewage treatment works and the latest addition, the waste-to-energy plant.

In 2015 the ferry service connecting Dún Laoghaire with Holyhead was closed, ending a connection between the two ports that had been in existence since the 1830s. The connection had begun when the paddle steamers bringing the mails to Dublin had transferred from Howth Harbour, which was too shallow to accommodate the ships, which were increasing in size. The changeover to screw propulsion came in 1896 with the introduction of four vessels, the *Ulster*, *Munster*, *Leinster* and *Connaught*, owned by the City of Dublin Steampacket Company.[6] The *Leinster* was torpedoed in 1918, as described in Chapter 10. In the 1960s dramatic changes took place with the introduction of car ferries on the route and in 1995 the world's largest fast craft, the HSS *Stena Explorer* began to run between Dún Laoghaire and Holyhead, cutting the crossing time to 90 minutes, less than half the time taken by conventional ships. This service peaked in 1998, when it carried 1.7 million passengers, but competition from cheap flights, the abolition of duty-free shopping and a general drop in passenger and car numbers led to the service being limited to the summer season in 2010; it had a mere 200,000 passengers in 2014.[7] In a bid to fill the void in the business of the harbour the Dún Laoghaire Harbour Company developed plans to attract cruise ships to the harbour. This achieved some success with smaller cruise ships, including the 187-metre *Windsurf*, which became a regular visitor. However, the harbour lacked the capacity for the larger cruise liners. In 2015 the company submitted a planning application for permission to develop a cruise liner facility based at the old St Michael's Wharf in place of the HSS docking facility to handle liners of up to 340m in length. Following a great deal of controversy and a planning appeal, An Bord Pleanála granted planning permission for the proposal in November 2016, subject to a condition that limited the size of the ships to 250m.[8]

Water quality and waste disposal

Public awareness of water quality in Dublin Bay probably first arose at the end of the nineteenth century, when the consumption of shellfish became a major health risk (see Chapter 10). Up to the late eighteenth century all domestic waste, including human waste and ash from fires, was collected by operatives known as 'scavengers' and sold to farmers as fertiliser. With the advent of the flush toilet at the end of the century an increasing amount of waterborne waste found its way into water courses, though this was on a relatively small scale until the middle of the nineteenth century. With the introduction of the Vartry water supply scheme in 1868, the greater availability of piped water led to an increase in the amount of sewage that was carried in the drains originally designed to carry rainwater from the streets. While the extensive sewer network helped to clean up the dense residential areas of the city, it had a very negative impact on the River Liffey, to which the numerous sewers discharged. This contributed to high incidences of disease in the city, in comparison with other cities in the United Kingdom.[9] In 1892, Frederic W. Pim, president of the Dublin Sanitary Association, commented, in relation to the discharge of raw sewage from the towns of Kingstown and Blackrock:[10]

> I am sure that if the southern shores of our beautiful bay are not, within some comparatively short time, to become deserted by all to whom a choice of residence is free, means must be adopted by both Townships, either together or separately, to put a stop to the discharge of crude sewage on the foreshore west of Kingstown Harbour, which is now taking place in yearly growing volumes. Within my own memory, the bathing, which, forty years ago, was one of the chief attractions of the district, and from which the Dublin and Kingstown Railway reaped a handsome revenue, has been completely destroyed, and the flat sands from Salthill to Sandymount are being clothed with a foul and noisome deposit which, perhaps, only the beneficent action of the east winds in spring prevents from becoming a source of fatal pestilence.

The issue here was the failure of Kingstown township to co-operate with Blackrock township in providing a joint drainage scheme, though this was resolved in 1893, when the two townships obtained an Act of parliament to allow for the construction of a substantial holding tank at Salthill, which would be discharged on the ebb tide through a long outfall pipe at the back of the West Pier.[11] Between 1895 and 1906 the city was catered for with the implementation of the Dublin Main Drainage Scheme, including the provision of sewers along each side of the Liffey through the city, intercepting every foul sewer and diverting its contents to a new pumping station at Ringsend.[12]

Liquid waste was discharged into the estuary, while the remaining sludge was loaded onto a specially designed ship, MV *Shamrock*, to be discharged 6 miles out in the bay.[13] The original 1906 sludge transport vessel was replaced in 1958 by MV *Seamróg II*, which became more and more incapable of dealing with ever-increasing loads. A new jetty was built and *Seamróg II* was replaced by the *Sir Joseph Bazalgette* in 1983. Sea dumping ceased in December 1999 and the *Sir Joseph Bazalgette* was sold. Dublin Corporation had purchased the latter ship from the Greater London Council, and had intended to change the ship's name but decided not to do so when they discovered that Sir Joseph Bazalgette had designed the early sewer system for Dublin city.[14]

Despite repeated improvements in the treatment of sewage effluent, microbiological quality has remained a constant preoccupation to the present day. Regular monitoring for the presence of indicator

A dead great northern diver on Sandymount Strand *(Richard Nairn)*

organisms of enteric pathogens is regarded as the most practical tool to guard the health of bathers and all who participate in water-contact sports.[15] Monitoring of bathing waters is called for throughout Europe, and assessed by the European Commission. Even higher standards are recommended under the Blue Flag scheme, organised by An Taisce. On the whole, public health risks from use of the water in Dublin Bay are greatly reduced.

The other key aspect of water quality is eutrophication. In brief, this means deciding which mineral nutrient controls primary production in a water body, determining if the current state of production is satisfactory, and if it is not, seeking a remedy. In lakes and fresh waters generally it has been found that the phosphate ion is the limiting factor to algal growth. Estuaries and coastal waters are phosphate-saturated, and nitrogen is the key limiting factor.[16] Nitrogen removal is now a key process in the sewage treatment process at Ringsend.

Two historical episodes of contamination in the bay make salutary reading. The first concerns the 'Irish Sea Bird Wreck', when thousands of seabirds, mainly guillemots, were washed up dead and dying on Irish Sea coasts, including Dublin Bay, in the winter of 1969.[17] Investigations revealed high, but sublethal, concentrations of toxic polychlorinated-biphenols (PCBs). These originated from a licensed dump, where they were tipped at very low concentrations off the Clyde estuary in Scotland. The contaminants came from heavy electrical industry, building and recommissioning heavy transformers. PCBs are used in the switch gear, and become contaminated. However, from low concentrations at discharge, the ecosystem processes of transfer from phytoplankton to zooplankton to fish to seabirds led to a tenfold increase in concentration at each step. Hence the birds were greatly weakened. The *coup de grâce* was a series of severe storms in the winter of that year which weakened the birds, prevented them from feeding and forced them to mobilise body fat containing the lethal chemicals. This was an isolated event but it illustrates how apparently remote sources of pollution can be transferred through food chains to devastate top predators. Biological concentration of materials, via the food chains, is always a counter argument to the view that 'dilution is the solution to pollution'!

The other case concerns the release of radio-isotopes from the nuclear fuel reprocessing plant at Sellafield in Cumbria. It is correct that radioactive caesium isotopes (caesium-134 and caesium-137) have been detected in Dublin Bay, but seawater is naturally radioactive because of a universally present isotope of potassium. This constitutes a background signal, while the caesium isotopes barely reach one tenth of this. We should be watchful of this situation, but there is currently no risk to recreational users of Dublin Bay.

Recreation

Although rarely acknowledged, Dublin Bay is one of the most heavily used stretches of coastline in Ireland. Enormous numbers of people enjoy the amenity of the bay each week either in a structured or casual way. In 1987, Jack O'Sullivan wrote a detailed review of recreational use of the bay[18] using the results of two extensive surveys by An Foras Forbartha[19] and Brady Shipman Martin[20] in the 1970s. In 1997 O'Sullivan[21] updated these findings and it is now possible to consider additional new uses of the bay. These findings make an interesting comparison with the present-day usage. At a rough estimate, 100,000 people are involved in recreational activities dependent on Dublin Bay at peak periods.

Most of the water sports activity is voluntary, with 12 yacht, boat and sailing clubs, eight of which have premises. There are also at least six coastal rowing clubs, and five sea angling clubs. There are several national water sports bodies, such as the Irish Sailing Association,

Walking on Sandymount Strand close to a flock of oystercatchers *(Richard Nairn)*

with a concentration of members in the Dublin area, even though they represent a national membership. The bay also has representative organisations for swimmers, anglers, kitesurfers, windsurfers, canoeists and kayakers. There are two well-established links golf courses with clubhouses on Bull Island.[22]

Enjoying beaches and dunes

There is no doubt that the beaches of Dublin Bay are its prime recreational attractions during any period of fine weather. The 5.5km Dollymount Strand is the longest stretch of recreational beach but, on a sunny day, all areas of exposed sand are occupied by those enjoying beach recreation. Even less prepossessing areas, such as those adjacent to the Poolbeg power station, are often quite busy. A great deal of discussion has taken place over the years since 1977 concerning the benefits and impacts of beach recreation. It seems that under present conditions very little ecological harm results from such use. However, certain types of human disturbance can be a problem for seals (Chapter 3) and sensitive birds that use the shorelines (Chapter 6).

The provision of car parking close to Sandymount Strand, and the current restrictions to car movement on Dollymount Strand, minimise beach damage and injury to people. The issue of beach litter is not easy to manage. On one hand, the twice-daily tidal cycle deposits a regular tideline of floating debris. This progresses up the beach as

Sand yachts and kitesurfers on Dollymount Strand *(John Fox)*

tide height increases in the neap–spring tide sequence. The amount of debris varies greatly according to local currents. Marine debris at least 50cm deep and many metres wide can accumulate at Merrion Gates. This material is offensive to beach recreational users, but may be the nucleus for further dune growth in appropriate situations. On the other hand, litter associated with recreational use is inevitable, despite anti-litter campaigns. This situation has led local authorities to undertake mechanical beach-cleaning activities in the name of health and safety. These should be restricted to minimal essential activity in preparation for particular peak recreational activity. Maintaining maximum sand mass in the beach–dune system is a priority task.

Swimming

In the eighteenth century, swimming in seawater became a popular pastime and this led in the nineteenth century to the construction of public seawater baths at Dalkey, Sandycove, Dún Laoghaire, Salthill, Seapoint, Blackrock, Merrion, Sandymount, Irishtown and Clontarf. These generally operated by allowing water to enter on one high tide and holding it in concrete pools over the tidal cycle. Some of these pools were used for sports such as water polo and swimming races. The earliest of these was Cranfield Baths, which opened at Sandymount in 1791, though there were various bathing places along the shore prior to this, without enclosed baths. Kingscourt Baths at Clontarf were established

Swimming race
(Karl Partridge)

in 1833; they were separated from the coast by Clontarf Road, so there must have been pipes extending beneath the road to fill the baths.[23] These baths closed in about 1863 and in 1879 a company was formed to open baths opposite Castle Avenue. These were located about 50m offshore and were accessed by means of a bridge or pier. A similar approach was taken with the baths at Strand Road, Merrion, which were accessed via a cast-iron pier, known as Merrion Promenade Pier, on which there were amusements such as band recitals and fancy dress events. The baths at Merrion and those at Clontarf were concrete basins that filled with seawater. Blackrock Baths, built in the late 1880s by a private company, were adjacent to the shore and, unlike the others, did not have a pier. These baths were acquired in 1926 by Blackrock Urban District Council, which enlarged and improved them to competition standard, including a 50m pool and diving boards. The swimming and diving events of the 1928 Tailteann Games were held in the baths.[24] Clontarf Baths closed in the 1990s, Merrion in the 1920s and Blackrock in the 1980s.

Swimming in the open sea became popular at some well-known spots such as Sandycove, Salthill, Seapoint, South Wall, Bull Wall, Sutton and Howth. In 1875 *The Freeman's Journal* announced that Dublin Swimming Club would hold its annual swimming races in Salthill Baths. This appears to be have been a very colourful affair with a festive atmosphere: it included fancy dress and even a water polo match played with ball and mallets on 'horses' made out of sealed casks with artificial heads and tails! This kind of atmosphere seems to have prevailed at all 'athletics in aqua' or 'water carnivals' held around Dublin Bay at the time. The Half Moon Swimming Club, whose clubhouse is still located on the Great South Wall, was founded in 1898 and was originally known as the Poolbeg Bathers' Association. The building once held an army gun battery with the gun turret mounted in a half-moon shape. Today the club hosts four open-sea swimming events during the summer months and is an active participant in water polo competitions.

The Forty Foot bathing place at Sandycove was once exclusively a male bathing place and a gentlemen's swimming club was established

Crowds swimming at Seapoint
(Richard Nairn)

to help conserve the area. Owing to its relative isolation and gender-specific nature, men were allowed to swim nude, but in the 1970s, during the women's liberation movement, a group of female equal-rights activists plunged into the waters and now it is also open to women and children. Casual beach swimming at such places as Dollymount, Sandymount, Seapoint and Sandycove is very weather-dependent but there does appear to have been a decline in sea swimming with the expansion of indoor heated facilities. A survey of water-based leisure activities in Ireland found that one third fewer people took part in sea swimming in 2003 than in 1996. While environmental concerns about 'pollution' were cited by 19 per cent of swimmers, 'lack of facilities' was seen as the most negative issue.[25]

Walking

The shorelines of Dublin Bay offer wonderful opportunities for physical exercise and fresh air close to a heavily populated area. The long piers that protect the harbours in Dún Laoghaire, Dublin and Howth are among the most heavily used walking locations. A study in 1974 found that Dún Laoghaire East Pier and Howth East Pier had peaks of 3,500 and 2,600 pedestrians respectively in a single day.[26] The South Wall, the Bull Wall and Clontarf Promenade in the city are also popular walking areas for people and their dogs.

Cyclists and walkers on the seafront at Clontarf (John Fox)

Cycling

The coastal roads and paths along the northern shore of the bay, between Sutton and Fairview, are popular cycling routes both for leisure use and for commuters heading for the city centre. Estimates of the number of cyclists are scarce, but anyone standing on the Clontarf seafront at rush hour will be impressed by the constant stream of passing bikes. Coastal roads and cycle paths are currently accessible by bike around parts of Howth Head, from Sutton to Fairview, from Irishtown to Merrion Gates and from Dún Laoghaire to Dalkey. The local authorities and National Transport Authority have a plan to link all the coastal sections together in a single cycleway, together with a coastal path, called the East Coast Trail.[27]

Golf

A large proportion of the sand dunes at the Bull Island are occupied by two popular golf links. The Royal Dublin Golf Club is the older of the two and is a private club for members only. St Anne's Golf Club is open

St Anne's Golf Club on Bull Island *(John Fox)*

to all comers but also has a membership. Together, on a fine day at the weekend, they can provide playing facilities for hundreds of golfers. The Royal Dublin has already hosted the Irish Open Golf Championship, attracting thousands of spectators.

Nature study and birdwatching

Dublin Bay has been a popular location for naturalists since Victorian times. The ornithologist Alexander Williams wrote in 1908, 'To many of the town dwellers perhaps the large number of aquatic birds to be seen about the city will attract most attention, and the seashore stretching from Clontarf to Howth, and from the South Wall to Kingstown, presents an ever-changing field for observation.'[28] Today, BirdWatch Ireland has over 4,200 members in Dublin city and county and a proportion of these frequently watch birds on the bay. Several Dublin branches run regular outings in the coastal area with an average turnout of 60 people per visit. Occasional public events are also organised by BirdWatch Ireland

Birdwatching guide to Bull Island *(courtesy of BirdWatch Ireland and Dublin City Council)*

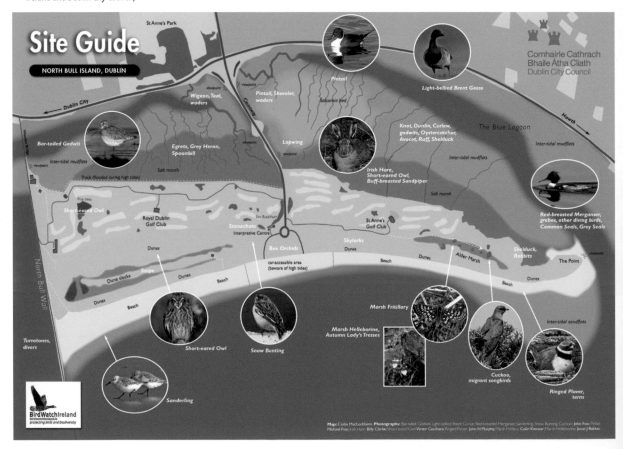

at Bull Island and it is estimated that these have attracted more than 3,000 people over several years.

The Dublin Naturalists' Field Club was founded in 1886 and early members included Robert Lloyd Praeger and Nathaniel Colgan. It has the general aim of promoting an interest in all branches of natural history and organises up to 60 field outings per year. The *Flora of County Dublin*[29] was published by the Field Club in 1998 and it is the most detailed county survey of plants ever carried out in Ireland. The Field Club is currently working on a revised *Flora of Howth*. Bull Island Interpretative Centre, built by Dublin Corporation (now Dublin City Council) contains displays on the history and nature of the island and provides a base for the staff who manage the public areas of this important nature reserve.

Cruising tours

In 2013 a new service was launched on the bay. A passenger vessel, the *St Bridget*, began summer cruises from Dún Laoghaire to Dublin to Howth. This proved highly popular, with 80 per cent of the passengers from Ireland and 20 per cent overseas tourists. By 2015 the vessel was carrying an annual total of 30,000 people on cruises between April and October. Viewing the bay from the comfort of a ship has turned out to be a novel experience for many people as fewer of us use ferries regularly. In 2016 guides were employed on board the *St Bridget* to give visitors an

Cruise ship passing Ireland's Eye
(courtesy of Dublin Bay Cruises)

introduction to Dublin Bay Biosphere. The cruise route takes in close views of Dalkey Island, the entrance to Dublin Port, Howth Head cliffs and Ireland's Eye as well as opportunities to see seals, porpoises and seabirds in their natural habitats.

Sailing

Dublin Bay has the largest single concentration of leisure sailors in Ireland, with nine clubs based in Dún Laoghaire, Poolbeg, Clontarf, Kilbarrack, Sutton and Howth, with a combined membership of between 6,500 and 7,000. Racing from Dún Laoghaire is mainly organised by Dublin Bay Sailing Club and there are other common organisations, such as the Irish Cruising Club, that have large memberships in the Dublin area. In addition, the biennial Dún Laoghaire Regatta is now the largest sailing event in Ireland, hosting five national championships and three regional titles; 3,000 sailors in over 400 boats take part in 29 classes. The National Sailing School is based in Dún Laoghaire Harbour.

Yachts moored in Dún Laoghaire Harbour
(Richard Nairn)

Sail boards and kitesurfing

Modern developments in water sports have made the bay available to a wider range of enthusiasts for a much smaller investment in equipment. A sail board is little more than a surfboard with a single plastic sail balanced by the sailor who stands on the board. The lack of friction between the board and the water surface allows these sailors to reach speeds of up to 30km/h in high winds. Speed is also the main attraction of the new sport of kitesurfing, which involves a short board with the surfer strapped into a harness below a large plastic kite. The friction is often so low that the surfer leaves the water surface altogether and the sport becomes a mixture of surfing and flying. This sport has become so popular and accessible that an annual festival of kitesurfing, the 'Battle of the Bay', is staged each year on Dollymount Strand.

Angling

Sea angling is quite a different sport from river and lake fishing in that anglers have to contend with many more variables, such as tides, winds and different shore types. Dublin Bay offers a variety of sea angling opportunities on beaches, piers and from chartered boats. Howth Harbour is the best place to find a deep-sea angling boat to try fishing on one of the many wrecks around the Dublin coast. Shore angling on Howth Head at Balscadden can be rewarded with mackerel, plaice, dogfish, whiting and codling, while the rough ground at Red Rock is a good place for bass.

Evening tides on Dollymount Strand in midsummer and autumn are good for bass, flounder and codling. On the south side of the Bay, Poolbeg lighthouse and Dún Laoghaire West Pier are popular with

Kitesurfing at Poolbeg
(John Fox)

Sailing and angling boats at
Bullock Harbour (Richard Nairn)

anglers for much of the year, with dab, plaice, conger and bass the main targets. In summer, mackerel and pollack are regularly taken here.[30] Small boats are available for hire in Bullock Harbour and Coliemore Harbour in Dalkey.

Rowing

The long tradition of rowing is now carried on through the east coast rowing clubs that are based around the old Dublin pilot stations of Ringsend, East Wall, Dún Laoghaire, Dalkey and Bray. Organised by the East Coast Rowing Council each year, a summer schedule of regattas are held from Ringsend to Wicklow. On average over 225 rowers are actively involved in club racing in Dublin Bay during the summer, and competitions may attract between 350 and 400 entrants. The traditional design is retained in the racing boats. Present-day racing skiffs are 25 feet (roughly 7.5m) long, clinker-built double-enders. Each area races its own traditional boat, and they come together annually for the Irish coastal rowing championships, for which they now use an agreed one-design boat. Coastal rowing helps communities to maintain links with their maritime heritage.

Skiff racing on the Liffey in Dublin Port *(Karl Partridge)*

Sub-aqua diving

Dublin Bay and the Irish Sea are less attractive for sub-aqua diving than the west coast due to the poor visibility underwater. However, the bay is used for training large numbers of enthusiasts in the sport. The Irish Underwater Council has about 28 diving clubs in the Irish Sea area and many of these regularly use Dublin Bay. Some of these clubs have been diving Dublin Bay for over 50 years. The Dublin North clubs dive mainly out of Howth, but some use Malahide, Skerries and Rush, while the Dublin South clubs mostly operate out of Dún Laoghaire. In 2015 there were a total of over 400 active divers in the Dublin region, with a significant number of divers also using the numerous commercial operators in the bay. Some of these operate diving schools where a beginner can hire the necessary tanks and other equipment to learn the techniques of the sport. The most popular dive sites in Dublin Bay are Rockabill, Lambay, Ireland's Eye, Balscadden, Howth Head, the Muglins, Dalkey Island, Dalkey Sound and all the wrecks in Dublin Bay. There are a few shore dives and more obscure dive sites that clubs visit from time to time, and a lot of training dives take place at Dalkey Sound and Sandycove.

Protection of biodiversity

Dublin Bay already includes the greatest number of designations of any area of comparable size in Ireland. It was largely due to the efforts of Father Patrick Kennedy that Bull Island became Ireland's first bird sanctuary, designated under an order signed in 1931 (Chapter 6). In the 1970s it was listed as an Area of Scientific Interest, renamed Natural Heritage Area and then designated National Nature Reserve in the 1980s. The most significant designations were those under the European Union directives – Special Area of Conservation (SAC) and Special Protection Area (SPA) – and these took in a wider area of North Dublin Bay. Simultaneously, the SAC and SPA designations were applied to South Dublin Bay and later to the Tolka Estuary between Bull Island and the port. Howth Head and Dalkey Island also have both SAC and SPA designations and in 2013 a new, entirely marine, SAC was declared, which stretches from Rockabill (off Skerries) to Dalkey Island. Public pressure forced the government of the time to instigate Special Amenity Area Orders (SAAOs) for Bull Island and Howth Head in the 1990s.

John Fox at the nature reserve
sign on Bull Island
(Richard Nairn)

To add to this collection of confusing titles and acronyms the recognition in 1981 by UNESCO of Bull Island as a Biosphere Reserve was probably the greatest accolade as it conferred a global status on this humble island of sand and saltmarsh. Then, in 2015, the Biosphere recognition was extended to take in the whole of Dublin Bay with a core area to include the legally designated areas (SPA, SAC and SAAO); a buffer zone of highly modified habitats, such as the golf courses on Bull Island and public open spaces throughout the city; and a transition zone covering most of the hinterland and fringing marine areas. Six organisations – the three local authorities, Dublin Port Company, Fáilte Ireland (the Irish Tourist Board) and the National Parks and Wildlife Service – have agreed a memorandum of understanding giving a commitment, *inter alia*, to develop and implement a five-year conservation programme for key sites and species within the Biosphere Reserve, and to improve education and awareness of the significance of Dublin Bay in terms of natural heritage.

One could easily ask what difference this plethora of legal designations makes to the important flora and fauna of the bay – or, indeed, whether it is managed more sensibly or sustainably as a result. An early case study on the conservation needs of Bull Island in 1983 focused on the threats and conservation priorities of this unique area.[31]

Certainly, there could be more 'joined-up thinking' when it comes to management of the coastal zone, but this would require co-operation, consensus and, more important, compromise between a wide range of agencies and organisations. The new Biosphere project is a brave attempt to bring some of the key players together in a co-ordinated approach to Dublin Bay, reflecting its significant environmental, economic, cultural and tourism importance, and extending to over 300km². More than 300,000 people live within the newly enlarged Biosphere and the aim is to achieve co-ordinated management in a partnership of communities, NGOs and local and national governments. However, there are numerous other stakeholders who will need to be consulted on any new developments or policies. No new regulations are planned. The aims are to be achieved by people working together. It will take a very strong and determined team of professionals to get such disparate interests working in a common direction to implement any long-term objectives such as adapting to the impacts of climate change.

However, there are already several ways in which things have changed for the better. The EU Natura 2000 designations SAC and SPA now cover virtually all the intertidal and shallow marine areas of the bay as well as some key terrestrial areas such as the sand dunes, saltmarsh, cliffs and islands. These are transposed into Irish law and make any damage to these habitats by way of developments within the planning system much less likely. Water quality has improved markedly since the 1980s as a result of the removal of several disparate sewage discharges (Dún Laoghaire, Sutton and Howth) and the treatment at Ringsend of the majority of the waste water from Greater Dublin to a very high standard before it is discharged. Monitoring of the natural environment has improved. For example, the birds of the bay are now intensively monitored throughout the year by BirdWatch Ireland, supported by Dublin Port Company and the Biosphere Partnership. But there could be much more co-ordination and sharing of information, which would have benefits for management decisions and would also help to inform local people about their environment.

People's opinions on Dublin Bay do not always reflect reality. A recent opinion survey revealed that 73 per cent of people interviewed in the Greater Dublin area are proud of their coastline and 87 per cent of respondents agreed or strongly agreed with the statement 'Dublin Bay is important to me'.[32] While 54 per cent felt that Dublin Bay was doing well or very well in terms of its beaches, only 38 per cent of respondents agreed that water quality was good. For almost one third of people interviewed, 'the view' was the most important aspect of the bay, while pollution/litter/waste were the least favoured aspects for nearly half of the interviewees. About 15 per cent of those people interviewed visit the bay every day, while a further 27 per cent said that they visit about once a week. In 2015, Dublin City and County had a population of 1.27 million and more than 1.8 million people currently live in the Greater Dublin Area, a region comprising Dublin and the counties of Meath, Kildare and Wicklow. This figure is set to grow to 2.2 million by 2031.[33] A new survey of the number of people using the bay for various pursuits is seriously overdue and this would help with future planning. However, there is no doubting that the numbers of people in the bay are substantial. Considering this popularity, it is not surprising that any proposals for changing the bay come under intense scrutiny, and frequently organised opposition, when a development is seen as damaging the amenity that people currently enjoy. Difficult management decisions in future will be greatly helped by good information and consultation with the large number of users of Dublin Bay.

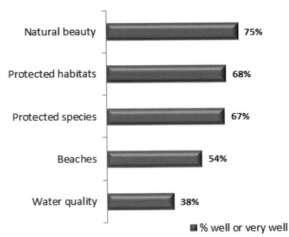

How do you think Dublin Bay is doing in terms of:

Natural beauty — 75%
Protected habitats — 68%
Protected species — 67%
Beaches — 54%
Water quality — 38%

■ % well or very well

Some results of a 2015 opinion survey of Dublin residents *(courtesy of Dublin City Council)*

People engaging with the bay

It is clear that large numbers of people currently visit and use Dublin Bay for a wide range of both passive and active recreation. Dubliners are aware of and, in most cases, proud of the bay, but there is a poor understanding of environmental pressures and changes. Threats are often seen as short term – a wind farm, a flood protection wall, an oil exploration licence – and there is little understanding of the long-term issues such as climate change, habitat loss and the indirect effects of

urban growth. Local communities need to feel that they have a voice in the protection and management of their environment, and some sections of the local population want to be directly involved in helping with this. There is a need to reconnect the city with its bay, both physically and psychologically. One of the most hopeful of recent developments is the establishment in 2015 of a Biosphere Partnership involving a number of the key authorities, and this will engage with a wide range of stakeholders and users of the Bay. The Biosphere is discussed further in Chapter 12.

People enjoying an event on Dollymount Strand *(John Fox)*

12 | The Future of the Bay

None of us can accurately predict the future, but we can learn from the past and the present to help us prepare for coming changes. Dublin Bay has changed radically over the last two centuries. At the start of the nineteenth century the modern Dublin Port and Dún Laoghaire Harbour, as we know them today, had not yet been built. There was no Bull Wall and no Bull Island. The Dublin and Kingstown railway, now occupied by the DART line, did not exist. Either side of the city stretched a coastline with farmland and small villages such as Sandymount and Clontarf. Sailing ships lined the quays in the city and fishing smacks set out from the village of Ringsend at the mouth of the Liffey to work the Irish Sea. Dublin Bay was a place where people worked hard – hauling the nets on fishing trawlers, raking the sands for shellfish, unloading cargos from ships in the docks, carting rocks to build new sea walls around the reclaimed land. Recreation, as we know it, was rare, at least for the vast bulk of poor city dwellers. Disease and hunger were commonplace and the port was the main exit gate for emigrants leaving the country for ever.

In the nineteenth century, when the British Empire encompassed much of the known world, life must have seemed unchanging from one generation to the next. But things were already changing fast. The industrial revolution, which spanned the eighteenth and nineteenth centuries, marked a major turning point in history. Almost every aspect of daily life was influenced by it in some way. Dublin had become the second city of the empire, after London, and industry was beginning to employ large numbers of people, supporting a growth in population. Huge quantities of coal were burnt to fuel this growth and the smoke that it produced hung over the city in a black cloud. Although nobody recognised it then, the release of greenhouse gases had begun in earnest.

A BIRD'S EYE VIEW OF DUBLIN
H.W. BREWER. 1890

Climate change and the bay

Climate change is the overriding environmental issue for the world today. It is already affecting weather patterns for Ireland, where there is much greater climate variability from decade to decade. For Dublin and eastern Ireland the coming decades will bring hotter, drier summers and stormier winters.[1] The sea temperature is rising steadily, affecting the Irish Sea's stocks of fish that were once a major source of food for the people of Dublin. Sea level is rising due to thermal expansion of seawater as the temperature rises, and to the melting of glaciers around the world.[2] Coastal flooding is already a reality for residents of some of the low-lying districts around the city. Images of people wading through floodwaters in Clontarf, Fairview or Sandymount as they try to protect their homes from the rising seawater are all too familiar.

Dublin City Council's strategy to protect the capital from future flooding is already out of date, according to the latest predictions by climate scientists. A new study suggests the city will be at risk from a combination of higher sea levels and storm surges of 3m or more by the end of the century. This is significantly above the median risk of 0.5m outlined in the Irish Coastal Protection Strategy (2013), drawn up by the Office of Public Works (OPW) and used by Dublin's local authorities. It is 'probable' that Dublin will see a 0.69m rise in sea levels by 2100, according to a 2015 paper by scientists at the Niels Bohr Institute in Denmark.[3] Professor John Sweeney, a scientist based at the Irish Climate Analysis and Research Unit in Maynooth University, has said he expects a sea level rise in the Dublin area of about 1m by 2100, based on modelling by the Intergovernmental Panel on Climate Change.[4] Across Europe, a sea level rise of about a metre will directly threaten 13 million

A bird's-eye view of Dublin city with the bay in the background, 1890 *(H.W. Brewer)*

265

people.[5] The resulting land loss will impinge on expanding urban areas, inundate agricultural land and eradicate coastal wetlands that offer a measure of protection against serious storms and flooding. It has been estimated that approximately 350 square kilometres in Irish cities is vulnerable from a 1m rise in sea levels, with potential economic costs related to property insurance claims likely to be in the region of €339 million in Dublin alone.[6]

Clontarf seafront during tidal flooding *(John Fox)*

Protecting the city

The human cost of rising sea levels will undoubtedly be high as residential areas are flooded and large numbers of people need to be rehoused. Major sea defences will be needed to protect vital infrastructure such as the ports and harbours, the port tunnel, the rail lines, as well as the historic parts of Dublin's quays. Professor Robert Devoy of University College Cork has suggested some solutions for the future management of the Dublin coasts to respond to coastal flooding. These might include 'hard-engineered', high-cost solutions (e.g., sea walls, barrages), 'soft', lower-cost techniques (e.g., sand traps and dune planting), or a combination of the two. He has also suggested planned coastal property retreat and compensation for property buy-up, plus a rigorous planning regulation for vulnerable coastal environments (i.e. low-lying, 'soft' sedimentary coasts). Rapid response defence techniques, tuned to storm/disaster early warning systems, will be needed to deal with imminent storms coinciding with high tides. Perhaps a combination of all three measures will be needed, as appropriate to different sections of the coast and the functioning of coastal systems.[7] To meet the impacts of certain future flooding events, central government and the local authorities need to agree on the best approach to adopt, to avoid the worst effects of climate change impacts on coasts.[8] While many environmental factors are interlinked with global climate change, some factors will be minimally affected, in particular the long-term flows of fine-sized sediment from river catchments, coasts and sand from the floor of the Irish Sea.

An easterly storm hits the seafront at Dún Laoghaire (*John Coveney*)

Coastal squeeze and habitat loss

For the natural habitats there will also be great changes. As the low water mark creeps ever closer to the hard coastline of sea walls, railway embankments and rocky shores, the coastal zones will be squeezed into ever smaller areas. Exposed areas of sand and mudflat will be reduced. Sea walls always destroy sandy beaches in the long term but, perversely, these measures are still used as the primary solutions to beach erosion in many places in the world.[9] In north Dublin Bay, saltmarsh areas will be inundated and become progressively narrower as sea level rises. However, evidence from the USA shows that coastal marshes can grow upwards in response to gradual sea level rise.[10, 11] Pioneer sand dunes that currently build up each summer at the north end of Bull Island and in Merrion Strand will be replaced by beach erosion. All sand dune areas will suffer saltwater penetration into the water table. Overall, we will lose large parts of the natural habitats that have survived for centuries alongside urban development.

Added to sea level rise is an increasing frequency of significant storms. The exact wind direction behind storm surges is of great importance. They will undoubtedly recur more frequently as more energy is transferred to the ocean–atmosphere system. But will Dublin

Wave height in Dublin Bay modelled for an easterly storm at spring high water *(courtesy of Adrian Bell, RPS Group)*

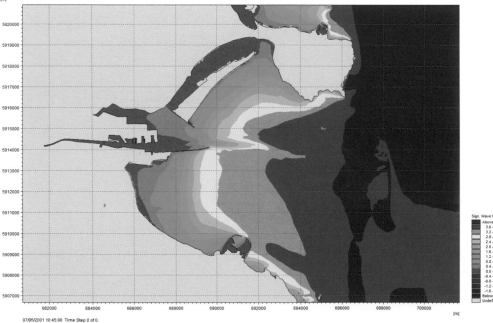

07/05/2001 10:45:00 Time Step 0 of 0.

Bay be protected, in its east-facing location, from the most extreme Atlantic storms and changing wave climate? This should not be taken for granted and European trends in weather patterns may indicate what is in store. Surges adding a metre to the height of high spring tides have been experienced recently. The resultant local flooding alone is enough reason to implement appropriate flood-protection schemes. The effect of such surges on sand dunes is no greater today than in the past century. But if their frequency increases markedly, as part of the pattern of climate and sea level changes, and without compensatory summer growth, then long-term retreat of beach–dune systems will result. Saltmarshes are not subject to disturbance by storms, because of their inherently protected position, but sea level rise will certainly affect them.

Impacts of climate change on wildlife

And what of the plant and animal populations that live in these habitats? Some rare species, such as the orchids that survive in the alder marsh at Bull Island, will certainly disappear as seawater enters the water table. The great diversity of plants in the saltmarshes will be reduced as natural vegetation narrows to a strip between the low water mark and

Roosting waders and gulls on Sandymount Strand *(John Fox)*

the edge of the golf courses, which themselves are likely to be regularly flooded by seawater. Some of the pioneer plants of saltmarshes, such as glasswort and cordgrass, will be severely reduced as the lower levels of the mudflats are eroded. We can expect parts of the Tolka Estuary and Sandymount Strand to become permanent shallow water, changing the invertebrate life that depends on the rise and fall of the tides each day.

This reduction in intertidal foraging areas will significantly reduce the important waterbird populations in Dublin Bay as most of them depend for feeding and roosting on the sand and mudflats. Brent geese will be forced to move to feed on parks and sports pitches earlier and earlier each winter. Already there is evidence that climate change is reducing the frequency of sea ice in the Baltic countries, allowing migratory birds such as wigeon to stop short of Ireland in their annual southward journeys from the Arctic. We may find that brent geese, and many other birds such as golden plover and redshank, increasingly overwinter in Iceland and no longer need to come to Dublin Bay. With the decline of northern species, their place may be taken by birds that we associate with the Mediterranean countries today. Mediterranean gulls and little egrets have both become common here in the last decade and, as the temperatures rise, we might expect to see more exotic heron species such as cattle egrets and perhaps even flamingos feeding in the remaining parts of Dublin Bay. We are already seeing changes in the fish stocks of the Irish Sea due to temperature changes and overfishing, so it is quite likely that the seabirds and cetaceans will respond either by changing their diet or by moving elsewhere.

The long-term trend in sea temperature is more difficult to predict. Dublin is already, anomalously for its latitude, warmed by the Gulf Stream. Should a greater flow of cold Arctic water into the North Atlantic displace the warm current, a fall in sea temperature throughout western Europe may occur. If warming of the sea continues, as it has done for the last 50 years, we may expect slow migration of marine species northwards. Ecologically this is part of a continuing change that has oscillated since the retreat of the last glaciation 13,000 years ago. The coastal waters surrounding Britain and Ireland became warmer during the twentieth century and, according to the UK Climate Impact Programme predictions, average annual temperatures may rise a further 2°C by 2050.[12] This warming is part of a global rise in sea and air surface temperatures that will cause changes in the abundance and distribution of species. Initially, there will not be a wholesale movement northwards of marine species because many additional factors will influence the responses of the different organisms. How will the marine fauna of Dublin Bay respond?

Some predominantly northern species, such as the horse mussel, may decline, reducing their value as rich habitats for marine life. Others, characterised by southern species, for example the sea fan and the alcyonacean *Alcyonium glomeratum*, may increase in extent. Climate change and overfishing together already appear to be causing ecosystem instability and may benefit organisms such as jellyfish. In the Irish Sea, an increase in jellyfish abundance was recorded during juvenile fish surveys over a 16-year period (1994–2009). Jellyfish numbers rose with increasing sea surface temperature and with decreasing spring rainfall amounts. Before 1970 the herring stock in the northern Irish Sea declined rapidly to a low level, potentially stimulating structural change in the ecosystem. In 1985, there was a significant decrease in abundance of copepods – tiny animals in the plankton – and in 1989 a big increase in the density of phytoplankton, suggesting a shift in balance of primary production during the 1980s. Subsequent overexploitation of cod and related fish, coupled with warmer temperatures and the poor recruitment of young fish to the populations, led to the rapid decline in cod stocks from 1990. While the biomass of sprat has decreased in the last decade, the herring stock has recovered partially. Reductions in fishing pressure on the seabed since 2000, intended to stimulate cod recovery, appear to have facilitated further rises in haddock stocks. Since the 1980s, sea temperatures have increased, the fish community has altered and jellyfish abundance has risen such that jellyfish and haddock may now play an increasingly important role in the ecosystem.[13]

Compass jellyfish stranded on the beach *(Richard Nairn)*

Changes in water quality

The last few decades have seen progressive improvements in the quality of water in Dublin Bay with better treatment of waste water and reduction of toxic discharges into the rivers that feed the bay. This contrasts dramatically with the late nineteenth century, when raw sewage was released into the Liffey, and even in the mid-twentieth century parts of the inner estuary were considered abiotic (or devoid of life). The city of Dublin will continue to grow and discharge waste water into the bay. As we saw in Chapter 11, some 1.8 million people currently live in the Greater Dublin Area (Dublin, Meath, Kildare and Wicklow), and this figure is predicted to grow to 2.2 million by 2031.

While EU Directives on water quality are in force, waste water will have to be treated effectively.

The lower Liffey and Tolka estuaries were first designated as 'sensitive' areas under the Urban Waste Water Treatment Directive in 2001. This requires that nutrients be removed from the final effluent at Ringsend before discharge into the lower Liffey estuary. In 2012 an advanced secondary treatment technology, known as aerobic granular sludge, became available at a scale appropriate for the Ringsend plant. The latest proposal in 2017 – to use this technology to treat Dublin's waste water – offers significant advantages over conventional secondary treatment with biological nutrient removal (of both nitrogen and phosphorous).

Ringsend Waste Water Treatment Works in the foreground *(courtesy of Peter Barrow)*

Recent and future battles for the bay

We have seen in earlier chapters how Dublin Bay was central to the development and growth of the capital city, how it still forms a vital 'lung' for the people of the area and how it provides a natural envelope for the city. But it is also a fragile place, easily damaged by inappropriate development, mismanagement or neglect. The bay needs to be managed in a sustainable way so that it can go on providing the essential functions of a sea within a city. Writing in 1987, Anne Brady evaluated the political and administrative systems governing Dublin Bay.[14] Her conclusion was that 'the continued growth and development of the Bay as a resource can plainly no longer continue without the objectives of one body being achieved at the expense of another.' As an example she cited the loss of seaside amenity as the price of successful port activity. Three decades later Dublin Port is highly successful, but few people would agree that the seaside amenity of Dublin Bay has been compromised as a result. Brady also believed that successful development of harbour marinas would mean traffic congestion onshore. Since then successful yacht marinas have been developed in Dún Laoghaire, Poolbeg and Howth,

Storm-driven waves flood the seafront at Clontarf (*John Fox*)

but there has been no resulting traffic congestion. However, Brady did highlight the large number of organisations and interest groups that seek to use the bay for a variety of purposes and the potential conflicts that can arise.

Not all users of Dublin Bay are likely to agree about what needs to be done. For example, the proposals of Dublin City Council to erect flood defences along the seafront from Fairview to Clontarf were rejected by a majority of local residents. In 2008 the council had secured planning permission to build flood defences up to 2.75m high, involving earthen embankments and walls. Following objections from local residents, the council offered to reduce the height of the protective embankment to 2.17m, the lowest height permitted by An Bord Pleanála. Despite having been hit by an 'extreme tidal event' in February 2002 and a less severe one in October 2004, both of which caused damage to homes and businesses, residents even opposed this reduced barrier. Serious concerns were raised by the local community and local public representatives in relation to the loss of views of the sea and Dublin Bay, the potential safety and security of people walking on the seaside walkway, and their ability to enjoy the amenity. In 2014, the council proposed a 'dual flood defence' comprising the existing sea wall and a secondary defence as close as possible to Clontarf Road. The promenade would be 'sacrificed to flood waters in extreme events' and its length and grass surface used to contain floodwaters and absorb wave energy. The car parks and all the flood gates would be closed following warnings of very high tides, which are normally issued two days in advance. The controversy rumbles on and coastal residents in the low-lying areas still keep sandbags in their gardens for individual attempts to save their houses in the next flooding event. A more far-sighted and comprehensive solution is surely required.

In 2012, the government issued a foreshore licence for a single exploratory well for oil to be drilled in the Kish Basin in the outer part of Dublin Bay. This generated a protest group called Dublin Bay Concern. It organised a public meeting in Dún Laoghaire, attended by almost 600 objectors, which called for a judicial review to have the licence overturned. The protesters wanted an environmental impact assessment to be undertaken before any drilling was allowed, and for the government to reconsider the proximity to the Dublin coastline of any exploratory drilling. According to Dublin Bay Concern, drilling would cause environmental damage that could spread all along the coast of Dublin, contaminating shellfish and devastating that export industry. In 2013, plans for the exploratory well were put on hold after Providence Resources plc announced that it was surrendering its foreshore licence because elements of an EU directive on environmental impact assessments (EIAs) 'were not transposed correctly in 1999 by the Irish government'. The voluntary conservation body An Taisce had challenged the granting of the licence in the High Court. It alleged that the government acted unlawfully in awarding the licence without an EIA, which, An Taisce argued, was required under EU law.

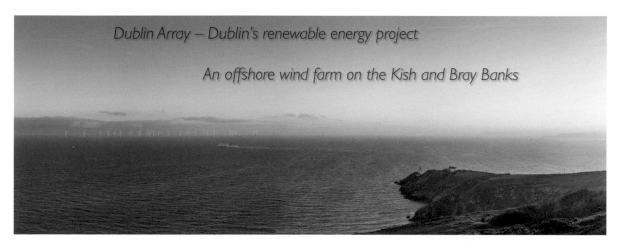

Dublin Array – Dublin's renewable energy project

An offshore wind farm on the Kish and Bray Banks

In 2013, an application was lodged for a foreshore licence to build an offshore wind farm on the Kish and Bray Banks off Dublin Bay. To be known as the Dublin Array, the proposed development would comprise up to 145 wind turbines with a maximum blade tip height of 160m above mean sea level and associated infrastructure including the turbine foundations, subsea cabling and offshore substation. It was to be located within an area of 54 square kilometres in water depths ranging from 2m to 30m. The proposal was viewed with concern by residents, especially those in the coastal areas of south Dublin and north Wicklow. The environmental impact statement accompanying the application identified some of the potential effects. Both the installation of turbines and the laying of cables would have the capacity to damage remains of shipwrecks, of which 48 have been recorded on the banks since the mid-eighteenth century. Potential impacts on fish communities include the effects of noise and vibration, electromagnetic field (EMF) and changes in water quality. The construction noise associated with installing

Artist's impression of a wind farm on the Kish Bank as viewed from Howth Head *(Dublin Array and Innovation Media Ltd)*

275

the foundations for the turbines was identified as having the greatest potential to cause significant impact on fish. BirdWatch Ireland was concerned about the potential for seabirds colliding with the operating turbines. While a licence for the Dublin Array has not yet been granted, there is a need for a policy on future renewable energy generation in Dublin Bay.

In 2012, residents on both sides of the bay objected to the proposal to pump Dublin's treated waste water from the upgraded Ringsend Treatment Works through a tunnel out to the Burford Bank. Even though planning permission was granted after an appeal hearing for the extension, the tunnel element of the project was later abandoned by the newly formed state agency Irish Water. In 2015, another controversy erupted when Dublin Port Company applied to the Environmental Protection Agency (EPA) for a licence to dump a large amount of dredged sand from the shipping channel in a long-established disposal site near the Burford Bank about 15km from the port. This dredging operation was required as part of the permitted redevelopment of the Alexandra Basin area of the port, as the size of modern shipping now requires depths of up to 10m at low water. Both Dublin Port and Dún

A cruise ship turning into its berth in Dublin Port
(Richard Nairn)

Laoghaire Harbour were proposing to deepen their navigations in rival bids to capture more business from larger vessels, including the lucrative cruise ships. An Taisce voiced concern over this application in a submission to the EPA asking that the cumulative effects of both dredging and dumping schemes be examined. Both schemes received planning permission but there are significant limits placed on the size of the vessels that may enter Dún Laoghaire Harbour. Despite the fact that the material to be dredged and moved to the outer bay is mainly clean sand, similar to that already on the dump site, it appears that any proposal for development in the bay must now run a gauntlet of media misinformation and public protest.

Among the most vigilant organisations in the bay are the various residents' associations from Howth to Dalkey, numerous recreational clubs and associations representing water sports and activities such as sailing, rowing, kitesurfing, angling, sub-aqua diving, and conservation bodies like BirdWatch Ireland, Coastwatch and An Taisce. A multiplicity of official bodies, each with its own agenda, also has an interest in Dublin Bay. The major ones are three coastal local authorities, Dublin Port Company, Dún Laoghaire Harbour Company, the Electricity Supply Board, Irish Water, Irish Rail and a wide range of government departments. To get a voluntary consensus on any one issue between the actors in this cast of interested parties is a difficult task.

Who will manage the bay?

Internationally, the process of reaching consensus between all the disparate interests in a section of coastline is widely known as Integrated Coastal Zone Management (ICZM). These challenges have been tackled in many other countries by setting up a co-ordinating body that has some teeth. This requires not only legislation but a commitment by government to dedicate funding and professional staff to achieve any meaningful results. In Ireland, ICZM has been characterised by much talk and research over many decades, but there has been little action to change the status quo. As long ago as 1997, the government commissioned consultants Brady Shipman Martin to prepare a Coastal Zone Management Policy for Ireland.[15] This resulted in a short-lived ICZM unit in a government department, but little action on the ground. As sea level rises and increased storm surges put pressure on the coastal zone, there is less room for manoeuvre. Time is running out for action to adapt to the real and imminent threats from climate change.

In 2002 the Heritage Council commissioned a review of ICZM in Ireland.[16] National case studies from the UK, Norway, New Zealand and Australia were selected for specific review for comparison against the status of ICZM in Ireland. Coastal management in Ireland is characterised by a sectoral approach to resource exploitation and management. Among these activities are shipping, fishing, aquaculture, oil and gas exploitation, aggregate and mineral extraction, conservation, tourism and dumping. Unless decision-makers facilitate the development and implementation of an integrated management strategy for the coastal area, by adopting a broad perspective and a multi-sectoral approach, the policies that prevail will continue to be driven by sectoral interests. This will place sustainable development of the coast beyond the reach of current and future generations. In order to promote sustainable development of its marine environments, including its coastal zones, the European Commission adopted in 2014 a proposal for a Directive establishing a framework for maritime spatial planning (MSP) and integrated coastal management (ICM) consistent with the principles and elements of the Barcelona Convention on ICZM, ratified by the EU in 2010. While elements of the proposed earlier EU legislation have now been adopted as a Directive for MSP, the ICM elements have been dropped. The eye has been taken off the ball by the preoccupation of the EU and the Irish government with a less controversial MSP approach, as part of the push to exploit marine resources (oil and gas, renewable energies, fish populations and seabed minerals). This raises the key question: how and by whom is future planning for Ireland's coasts being developed?

Dublin Bay Biosphere logo

Dublin Bay Biosphere

One ray of hope for Dublin Bay comes not from the European Union but from the United Nations. UNESCO, the global organisation that

Walking the cliff path at Howth Head *(John Fox)*

stands for educational, scientific and cultural values, recognised in 2015 that Dublin Bay is a 'Biosphere'. In ecological terms, the biosphere is the global ecological system integrating all living beings and their relationships, including their interaction with the physical environment. If this complicated definition is to be appropriate to Dublin Bay it is worth considering how UNESCO came to use the term 'biosphere'. Launched in 1971, the Man and the Biosphere Programme (MAB) is an intergovernmental scientific programme that aims to establish a scientific basis for improving relationships between people and their environments. Still in place over four decades later, MAB combines the natural and social sciences, economics and education to improve human livelihoods and the equitable sharing of benefits, and to safeguard natural and managed ecosystems, thus promoting innovative approaches to economic development that are socially and culturally appropriate, and environmentally sustainable. The programme for the Biosphere includes contributing to the Climate Change Action Plans for the Dublin Local Authorities, a co-ordinated approach across the four Dublin local authorities. The Biosphere Partnership has joined in a UCD-led consortium that is undertaking research to address faecal contamination of rivers and bathing waters and assess the impact of climate change-driven effects on water pollution in the bay. A project has been organised with the Dogs Trust on managing the impacts of dogs on biodiversity at Bull Island. The Biosphere team is also working with community groups, such as Comhairle na nÓg, to raise awareness of the bay among young people who will be the responsible adults of the future.

Improving relationships between people and their environment has already started; there is much greater awareness of the importance of the bay in the lives of ordinary people. An opinion survey in 2014 on what the natural environment means to local people found that Bull Island was recognised as a Biosphere reserve by 49 per cent of Dubliners, while only 7 per cent of respondents recognised the term 'Natura 2000', the title of the EU Commission network of international conservation areas.[17] Awareness of the issues is a prerequisite for political support to protect natural areas, which normally requires finance and staff resources at a local authority or national level. This awareness of the key role of Dublin Bay in the life of the city has started with the Biosphere managers interacting with local communities. Inviting local people to become involved with the management and protection of the shorelines is a valuable investment for the future. This could include volunteer schemes such as wardening the more natural core areas to protect sensitive wildlife such as roosting birds, breeding hares or seals from uncontrolled dogs or unnecessary disturbance. If local community groups such as residents' associations, youth groups, school classes and business organisations get directly involved in practical action it will generate a core of committed individuals to deal with the bigger threats of climate change that require coordinated action to save vital infrastructure and the homes of ordinary people.

A glimpse into the future

Nobody can say exactly how the bay will change over the coming century, with so many variables, from climate change and economic fluctuations to political priorities and frequently changing public opinion. Given the importance of Dublin Bay in the lives of local residents (see Chapter 11), there is a surprising lack of awareness of the threats posed by climate change in the near future. As thousands of people across the globe march in rallies calling for action on climate change and the effects of global warming become increasingly obvious, most Irish people seem to be living either in ignorance or in denial of these issues. Given our increasing knowledge about climate change, why do so many fail to take

People enjoying the East Pier in Dún Laoghaire *(Richard Nairn)*

action or even to show any interest in the subject? The author George Marshall argues that we have failed to engage the emotional side of our minds with this issue and that, if our personal happiness depended on it, we would all back positive action to respond to climate change.[18] If we continue to ignore the issue we will be very unhappy indeed! Naomi Klein is more blunt in her contention that we continue to avoid meaningful actions to lower emissions because such requirements are 'extremely threatening to an elite minority that has a stranglehold over our economy, our political process, and most of our media outlets'.[19] Perhaps it takes several large dramatic events or disasters, such as the flooding that occurred in Sandymount in January 2014, to shake people out of their apathy and produce some action from public representatives.

The setting-up in 2016 of a new governance for the environment, in the form of the Department of Communications, Climate Action and the Environment (DoCCAE) is a step in the right direction, but, again, not without its administrative problems. This is complemented by the formation of the National Climate Council and the National Risks and Adaptation Committee, together developing policies and planning for climate warming under Ireland's new Climate Act (2015). But urgent actions are required *now* rather than waiting for these organisations to deliberate further.

Future proposals for development in the bay, from dredging and wind farms to shoreline protection and port development, will all need to be 'climate-proofed', a process to ensure that any new structures are sustainable in the long term, given the certainty of rising sea levels, increased storminess and repeated coastal flooding. 'Climate-smart' conservation measures will also be needed to protect and restore some of the most valuable natural features.[20] New techniques of proactive management, such as dune creation and managed realignment of the coastline, will have to replace the existing policy of 'do nothing' or the habitats will be squeezed between rising sea levels and the hard coastal defences.

Considering the strategic national importance of the bay, a strong and well-staffed partnership will be needed to co-ordinate all the agencies involved in coastal development and managing recreational pressures on the natural environment. This could evolve through the new Dublin Bay Biosphere Partnership, launched in 2015, as this was the first time that national and local government, together with Dublin Port Company, sought to collaborate in protecting the bay. This partnership should also develop both monitoring programmes and long-term strategies that will guide other policies and key decisions

A container ship enters Dublin Port watched by sea anglers around the Poolbeg Lighthouse. Howth Head is in the background. *(John Fox)*

in the area, such as local authority development plans and port master plans. Achieving public support and confidence in these strategies will be vital if they are to progress beyond paper proposals.

The many faces of Dublin Bay

One of the best locations to appreciate the importance of Dublin Bay is the Great South Wall that guards the southern entrance to the port. On a fine summer's evening, you can walk out along the 3km of sea wall on the granite blocks that have survived centuries of storms here. The decision to build the wall was taken three centuries ago and the early structures were stabilised by driving wooden stakes into the sandbanks at low tide. Today, the piping calls of oystercatchers drift in from the edge of the tide on the huge sandflats of Sandymount Strand, and you may be lucky enough to see the fin of a porpoise rising from the waters. Kitesurfers are visible on the north side of the bay at Dollymount Strand, with lines of sea anglers around the lighthouse and great flocks of white-sailed yachts outside Dún Laoghaire Harbour on the south side.

A steady stream of ships – giant ferries, container ships and cruise vessels – enters and leaves the Liffey estuary where the Vikings arrived in their wooden longships a thousand years before. Reaching the iconic red Poolbeg Lighthouse, you are in the centre of the bay, with Howth Head and Dalkey Island clearly visible on either side. Looking back to the west, the whole vista of Dublin city comes into view, backed by the familiar Dublin mountains and the Sugarloaf peak in Wicklow. This is a good place to contemplate how Dublin Bay, celebrated a century ago by one of our most famous writers, James Joyce, might look in another hundred years.

Nature and history have combined to mould Dublin Bay into the key resource that we enjoy and ultimately depend upon. There are many threats to this resource, but only some of these can be managed or mitigated. Throughout its long and chequered history the natural ecosystem of the bay has shown remarkable resilience. While it is not pristine, it is still in reasonably good shape. Dublin Bay faces an uncertain future. In making decisions about its management we should learn from the mistakes of the past and the lessons that nature and history teach us. At the heart of policy should be the objective, 'Do not knowingly damage the Biosphere'. We have choices to make about the future and we should face them before they are made for us.

Appendix: Scientific names of species mentioned in the text

Common Name Scientific name

Alcyonacean *Alcyonium glomeratum*
Alder *Alnus glutinosa*
Arctic Skua *Stercorarius parasiticus*
Arctic tern *Sterna paradisaea*
Ash *Fraxinus excelsior*
Atlantic salmon *Salmo salar*

Baltic tellin *Macoma balthica*
Bar-tailed Godwit *Limosa lapponica*
Barn swallow *Hirunda rustica*
Barnacle goose *Branta leucopsis*
Barrel jellyfish *Rhizostoma octopus*
Bass *Dicentrarchus labrax*
Beadlet anemone *Actinia equina*
Beaver *Castor fiber*
Bell heather *Erica cinerea*
Betony *Stachys officinalis*
Birch *Betula pubescens*
Bird's-foot *Ornithopus perpusillus*
Black guillemot *Cepphus grylle*
Black redstart *Phoenicurus ochruros*
Black tern *Chlidonias niger*
Black-headed gull *Chroicocephalus ridibundus*
Black-legged kittiwake *Rissa tridactyla*
Black-tailed godwit *Limosa limosa*
Black-throated Diver *Gavia arctica*
Blackbird *Turdus merula*

Blackthorn *Prunus spinosa*
Bladder wrack *Fucus vesiculosus*
Blonde ray *Raja brachyura*
Bloody cranesbill *Geranium sanguineum*
Blue mussel *Mytilus edulis*
Borrer's saltmarsh grass *Puccinellia fasciculata*
Bottlenose dolphin *Tursiops truncatus*
Bristleworm *Scoloplos armige*
Brown bear *Ursus arctos*
Brown crab *Cancer pagurus*
Brown rat *Rattus norvegicus*

Channel wrack *Pelvetia canaliculata*
Coalfish (saithe) *Pollachius virens*
Cockle *Cerastoderma edule*
Cod *Gadus morhua*
Common broom *Cytisus scoparius ssp. maritimus*
Common European limpet *Patella vulgata*
Common goldeneye *Bucephala clangula*
Common guillemot *Uria aalge*
Common gull *Larus canus*
Common kestrel *Falco tinnunculus*
Common pochard *Aythya ferina*
Common redshank *Tringa totanus*
Common Scoter *Melanitta nigra*
Common shelduck *Tadorna tadorna*
Common snipe *Gallinago gallinago*

Appendix: Scientific names of species mentioned in the text

Common starling *Sturnus vulgaris*
Common teal *Anas crecca*
Common tern *Sterna hirundo*
Common woodlouse *Armadillidium
    vulgare*
Compass jellyfish *Chrysaora hysoscella*
Cordgrass *Spartina anglica*
Cuckoo ray *Raja naevus*
Curlew *Numenius arquata*
Curlew sandpiper *Calidris ferruginea*

Dab *Limanda limanda*
Devil's-bit scabious *Succisa pratensis*
Dog whelk *Nucella lapillus*
Dove's-foot cranesbill *Geranium molle*
Dublin Bay prawn *Nephrops norvegicus*
Dunlin *Calidris alpina*

Early forget-me-not *Myosotis
    ramosissima*
Eelgrass *Zostera noltii*
European curlew *Numenius arquata*
European golden plover *Pluvialis
    apricaria*
European gorse *Ulex europeus*
European herring gull *Larus argentatus*
European shag *Phalacrocorax aristotelis*

Feral (wild) goat *Capra hircus*
Feral pigeon *Columba livia*
Flounder *Platichthys flesus*
Fulmar *Fulmaris glacialis*

Glasswort *Salicornia europea*
Glaucous gull *Larus hyperboreus*
Goosander *Mergus merganser*
Great black-backed gull *Larus marinus*
Great cormorant *Phalacrocorax carbo*
Great crested grebe *Podiceps cristatus*
Great northern diver *Gavia immer*
Great ringed plover *Charadrius hiaticula*
Great spotted woodpecker *Dendrocopos
    major*
Greater scaup *Aythya marila*

Greater sea-spurrey *Spergularia media*
Green crab (shore crab) *Carcinus maenas*
Green-winged orchid *Orchis morio*
Grey gurnard *Eutrigla gurnardus*
Grey seal *Halichoerus grypus*
Grey heron *Ardea cinerea*
Grey thick-lipped mullet *Chelon labrosus*
Gut weed *Enteromorpha intestinalis*

Haddock *Melanogrammus aeglefinus*
Hairy violet *Viola hirta*
Hairy woodlouse *Eluma purpurascens*
Harbour porpoise *Phocoena phocoena*
Harbour seal *Phoca vitulina*
Hazel *Corylus avellana*
Heather (ling) *Calluna vulgaris*
Herring *Clupea harengus*
Horse mussel *Modiolus modiolus*
House martin *Delichon urbicum*
House mouse *Mus musculus*
Hoverfly *Sphaerophoria batava*
Humpback whale *Megaptera
    novaeangliae*

Iceland gull *Larus glaucoides*

Knotted wrack *Ascophyllum nodosum*

Laver spire shell *Hydrobia ulvae*
Lesser sandeel *Ammodytes tobianus*
Lesser-spotted dogfish *Scyliorhinus
    caniculus*
Little stint *Calidris minuta*
Little tern *Sternula albifrons*
Lobster *Homarus gammarus*
Long-tailed field mouse *Apodemus
    sylvaticus*
Lugworm *Arenicola marina*
Lyme grass *Leymus arenarius*

Mackerel *Scomber scombrus*
Magpie *Pica pica*
Mallard *Anas platyrhynchos*
Marram grass *Ammophila arenaria*

Marsh fritillary *Euphydryas aurinia*
Marsh harrier *Circus aeruginosus*
Marsh helleborine *Epipactis palustris*
Meadow pipit *Anthus pratensis*
Mediterranean gull *Larus melanocephalus*
Merlin *Falco columbarius*
Minke whale *Balaenoptera acutorostrata*
Moon jellyfish *Aurelia aurita*
Moss carder bumblebee *Bombus muscorum*
Mountain (Irish) hare *Lepus timidus hibernicus*

Native oyster *Ostrea edulis*
Nilsson's pipefish *Syngnathus rostellatus*
Northern gannet *Morus bassanus*
Northern pintail *Anus acuta*
Northern shoveler *Anas clypeata*

Osprey *Pandion haliaetus*
Otter *Lutra lutra*
Oystercatcher *Haematopus ostralegus*

Pale-bellied brent goose *Branta bernicla hrota*
Peppery furrow shell *Scrobicularia plana*
Peregrine *Falco peregrinus*
Periwinkle *Littorina saxatilis*
Plaice *Pleuronectes platessa*
Pollack *Pollachius pollachius*
Portuguese man o' war *Physalia physalis*
Purple sandpiper *Calidris maritima*

Rabbit *Oryctolagus cuniculus*
Ragworm *Hediste diversicolor*
Razorbill *Alca torda*
Razorshell *Ensis ensis*
Red fescue *Festuca rubra*
Red gurnard *Chelidonichthys cuculus*
Red knot *Calidris canuta*
Red squirrel *Sqiurus vulgaris*
Red-breasted merganser *Mergus serrator*
Red-tailed bumblebee *Bombus lapidarius*

Red-throated diver *Gavia arctica*
Ring-billed gull *Larus delawarensis*
Roseate tern *Sterna dougallii*

Saltmarsh grass *Puccinellia maritima*
Saltmarsh rush *Juncus gerardi*
Sand couch grass *Elytrigia juncea*
Sand goby *Pomatoschistus minutus*
Sand mason worm *Lanice chonchilega*
Sand smelt *Osmerus eperlanus*
Sandeel *Ammodytes marinus*
Sanderling *Calidris alba*
Scaldfish *Arnoglossus laterna*
Sea arrowgrass *Triglocin maritima*
Sea buckthorn *Hippophae rhamnoides*
Sea campion *Silene uniflora*
Sea club-rush *Scirpus maritimus*
Sea lavender *Limonium humile*
Sea lettuce *Ulva latissima*
Sea lettuce *Ulva lactuca*
Sea milkwort *Glaux maritima*
Sea pink/sea thrift *Armeria maritima*
Sea plantain *Plantago maritima*
Sea purslane *Halimione portulacoides*
Sea rocket *Cakile maritima*
Sea rush *Juncus maritimus*
Sea sandwort *Honkenya peploides*
Sea trout *Salmo trutta*
Sea-clubrush *Scirpus maritimus*
Serrated wrack *Fucus serratus*
Sheep's bit *Jasione montana*
Shipworm *Toredo navalis*
Shore crab (green crab) *Carcinus maenas*
Short-eared owl *Asio flammeus*
Skylark *Alauda arvensis*
Slavonian grebe *Podiceps auritus*
Smooth-hound *Mustelus mustelus*
Snow bunting *Plectrophenax nivalis*
Song thrush *Turdus philomelos*
Spider crab *Hyas araneus*
Spider-hunting wasp *Pompilus cinereus*
Spiral wrack *Fucus spiralis*
Spotted (Homelyn) ray *Raja montagui*

Appendix: Scientific names of species mentioned in the text

Sprat *Sprattus sprattus*
Spring squill *Scilla verna*
Spurdog *Squalus acanthias*

Thin tellin shell *Tellina tenuis*
Thornback ray (roker) *Raja clavata*
Tufted duck *Anthya fuligula*

Velvet crab *Necora puber*

Western gorse (autumn gorse) *Ulex gallii*
Whelk *Buccinium undatum*

White satin moth *Leucoma salicis*
White-tailed sea eagle *Haliaeetus albicilla*
Whiting *Merlangius merlangus*
Wigeon *Anas penelope*
Wild boar *Sus scrofa*
Wild madder *Rubia perigrina*
Willow *Salix* sp.
Wolf *Canis lupus*
Woodcock *Scolopax rusticola*

Yorkshire fog *Holcus lanatus*

References

Chapter 1: Introduction

1.   Carson, R. (1955) *The Edge of the Sea*. Boston, MA: Houghton Mifflin.
2.   Foster, J.W. (ed.) (1997) *Nature in Ireland: A Scientific and Cultural History*. Dublin: Lilliput Press.

Chapter 2: The Coastal Environment

1.   Mansfield, M.J. (1992) 'Field studies of currents and dispersion', Technical Report 3, *Dublin Bay Water Quality Management Plan*. Dublin Corporation.
2.   Nolan, S.C. (1985) 'Carboniferous Geology of the Dublin Area'. Unpublished master's thesis, Trinity College Dublin.
3.   Naylor, D.F. (1965) 'Pleistocene and post-pleistocene sediments in Dublin Bay', *Scientific Proceedings of the Royal Dublin Society*, Series A, Vol. 2, 175–88.
4.   Farrington, A. (1929) 'The pre-glacial topography of the Liffey Basin', *Proceedings of the Royal Irish Academy* 38B, 148–70.
5.   Rhein, M., Rintoul, S.R., Aoki, S., Campos, E., Chambers, D., Feely, R.A., Gulev, S., Johnson, G.C., Josey, S.A., Kostianoy, A., Mauritzen, C., Roemmich, D., Talley, L.D. and Wang, F. (2013) 'Observations: Ocean' in Stocker, T.F., Qin, D., Plattner, G.-K., Tignor, M., Allen, S.K., Boschung, J., Nauels, A., Xia, Y., Bex, V. and Midgley, P.M. (eds), *Climate Change 2013: The Physical Science Basis*. Contribution of Working Group I to the Fifth Assessment Report of the Intergovernmental Panel on Climate Change. Cambridge UK and New York: Cambridge University Press.
6.   Gleeson, E., McGrath, R. & Treanor, M. (eds) (2013) *Ireland's Climate: The Road Ahead*. Dublin: Met Éireann.
7.   Costanza, R., D'Arge, R., de Groot, R., Farber, S., Grasso, M., Hannon, B., Limburg, K.,Naeem, S., O'Neil, R.V., Paruelo, J., Raskin, R.G., Sutton, P. and van den Belt, M. (1997) 'The value of the world's ecosystem services and natural capital', *Nature* 387, 253–60.

Chapter 3: Marine Life

1.   Hardy, A. (1956) *The Open Sea: Its Natural History*. New Naturalist Series. London. Collins.
2.   Gowen, R.J. and Bloomfield, S.P. (1996) 'Chlorophyll standing crop and phytoplankton production in the western Irish Sea during 1992 and 1993', *Journal of Plankton Research* 18, 1735–51.
3.   Hillis, J.P. (1974) 'Field observations on larvae of the Dublin Bay prawn *Nephrops norvegicus* (L.) in the Western Irish Sea', *Irish Fisheries Investigations Series B (Marine)*, pp. 1–25.
4.   O'Higgins, T.G. and Wilson, J.G. (2005) 'Impact of the River Liffey discharge on nutrient and chlorophyll concentrations in the Liffey estuary and Dublin Bay (Irish Sea)', *Estuarine, Coastal and Shelf Science* 64, 323–34.
5.   Dublin Corporation (1992) *Dublin Bay Water Quality Management Plan*. Technical Report No. 6: 'Studies on the benthos'. Dublin Corporation.
6.   Dublin Port Company (2014) *Alexandra Basin Redevelopment Project: Environmental Impact Statement*. Dublin: RPS.

7.   Berrow, S.D., Hickey, R., O'Brien, J., O'Connor, I. and McGrath, D. (2008) 'Harbour Porpoise Survey 2008: Report to the National Parks and Wildlife Service'. Irish Whale and Dolphin Group.

8.   Carson, R.L. (1951) *The Sea Around Us.* London: Staples Press.

Chapter 4: Shorelines

1.   Brafield, A.E. (1978) *Life in Sandy Shores.* Institute of Biology Studies in Biology no. 89. London: Edward Arnold.

2.   Nichols, A. R. (1899) 'A list of the marine mollusca of Ireland', *Proceedings of the Royal Irish Academy* 5, 477–662.

3.   Southern, R. (1910) 'The marine worms (*Annelida*) of Dublin Bay and the adjoining district', *Proceedings of the Royal Irish Academy* 28, B(6), 215–46.

4.   West, A.B. (1977) 'The Fauna of the Intertidal Flats and Beach' in D.W. Jeffrey (ed.), *North Bull Island, Dublin Bay: A Modern Coastal Natural History.* Dublin: Royal Dublin Society.

5.   Wilson, J.G. (1982) 'The littoral fauna of Dublin Bay', *Irish Fisheries Investigations Series B* 26, 1–20.

6.   Roth, S. and Wilson, J.G. (1998) 'Functional analysis by trophic guilds of macrobenthic community structure in Dublin Bay, Ireland', *Journal of Experimental Marine Biology and Ecology* 222, 195–217.

7.   West, *op. cit.*

8.   Jeffrey, D.W. (1984) 'Bull Island: An Assessment of a Nature Conservation Resource' in *Nature Conservation in Ireland: Progress and Problems.* Dublin: Royal Irish Academy.

9.   Adeney, W.E. (1908) 'Effect of the New Drainage on Dublin Harbour' in *Handbook of the Dublin District British Association*, pp. 387–8. Dublin.

10. Jeffrey, D.W., Brennan M.T., Jennings E., Madden B. and Wilson J.G. (1995) 'Nutrient sources for in-shore nuisance algae: the Dublin Bay case', *Ophelia* 42, 147–61.

11. Pitkin, P.H. (1977) 'Distribution and Biology of Algae' in D.W. Jeffrey (ed.), *North Bull Island, Dublin Bay: A Modern Coastal Natural History.* Dublin: Royal Dublin Society.

12. Jeffrey, D.W., Madden, B. and Rafferty, B. (1993) 'Beach fouling by *Ectocarpus siliculosus* in Dublin Bay', *Marine Pollution Bulletin* 26, 51–3.

13. Jennings, E. (1991) 'The Seasonal Biomass and Nitrogen and Phosphorus Turnover of the Seagrass *Zostera noltii*', BAMod thesis, Botany Department, Trinity College Dublin.

14. Madden, B. (1984) 'The Nitrogen and Phosphorus Turnover of the *Salicornia* Flat at Bull Island, Dublin Bay', BAMod thesis, Botany Department, Trinity College Dublin.

15. Boyle, P.J. (1977) '*Spartina* on Bull Island' in Jeffery, D.W. (ed.), *North Bull Island, Dublin Bay: A Modern Coastal Natural History.* Dublin: Royal Dublin Society.

16. McCorry, M.J. (2001) 'The Ecological Effects of *Spartina anglica* and its Control on the Mudflats and Saltmarsh at Bull Island, Dublin Bay', PhD thesis, National University of Ireland.

17. McCorry, M.J. and Otte, M.L. (2000) 'Ecological effects of *Spartina anglica* on the macro-invertebrate infauna of the mud flats at Bull Island, Dublin Bay, Ireland', *Web Ecology* 2, 71–3.

18. Crowley, M. 2003. 'Variations in the size-class and micro-habitat of the blue mussel *Mytilus edulis* and the effects on associated faunal assemblages.' Unpublished BSc Thesis. University College Dublin.

19. Keenan, E. 2008. 'The effect of coastal urban structures on selected species on rocky shores.' Unpublished BSc Thesis. University College Dublin.

20. Firth, L.B., Thompson, R.C., Bohn, K., Abbiati, M., Airoldi, L., Bouma, T.J., Bozzeda, F., Ceccherelli, V.U., Colangelo, M.A., Evans, A., Ferrario, F., Hanley, M.E., Hinz, H., Hoggart, S.P.G., Jackson, J.E., Moore, P., Morgan, E.H., Perkol-Finkel, S., Skov., M.W., Strain, E.M., van Belzen, J. and Hawkins, S.J. (2014) 'Between a rock and a

hard place: environmental and engineering considerations when designing coastal defence structures', *Coastal Engineering* 87, 122–35. Additional information sourced from Aberystwyth University website.

21. Healy, B. (1977) 'The Bull Wall' in D.W. Jeffrey (ed.), *North Bull Island, Dublin: A Modern Coastal Natural History*. Dublin: Royal Dublin Society.

Chapter 5: Coastlands

1. Curtis, T.G.F. (1991) 'A Site Inventory of the Sandy Coasts of Ireland' in M.B. Quigley (ed.), *A Guide to the Sand Dunes of Ireland*. Galway: European Union for Dune Conservation and Coastal Management.

2. Fay, P. (1986) 'The Sand Dune Succession on Bull Island, Dublin Bay, with Emphasis on Nitrogen Nutrition', BA thesis, Trinity College Dublin.

3. Fay, P. (1992) 'On the Nitrogen Cycle in Young Sand Dunes', PhD thesis, Trinity College Dublin.

4. Moore, J.J. (1977) 'Vegetation of the Dune Complex' in D.W. Jeffrey, *North Bull Island, Dublin Bay: A Modern Coastal Natural History*. Dublin: Royal Dublin Society.

5. Devaney, F. (2008) 'The Alder Marsh: Ecohydrology and Restoration Prospects of a Desiccating Dune Slack', PhD thesis, University College Dublin.

6. Willis, A.J. (1963) 'Braunton Burrows: the effects on the vegetation of the addition of mineral nutrients to the dune soils', *Journal of Ecology* 51, 353–74.

7. Fay, P. (1992) 'On the Nitrogen Cycle in Young Sand Dunes', PhD thesis, Trinity College Dublin.

8. Fay, P.J and Jeffrey, D.W. (1995) 'The Nitrogen Cycle in Sand-dunes' in D.W. Jeffrey, M.B. Jones and J.H. McAdam (eds), *Irish Grasslands: Their Biology and Management*, Dublin: Royal Irish Academy, pp. 151–66.

9. Speight, M.C.D. (1977) 'Invertebrates of the Dunes and Grassland' in D.W. Jeffrey (ed.), *North Bull Island, Dublin Bay: A Modern Coastal Natural History*. Dublin: Royal Dublin Society.

10. McCorry, M. and Ryle, T. (2009) *A Management Plan for Bull Island. Dublin: Dublin City Council.*

11. Fitzpatrick, Ú., Murray, T.E., Byrne, A., Paxton R.J. and Brown, M.J.F. (2006) *Regional Red List of Irish Bees*. Dublin: Higher Education Authority.

12. O'Rourke, A. (2014) 'Conservation of Fixed Dune Pollinators: An Investigation into Key Forage Resources and Landscape Requirements', MSc thesis, Trinity College Dublin.

13. Praeger, R.L. (1937) *The Way that I Went*. Dublin: Hodges Figgis.

14. O'Mahony, E. (1935) 'The North Bull house mouse', *Irish Naturalists' Journal* 5, 291.

15. Fairley, J.S. (1971) 'A critical reappraisal of the status in Ireland of the eastern house mouse, *Mus musculus orientalis* Cretzchmar', *Irish Naturalists' Journal* 17, 2–5.

16. Pearson, P. (1998) *Between the Mountains and the Sea: Dún Laoghaire-Rathdown County*. Dublin: O'Brien Press.

17. Liversage, G.D. (1968) 'Excavations at Dalkey Island, Co. Dublin, 1956–59', *Proceedings of the Royal Irish Academy* 66C, 53–233.

18. *Dalkey Islands Conservation Plan 2013–2023*. Dún Laoghaire-Rathdown County Council.

Chapter 6: Birds

1. Cabot, D. and Nisbet, I. (2014) *Terns*. London: HarperCollins.

2. Nairn, R. (2005) *Ireland's Coastline: Exploring its Nature and Heritage*. Cork: The Collins Press.

3. Rutty, J. (1772) *Essay towards a Natural History of the County of Dublin*. Dublin.

4. Thompson, W. (1849–51) *The Natural History of Ireland*. London: Reeves.

5. Watters, J.J. (1853) *The Natural History of the Birds of Ireland*. Dublin and London.

6. Ledbetter, G.T. (2010) *Privilege and Poverty: The Life and Times of Irish Painter and Naturalist Alexander Williams RHA (1846–1930)*. Cork: The Collins Press.

7. Hutchinson, C.D. (1975) *The Birds of Dublin and Wicklow*. Dublin: Irish Wildbird Conservancy.

8. Nairn, R. (2014) 'Alexander Williams: a forgotten Dublin ornithologist', *Irish Birds* 9, 59–62.

9. Williams, A. (1908) 'Bird life in Dublin Bay: the passing of Clontarf Island', *Irish Naturalist* 17, 165–71.

10. Blake-Knox, H. (1866) 'The migratory and wandering birds of the County Dublin with the times of their arrival and departure', *Zoologist* 24, 220–7, 295–307, 479–83.

11. Barrington, R.M. (1900) *The Migrations of Birds as Observed at Irish Lighthouses and Lightships*. Dublin and London.

12. Barrington, R.M. (1908) 'Birds', in *Handbook to the City of Dublin and the Surrounding District*. Dublin: British Association, pp. 113–19.

13. Kennedy, P.G. (1953). *An Irish Sanctuary: Birds of the North Bull*. Dublin.

14. Hutchinson, C.D. (1979) *Ireland's Wetlands and their Birds*. Dublin: Irish Wildbird Conservancy.

15. Hutchinson, C.D. and Keys, J.M. (1973) 'The Numbers of Wildfowl on the Bull Island, Co. Dublin', in *Irish Bird Report 1972*. Irish Wildbird Conservancy, pp. 35–43.

16. Hutchinson, C.D. (1975) *The Birds of Dublin and Wicklow*. Dublin. Irish Wildbird Conservancy.

17. Jeffrey, J.W. (ed.) (1977) *North Bull Island, Dublin Bay: A Modern Coastal Natural History*. Dublin: Royal Dublin Society.

18. Brunton, M., Convery, F.J. and Johnson, A. (eds) (1987) *Managing Dublin Bay*. Dublin: Resource and Environmental Policy Centre, University College Dublin.

19. Ó Briain, M. (1987) 'The Waterfowl of Dublin Bay' in M. Brunton, F.J. Convery and A. Johnson (eds), *Managing Dublin Bay*. Dublin: Resource and Environmental Policy Centre, University College Dublin.

20. Crowe, O. (2006) 'A Review of the Wintering Waterbirds of Dublin Bay 1994/95 – 2003/04' in BirdWatch Ireland, *Irish East Coast Bird Report 2002*. Kilcoole, Co. Wicklow.

21. Boland, H. and Crowe, O. (2012) *Irish Wetland Bird Survey: Waterbird Status and Distribution 2001/02 to 2008/09*. Kilcoole, Co. Wicklow: BirdWatch Ireland.

22. Crowe, O., Boland, H. and Walsh, A. (2012) 'Irish Wetland Bird Survey: results of waterbird monitoring in Ireland in 2010/11', *Irish Birds* 9, 397–410.

23. Tierney, N., Whelan, R., Boland, H. and Crowe, O. (2017) *Dublin Bay Birds Project Synthesis 2013–2016*. Kilcoole, Co. Wicklow: BirdWatch Ireland.

24. Ó Briain, M., Carruthers, T.D. and Sheridan, V. (1986) 'Transitory staging of Brent Goose in Ireland', *Irish Birds* 32, 286.

25. Ó Briain, M. (1991) 'Use of a *Zostera* bed in Dublin Bay by Light-bellied Brent Geese, 1981/82 to 1990/91', *Irish Birds* 4, 299–316.

26. Ó Briain, M. and Healy, B. (1991) 'Winter distribution of Light-bellied Brent Geese *Branta bernicla hrota* in Ireland', *Ardea* 79, 317–26.

27. Benson, L. (2009) 'Use of inland feeding sites by Light-bellied Brent Geese in Dublin 2008–2009: a new conservation concern?', *Irish Birds* 8, 563–70.

28. Hutchinson, C.D. and Rochford, J.M. (1974) 'The Numbers of Waders on the Bull Island, Co Dublin' in *Irish Bird Report 1973*. Dublin: Irish Wildbird Conservancy.

29. Grant, J. D. (1982) 'A Study of the Winter Feeding Ecology of Common Wading Birds of the Bull Island, Dublin Bay', BSc thesis, University College Dublin.

30. Quinn, J.L. and Kirby, J.S. (1993) 'Oystercatchers feeding on grassland and sand flats in Dublin Bay', *Irish Birds* 5, 35–44.

31. Quinn, J.L. (1988) 'The Ecology of Oystercatchers on Estuaries and Grasslands in Dublin Bay', BSc thesis, University College Dublin.

32. Tierney *et al.* (2017) *op.cit.*

33. Phalan, B. and Nairn, R.G.W. (2007) 'Disturbance to waterbirds in South Dublin Bay', *Irish Birds* 8, 223–30.

34. Mathers, R.G., Watson, S., Stone, R. and Montgomery, W.I. (2000) 'A study of the impact of human disturbance on Wigeon *Anas Penelope* and Brent Geese *Branta bernicla hrota* on an Irish sea loch', *Wildfowl* 51, 67–81.

35. Burton, N.H.K., Evans, P.R. and Robinson, M.A. (1996) 'Effects on shorebird numbers of disturbance, the loss of a roost site and its replacement by an artificial island at Hartlepool, Cleveland', *Biological Conservation* 77, 193–201.

36. Fox, J. (2014) 'The Effects of Recreational Activity on the Low Tide Feeding Ecology of Oystercatchers (*Haematopus ostralegus*) on the sand flats, at Poolbeg , Dublin Bay, Dublin', unpublished field ecology thesis, University College Cork.

37. Merne, O.J., Madden, B., Archer, E. and Porter, B. (2009) Abundance of non-breeding gulls in Dublin Bay, 2006–2007', *Irish Birds* 8, 549–62.

38. Merne, O.J. and Madden, B. (2000) 'Breeding seabirds of Ireland's Eye, Co. Dublin', *Irish Birds* 6, 495–506.

39. Newton, S., Lewis, L. and Trewby, M. (2015) 'Results of a Breeding Survey of Important Cliff-nesting Seabird Colonies in Ireland 2015'. BirdWatch Ireland Report commissioned by the National Parks & Wildlife Service, 72pp.

40. Newton, S.F., Harris, M. and Murray, S. (2015) 'Census of Gannet *Morus bassanus* colonies in Ireland in 2013–2014', *Irish Birds* 10, 215–20.

41. Nairn, R. (2005) *op. cit.*

42. Tierney, N. (2014) 'Importance of Sandymount Strand in Dublin Bay as a post-breeding tern roost', *Irish Birds* 10, 124.

43. Tierney, N., Whelan, R. and Valentin, A. (2016) Post-breeding aggregations of roosting terns in South Dublin Bay in late summer. *Irish Birds* 10, 339–344.

44. Merne, O.J., Madden, B., Archer, E. and Porter, B. (2008) 'Autumn roosting by terns in south Dublin Bay', *Irish Birds* 8, 335–40.

45. Newton, S.F. and Crowe, O. (1999) 'Kish Bank: A Preliminary Assessment of its Ornithological Importance', BirdWatch Ireland Conservation Report 99/8.

Chapter 7: Settlers on the Shore

1. Edwards, R. and Brooks, A. (2008) 'The Island of Ireland: Drowning the Myth of an Irish Land-bridge?', in J.L. Davenport, D.P. Sleeman and P.C. Woodman (eds), *Postglacial Colonisation Conference: Mind the Gap 2006*; *Irish Naturalists' Journal*, special supplement, 19–34.

2. *Ibid.*

3. Woodman, P.C. (1974) 'Mount Sandel Mesolithic Settlement', in T.G. Delaney (ed.), *Excavations 1973*. Belfast: Ulster Museum; and Woodman, P.C. (1985) *Excavations at Mount Sandel 1973–77*. Belfast.

4. Lamb, H.H. (1998) *Weather, Climate and Human Affairs*. London: Routledge.

5. Praeger, R. L. (1896) 'A submerged pine forest', *Irish Naturalist* 20, 155–60.

6. O'Sullivan, A. (2001) *Foragers, Farmers and Fishers in a Coastal Landscape: An Intertidal Archaeological Survey of the Shannon Estuary*, Discovery Programme Monograph 5. Dublin: Royal Irish Academy.

7. Mitchell, F. and Ryan, M. (1997) *Reading the Irish Landscape*. Dublin: Town House and Country House.

8. D'Arcy, G. (1999) *Ireland's Lost Birds*. Belfast and Dublin: Four Courts Press.

9. Edwards and Brooks, *op.cit.*

10. This text is available at Irish Archaeology's website: http://irisharchaeology. ie/2011/05/dublin-the-prehistoric-city/.

11. McQuade, M. and O'Donnell, L. (2009) 'The excavation of late Mesolithic fish trap remains from the Liffey Estuary, Dublin, Ireland', in S. McCartan, R. Scheulting, G. Warren and P. Woodman (eds), *Mesolithic Horizons*. Oxbow, pp. 889–94.

12. *Ibid.*

13. Melanie McQuade, personal comment.

14. McQuade, M. and O'Donnell, L. (2007) 'Late Mesolithic fish traps from the Liffey estuary, Dublin, Ireland', *Antiquity Journal* 81: 313.

15. McQuade, M. (2008) 'Gone fishin': an update on the discovery of evidence for 3,000 years of prehistoric trap fishing along the Liffey estuary', *Archaeology Ireland* 22: 83, 8–11.

16. Irish Archaeology, http://irisharchaeology.ie/2011/05/dublin-the-prehistoric-city/.

17. O'Sullivan, *op. cit.*

18. O'Sullivan, A. and Breen, C. (2007) *Maritime Ireland: An Archaeology of Coastal Communities*. Stroud, Gloucestershire: Tempus.

19. Liversage, G.D. (1968) 'Excavations at Dalkey Island, Co. Dublin, 1956–1959', *Proceedings of the Royal Irish Academy* 66C, 55–233.

20. Mitchell, G.F. (1956) 'An early kitchen midden at Sutton, Co. Dublin', *Journal of the Royal Society of Antiquaries in Ireland* 86, 1–26.

21. Mitchell, F. (1993) *The Way that I Followed*. Dublin: Country House.

22. Nairn, R. (2005) *op. cit.*

23. Woodman, P.C., Anderson, E. and Finlay, N. (1999) *Excavations at Ferriter's Cove, 1983–95: Last Foragers and First Farmers in the Dingle Peninsula*. Bray, Co. Wicklow.

24. Dolan, B. and Cooney, G. (2010) 'Lambay lithics: the analysis of two surface collections from Lambay, Co. Dublin', *Proceedings of the Royal Irish Academy, Section C: Archaeology, Celtic Studies, History, Linguistics, Literature* 110C, 1–33.

25. Mitchell and Ryan, *op. cit.*

26. Irish Archaeology, http://irisharchaeology.ie/2011/05/dublin-the-prehistoric-city/.

27. *Ibid.*

28. *Ibid.*

29. Melanie McQuade, personal comment.

30. O'Sullivan and Breen, *op. cit.*

31. Harrison, S.H. and Ó Floinn, R. (2014) *Viking Graves and Grave-Goods in Ireland* (*Medieval Dublin Excavations 1962–81*, Series B). Dublin: National Museum of Ireland.

32. Simpson, L. (2005) 'Viking warrior burials in Dublin: is this the longphort?', in S. Duffy (ed.) *Medieval Dublin* VI. Dublin: Four Courts Press.

33. O'Sullivan, A. (2001) *op. cit.*

34. *Dublin to 1610*, in *Irish Historic Towns Atlas*. Dublin: Royal Irish Academy.

Chapter 8: Built Landscape

1. Gilbert, J.T. (1898) *Calendar of Ancient Records of Dublin* vol. VII, pp. 30–4.

2. *Ibid.*, (1896)vol. VI, pp. 512–13; vol. VII, pp. 77–80, 84–5.

3. Until 1752 the year began on 25 March. To clarify dates, it is normal to refer to dates between 1 January and 24 March by giving both years, as with 1714/15.

4. *Ibid.*, vol. VI, pp. 516–17, 533–4.

5. McEntee, Don and Corcoran, Michael (2016) *The Rivers Dodder and Poddle*. Dublin: Dublin City Council, p. 89.

6. *Ibid.*, p. 89.

7. *Ibid.*, pp. 89–91; Cox, Ronald and Donald, Philip, 2013, *Ireland's Civil Engineering Heritage*. Cork: The Collins Press, pp. 152–3.

8. Delany, Ruth (1996) *The Grand Canal of Ireland*. Dublin: Lilliput Press, pp. 51–3.

9. De Courcy, J.W. (1996) *The Liffey in Dublin*. Dublin: Gill & Macmillan, p. 407.

10. Ball, Francis Elrington (1903) *A History of the County Dublin*, vol. 2. Dublin, p. 5.

11. *Ibid.*, p. 33.

12. Sandymount Community Services (1993) *A Social and Natural History of Sandymount, Irishtown, Ringsend*. Sandymount.

13. Hussey, M.O. (1971) 'Sandymount and the Herberts', *Dublin Historical Record*, 24 (3), 76.

14. Sandymount Community Services, *op. cit.*, p. 96.

15. British Parliamentary Papers (1834) *Second Annual Report of the Commissioners for the Extension and Improvement of Public Works in Ireland*. London.

16. Joyce, Weston St John (1939) *The Neighbourhood of Dublin*. Dublin: M.H. Gill & Son, p. 34.

17. *Ibid.*, p. 32.

18. O'Reilly, Patrick J. (1901) 'The Christian sepulchral leacs and free-standing crosses of the Dublin half-barony of Rathdown', *Journal of the Royal Society of Antiquaries of Ireland*, part 4, 31 (31 December), 386–7.

19. Rocque, John (1760) *An Actual Survey of the County of Dublin*. Dublin.

20. Lowth, C.F. (2002) 'James O'Connor, Fenian and the tragedy of 1890'. *Dublin Historical Record* 55 (2), 132–53.

21. Anon (1834) *Thirteen Views of the Dublin and Kingstown Railway*. Dublin: P. Dixon Hardy, p. 14.

22. Comments made in audience discussion after lectures; sources not known.

23. Rutty, J. (1772) *An Essay Towards a Natural History of the County of Dublin*, vol. 2. Dublin, p. 140.

24. *Statutes at Large Passed in the Parliaments Held in Ireland* (1765), vol. vii. Dublin: Boulter Grierson, p. 618.; De Courcy, J.W. (1996) *The Liffey in Dublin*. Dublin: Gill & Macmillan, p. 407.

25. Goodbody, Rob (2010) *The Metals: From Dalkey to Dún Laoghaire*. Dún Laoghaire-Rathdown County Council, p. 8.

26. British Parliamentary Papers (1823) *Abstract of the Answers and Returns ... an Act to provide for the taking of an Account of the Population of Ireland*, p. 18.

27. Goodbody, *op. cit.*, p. 54.

28. Murphy, Étain, 2003, *A Glorious Extravaganza: the History of Monkstown Parish Church*. Bray: Wordwell, pp. 47–53.

29. British Parliamentary Papers (1833) *Population Ireland, Abstract of answers and returns under the Population Acts ... enumeration 1831*, p. 20.

30. Gilligan, H.A. (1988) *A History of the Port of Dublin*. Dublin: Gill & Macmillan, pp. 110, 119–20.

31. *Ibid.*, pp. 120–1.

32. Pearson, Peter (1981) *Dun Laoghaire-Kingstown*. Dublin: O'Brien Press, pp. 74, 78.

33. Date on memorial on Marine Parade, opposite Link Road.

34. Minutes of General Purposes Committee, Dún Laoghaire Urban District Council, 11 December 1936.

35. Power, Frank, and Pearson, Peter (n.d.) *The Forty Foot: A Monument to Sea Bathing*. Dublin: Environmental Publications, p. 54.

36. *Ibid.*, pp. 36–8.

37. *Irish Builder* (1868), pp. 195, 233.

38. Dowling, Noelle and Aran O'Reilly (eds) (2002) *Mud Island: A History of Ballybough*. Allan Library FÁS Project, p. 18.

39. Broderick, David (2002) *The First Toll Roads: Ireland's Turnpike Roads 1729–1858*. Cork: The Collins Press, pp. 163–4.

40. *Statutes at large passed in the Parliaments held in Ireland*, vol. XVI, 1796, p. 367.

41. de Courcy, J.W. (1996) *The Liffey in Dublin*. Dublin: Gill & Macmillan, p. 8.

42. *Ibid.*, pp. 8–9.

43. Thom, Alex & Co. (1908, 1909) *The Post Office Dublin Directory and Calendar.*

44. Mulligan, Fergus (1983) *One Hundred and Fifty Years of Irish Railways*. Belfast: Appletree Press, pp. 86–7.

45. Delany, Ruth (1995) *The Grand Canal of Ireland*. Dublin: Lilliput Press, p. 59.

46. Corcoran, Michael (2005) *Our Good Health: A History of Dublin's Water and Drainage*. Dublin City Council, pp. 89–90.

47. Lennon, Colm (2014) *That Field of Glory: The Story of Clontarf from Battleground to Garden Suburb*. Bray: Wordwell, pp. 146–7.

48. Rutty, John (1772) *An Essay Towards a Natural History of the County of Dublin*, vol. 1. Dublin, pp. 378–9, 385.

49. Berry, Henry F. (1902) *Sir Peter Lewys, Ecclesiastical, Cathedral and Bridge Builder and His Company of Masons, 1564–7*. Margate, p. 6.

50. Lennon, *op. cit.*, p. 146.

51. Lennon, *op. cit.*, p. 166.

52. Rutty, *op. cit.*, vol. 2, p. 139.

53. Griffith, Richard (1828) *Report on the Metallic Mines of the Province of Leinster in Ireland*. Dublin, p. 24.

54. Cole, A.J. Grenville (1922) *Memoir of Localities of Minerals of Economic Importance and Metalliferous Mines in Ireland*. Geological Survey of Ireland Memoir, pp. 105–6.

55. Lennon, *op. cit,* pp. 166–7.

56. Gogarty, Claire (2013) *From Village to Suburb: The Building of Clontarf since 1760*. Dublin: Clontarf Books, p. 183.

57. Dawson, T. (1976) 'The road to Howth', *Dublin Historical Record,* 29 (4), 125.

58. Warburton, J., Whitelaw, J. and Walsh, R. (1818) *History of the City of Dublin*, vol. 2. London, pp. 1251–2.

59. Corcoran, Michael (2000) *Through Streets Broad and Narrow*. Leicester: Midland, pp. 13–14, 141.

60. Dawson, *op. cit.*, 127.

61. British Parliamentary Papers (1814–15), *Second Report of the Select Committee on Holyhead Roads*, p. 46.

62. *Report of the Commissioners of Holyhead Roads*, 21 September 1831, in British Parliamentary Papers, *Reports from Commissioners, 1831.*

63. Ball, F.E., (1917), *A History of the County Dublin, part 5, Howth and its Owners*, Dublin: reprinted 1979, Gill & Macmillan.

64. National Archives of Ireland, Office of Public Works papers, OPW/8/HOW/355.

65. Bolton, Jason, Carey, Tim, Goodbody, Rob and Clabby, Gerry (2012) *The Martello Towers of Dublin*. Dún Laoghaire-Rathdown County Council and Fingal County Council.

Chapter 9: Historical Maps

1.   Gilbert, J.T. (1891), *Calendar of Ancient Records of Dublin*, vol. II, p.168.

2.   Haliday, Charles (1881) *The Scandinavian City of Dublin*, p. 229n.

3.   Andrews, J.H. (1997) *Shapes of Ireland: Maps and their Makers, 1564–1839*. Dublin: Geography Publications, p. 137.

4.   Bonar Law, A. and Bonar Law, C. (2005) *A Contribution towards a Catalogue of the Printed Maps of Dublin City and County*, vol. 2: *Maps*. Shankill: The Neptune, p. 389; Haliday, *op.cit.*, p. 235.

5.   Petty, W. (1685) *Hibernia Deliniato*.

6.   Gilligan, H.A. (1988) *A History of the Port of Dublin*. Dublin: Gill & Macmillan, p. 14.

7.   Gilbert, J.T. (1896), *Calendar of Ancient Records of Dublin*, vol. VI, pp. 453, 542.

8.   *Ibid.*, vol. VI, pp. 485–86.

9.   de Courcy, J.W. (1996) *The Liffey in Dublin*. Dublin: Gill & Macmillan, pp. 333–4.

10. Haliday, *op. cit.*, p. 231n.

11. Gilbert, *op. cit.*, vol. VI, pp. 419–20; de Courcy, *op.cit.*, pp. 270–1.

12. Gilbert, *op. cit.*, (1898), vol. VII, pp. 30–4.

13. British Parliamentary Papers (1806) (292)(293)(294) *Accounts &c presented to the House of Commons, relating to the inland navigation of Ireland, and to the port of Dublin*, p. 93.

14. Gilbert, *op. cit.*, vol. VI, pp. 516, 533–4.

15. de Courcy, *op. cit.*, pp. 374–6.

16. Gilbert, *op. cit.*, (1902), vol. IX, pp. 225, 239, 250, 263.

17. O'Keeffe, P. and Simington, T. (2016) *Irish Stone Bridges*. 2nd edition, revised by Rob Goodbody, Naas: Irish Academic Press, p. 58.

18. Gilbert, *op. cit.*, vol. IX, p. 264.

19. Gilbert, *op. cit.*, (1903), vol. X, p. 363.

20. de Courcy, *op. cit.*, p. 378.

21. Gilbert, *op. cit.*, (1904), vol. XI, p. 85.

22. Gilligan, *op. cit.*, pp. 37–8.

23. British Parliamentary Papers, *op. cit.*, p. 72.

24. Daly, G. (1993) 'George Semple's charts of Dublin Bay, 1762', *Proceedings of the Royal Irish Academy, Section C: Archaeology, Celtic Studies, History, Linguistics, Literature*, 93C (3), 81–105.

25. Gilligan, *op. cit.*, p. 51.

26. Gilligan, *op. cit.*, p. 57–61.

27. Hyde Page, T. (1800) *Reports Relative to Dublin Harbour and Adjacent Coast*. Dublin.

28. Tidal Harbours Commission (1846), *Second Report of the Tidal Harbours Commission*, House of Commons Papers no. 692, p. 40a.

29. British Parliamentary Papers, *op. cit.*, p.64.

30. Gilligan, *op. cit.*, p. 90; 'William Chapman' in *Dictionary of Irish Architects 1720–1940*, www.dia.ie, accessed 4 December 2016.

31. Tidal Harbours Commission, *op. cit.*, pp. 40a–41a.

32. British Parliamentary Papers, *op. cit.*, pp. 67–77.

33. Tidal Harbours Commission, *op. cit.*, p. 41a.

34. R. Goodbody, R. (2006) '"A tax upon daylight": window tax in Ireland', *Irish Architectural and Decorative Studies* 9, 89.

35. de Courcy, *op. cit.*, p. 53.

36. Goodbody, R. (2010) *The Metals: From Dalkey to Dún Laoghaire*, Dún Laoghaire-Rathdown County Council.

37. Tidal Harbours Commission, *op. cit.*, pp. 40a–41a.

Chapter 10: Maritime Heritage

1. Warburton, J., Whitelaw, J. and Walsh, R. (1818) *History of the City of Dublin*, vol. 2. London, p. 1249.

2. Williams, A. (1908) 'Bird life in Dublin Bay: the passing of Clontarf Island', *Irish Naturalist* 17, 165–71.

3. Flood, Donal T. (1977) 'Historical Evidence for the Growth of Bull Island', in D.W. Jeffrey (ed.), *North Bull Island, Dublin Bay: A Modern Coastal Natural History*. Dublin: Royal Dublin Society.

4. Kirwan, Richard (1806–10) 'A synoptical view of the state of the weather at Dublin for the years 1805–08', *Transactions of the Royal Irish Academy*, Science XI, 69.

5. Williams, *op. cit.*

6. *Ibid.*

7. *Ibid.*

8. Gunn, W.F. (1912) 'The Shelly Bank Dublin Bay', *Irish Naturalist* 21 (11), 223.

9. West, A.B., Partridge, J.K. and Lovitt, A. (1979) 'The cockle *Cerastoderma edule* (L.) on the South Bull, Dublin Bay: population parameters and fishery potential', *Irish Fisheries Investigations* Series B, no. 20. Dublin: Department of Fisheries and Forestry.

10. Wilkins, Noel, P. (2004) *Alive Alive O: The Shellfish and Shellfisheries of Ireland*. Kinvara, Co. Galway: Tír Eolas.

11. Rutty, J. (1772) *Essay towards a Natural History of the County of Dublin*. Dublin.

12. Reports of Inspectors (1894–1914) Annual Reports of the Inspectors of Irish Fisheries on the Sea and Inland Fisheries of Ireland for 1893–1913. Dublin: HMSO.

13. West *et al.*, *op. cit.*

14. Browne, T.J. (1904) 'Report on an enquiry into the conditions under which oysters and certain other edible molluscs are cultivated and stored on the coast of Ireland, with special reference to the question of the pollution of the shellfish layings by sewage matter', *Annual Report of the Local Government Board for Ireland 1903*. Dublin: HMSO.

15. West *et al.*, *op. cit.*

16. Dudley, E. (2009) 'A silent witness – Cork Street Fever Hospital', *Dublin Historical Record* 62 (1), 103–26.

17. McWeeney, E.J. (1904) 'Report on the bacterial examination of samples taken from shellfish layings', *Annual Report of the Local Government Board for Ireland 1903*. Dublin: HMSO.

18. Lowth, C.F. (2002) 'James O'Connor, Fenian and the tragedy of 1890', *Dublin Historical Record* 4 (2), 1 17.

19. Wilkins, *op cit.*

20. Rutty, *op. cit.*, vol. 2, pp. 375–8.

21. Browne, *op. cit.*

22. Act of parliament, 13–14 Geo III c. 41, sections xii and xiii. An act for reviving and continuing several temporary statutes, and to prevent the destructive practice of trawling for fish in the bay of Dublin.

23. Act of parliament, 17–18 Geo III, c. 36, section vi. An act for reviving and continuing several temporary statutes. Section vi relates to trawling in Dublin bay, to continue the ban until 24 June 1790.

24. Symes, E.P. (2000) 'The Torbay fishermen in Ringsend', *Dublin Historical Record*, 53 (2), 139–49.

25. W.J.C. (1881) 'A trawling excursion in Dublin', *Irish Monthly*, 9 (97), 371–4.

26. Lowth, C.F. (in preparation) *The Ringsend Sailing Trawlers: Fishing under Sail in the 19th Century*.

27. Mac Con Iomaire, M. (2005) *The History of Seafood in Irish Cuisine and Culture. Proceedings of the Oxford Symposium on Food and Cookery 2005*. Devon: Prospect Books, pp. 219–33.

28. *Ibid.*

29. Cooke, Jim (2005) *A Maritime History of Ringsend*. Dublin.

30. Magee, P., *op. cit.*

31. Sisk, H. (2012) *Dublin Bay: The Cradle of Yacht Racing*. Dublin: Peggybawn Press.

32. Archer, S. and Pearson, P. (1986) *The Royal St. George Yacht Club: A History*. Dún Laoghaire: Royal St George Yacht Club.

33. Long, B. (1993) *Bright Light, White Water: The Story of Irish Lighthouses and their People*. Dublin: New Island Books.

34. Gilligan, H.A. (1988) *A History of the Port of Dublin*. Dublin: Gill & Macmillan, p. 59.

35. *Ibid.*, p. 243.

36. Dublin Port Company (2014) *Alexandra Basin Redevelopment Environmental Impact Statement*. Cultural Heritage.

37. Brady, K. (2008) *Shipwreck Inventory of Ireland: Louth, Meath, Dublin and Wicklow*. Dublin: Stationery Office, pp. 215–98.

38. Hutchison, S. (2013) *Beware the Coast of Ireland*. Dublin: Wordwell Books.

39. *Ibid.*

40. Lowth, C.F. *The Boyd Disaster*. National Maritime Museum of Ireland website, www.mariner.ie/history-3/articles/people/the-boyd-disaster/.

41. Brady, *op. cit.*

Chapter 11: Using the Bay

1. Jeffrey, D.W. (ed.) (1977) *North Bull Island, Dublin Bay: A Modern Coastal Natural History*. Dublin: Royal Dublin Society.

2. Jeffrey, D.W. (1984) 'Bull Island: An Assessment of a Nature Conservation Resource' in *Nature Conservation in Ireland: Progress and Problems*. Dublin: Royal Irish Academy.

3. Goodwillie, R. (1987) 'Wildlife and Natural Areas – Conflicting Demands', in M. Brunton, F.J. Convery and A. Johnson (eds), *Managing Dublin Bay*. Dublin: University College Dublin.

4. McDonald, F. (2000) *The Construction of Dublin*. Dublin: Gandon Editions.

5. Quinn, Séan (2012) 'Sea Baths of South County Dublin', in Myles Reid, and Pádraig Laffan (eds), *Foxrock Miscellany*. Dublin: History Press Ireland, pp. 133–4.

6. Smyth, Hazel P. (1984) *The B & I Line: A History of the British and Irish Steam Packet Company*. Dublin: Gill & Macmillan, pp. 45, 59.

7. Taylor, Charlie (2015) 'Stena Line confirms end of Dun Laoghaire to Holyhead route', *Irish Times*, 4 February.

8. Kelly, Olivia (2016) 'Ruling restricts size of cruise liners in Dún Laoghaire Harbour', *Irish Times*, 4 November.

9. Pim, Frederic W. (1890) *The Growth of Sanitation in Dublin*. Dublin: R.D. Webb & Son, p. 30.

10. Pim, Frederic W. (1892) *Preventable Diseases: Why are they Not Prevented?* Dublin: R.D. Webb & Son, p. 17.

11. Corcoran, Michael (2005) *Our Good Health: A History of Dublin's Water and Drainage*. Dublin: Dublin City Council, pp. 84–5.

12. *Ibid.*, pp. 94–5.

13. O'Donnell, K. (1987) 'Residential and Industrial Sources of Pollution' in M. Brunton, F.J. Convery and A. Johnson (eds) *Managing Dublin Bay*. Dublin. University College Dublin.

14. Jack O'Sullivan, personal reminiscence.

15. Boyle, O.C., Masterson, B.F. and Stapleton, L. (1991) 'The Use of Indicator Organisms for the Protection of Recreational Users of Estuarine and Coastal Waters from Risks to Health', in D.W. Jeffrey and B. Madden (eds), *Bioindicators and Environmental Management*. London: Academic Press.

16. Jeffrey, D.W. (1998) 'General Concepts in Eutrophication', in J.G. Wilson (ed.), *Eutrophication in Irish Waters*. Dublin: Royal Irish Academy.

17. Holdgate, M.W. (1970) *The Seabird Wreck of 1969 in the Irish Sea*, a report by the Natural Environment Research Council.

18. O'Sullivan, J. (1987) 'Recreation', in M. Brunton, F.J. Convery and A. Johnson (eds), *Managing Dublin Bay*. Dublin: University College Dublin.

19. An Foras Forbartha (1975) *Survey of Outdoor Recreational Activities in Dublin City and County*. Dublin: An Foras Forbartha.

20. Brady Shipman Martin (1974) *Dublin Bay Amenity Study*. Dublin: Brady Shipman Martin.

21. O'Sullivan, J. (1987) 'Recreation', in John O'Sullivan and Séamus Cannon (eds), *The Book of Dun Laoghaire*. Dublin: Blackrock Teachers' Centre.

22. Nixon, W.M. (2014) 'Who runs Dublin Bay, the capital's waterborne playground?', *Afloat* magazine.

23. Gogarty, Claire (2014), *From Village to Suburb: The Building of Clontarf Since 1760*. Dublin: Clontarf Books, pp. 69–70, 109–10.

24. Quinn, Seán, *op. cit.*, pp. 127–37.

25. Marine Institute (2004) *A National Survey of Water-based Leisure Activities 2003*. Galway: Marine Institute.

26. O'Sullivan, J., *op. cit.*

27. National Transport Authority (2016) *Sandymount/Merrion to Blackrock Corridor Study: Public Consultation Document*. Dublin: National Transport Authority.

28. Williams, A. (1908) 'Bird life in Dublin Bay: the passing of Clontarf Island', *Irish Naturalist* 17, 165–70.

29. Doogue, D., Nash, D., Parnell, J., Reynolds, S. & Wyse Jackson, P. (1998). *Flora of County Dublin*. Dublin: Dublin Naturalists' Field Club.

30. Dunlop, N. and Green, P. (1992) *Sea Angling*. Dublin: Gill & Macmillan.

31. Jeffrey, D.W. (1984) 'Bull Island: An Assessment of a Nature Conservation Resource', in *Nature Conservation in Ireland: Progress and Problems*. Dublin: Royal Irish Academy.

32. Delve Research (2014) *Your Dublin, Your Voice: Survey of Opinion on Dublin Bay*. Unpublished report to Dublin City Council.

33. Dublin Chamber of Commerce (2015) *Economic Profile of Dublin*, http://www.dubchamber.ie/policy/economic-profile-of-dublin.

Chapter 12: The Future of the Bay

1. Gleeson, E., McGrath, R. and Treanor, M. (eds) (2013) *Ireland's Climate: The Road Ahead*. Dublin: Met Éireann.

2. Devoy, R.J.N. (2015) 'Sea-level Rise: Causes, Impacts and Scenarios for Change', in D. Sherman and J. Ellis (eds), *Coastal and Marine Hazards, Risks and Disasters*. Amsterdam: Elsevier, pp. 197–242.

3. Grinsted, A., Jevrejeva, S., Riva, R.E.M. and Dahl-Jensen, D. (2015) 'Sea level rise projections for northern Europe under RCP8.5', *Climate Research* 64, 15–23.

4. Professor John Sweeney, personal comment.

5.   Fagan, B. (2013) *The Attacking Ocean: The Past, Present and Future of Rising Sea Levels*. London: Bloomsbury.

6.   Flood, S. and Sweeney, J. (2012) 'Quantifying Impacts of Potential Sea Level Rise Scenarios on Irish Coastal Cities', in K. Otto-Zimmermann (ed.), *Resilient Cities 2: Cities and Adaptation to Climate Change*. Dordrecht: Springer.

7.   Sanchez-Arcilla, A., Garcia-Leon, M., Gracia, V., Devoy, R.J.N., Stanica, A. and Gault, J. (2016) 'Managing coastal environments under climate change: pathways to adaptation', *Science of the Total Environment* 572, 1336–52.

8.   McClatchey, J., Devoy, R.J.N., Woolf, D., Bremner, B. and James, N. (2014) 'Climate change and adaptation in the coastal areas of Europe's Northern periphery region', *Ocean and Coastal Management* 94, 9–21.

9.   Pilkey, O.H. and Cooper, J.A.G. (2014) *The Last Beach*. Durham and London: Duke University Press.

10. Stralberg, D., Brennan, M., Callaway, J.C., Wood, J.K., Schile, L.M., Jongsomjit, D., Kelly, M., Parker, V.T. and Crooks, S. (2011) 'Evaluating tidal marsh sustainability in the face of sea-level rise: a hybrid modeling approach applied to San Francisco Bay', *PLOS ONE* 6(11): e27388; doi: 10.1371/journal.pone.0027388.

11. Veloz, S.D., Nadav Nur, N., Salas, D., Jongsomjit, D., Wood, J., Stralnerg, D. and Ballard, G. (2013) 'Modelling climate change impacts on tidal marsh birds: restoration and conservation planning in the face of uncertainty', *Ecosphere* 4, 1–25.

12. Hiscock, K., Southward, A. Tittley, I. and Hawkins, S. (2004) 'Effects of changing temperature on benthic marine life in Britain and Ireland', *Aquatic Conservation*, 14, 333–362.

13. Lynam, C.P., Lilley, M.K.S., Bastian, T., Doyle, T.K., Beggs, S.E. and Hayes, G.C. (2011) 'Have jellyfish in the Irish Sea benefited from climate change and overfishing?', *Global Climate Biology 17, 767–82*.

14. Brady, A. (1987) 'The Political and Administrative System Evaluated', in M. Brunton, F.J. Convery and A. Johnson (eds), *Managing Dublin Bay*. Dublin: University College Dublin.

15. Brady Shipman Martin (1997). *Coastal Zone Management: A Draft Policy for Ireland*. Dublin: Government of Ireland.

16. Cummins, V., O Mahony, C. and Connolly, N. (2002). *Review of Integrated Coastal Zone Management and Principals of Best Practice*. Dublin: Coastal and Marine Resources Centre, Environmental Research Institute, Heritage Council.

17. Delve Research (2014). *op. cit.*

18. Marshall, G. (2014) *Don't Even Think About It: Why our Brains are Wired to Ignore Climate Change*. London: Bloomsbury.

19. Klein, N. (2014) *This Changes Everything: Capitalism vs. the Climate*. London: Allen Lane.

20. Stein, B.A., Glick, P., Edelson, N. and Staudt, A. (2014) *Climate-Smart Conservation: Putting Adaptation Principles into Practice*. Washington, DC: National Wildlife Federation.

Index